P9-DIJ-678

THE BANKRUPTING
OF AMERICA

Also by David P. Calleo

Beyond American Hegemony
The Imperious Economy
The German Problem Reconsidered

THE BANKRUPTING

OF AMERICA

How the Federal Budget Is Impoverishing the Nation

David P. Calleo

William Morrow and Company, Inc.
New York

Copyright © 1992 by David P. Calleo

All rights reserved. No part of this book may be reproduced or utilized in any form or by any means, electronic or mechanical, including photocopying, recording, or by any information storage or retrieval system, without permission in writing from the Publisher. Inquiries should be addressed to Permissions Department, William Morrow and Company, Inc., 1350 Avenue of the Americas, New York, N.Y. 10019.

It is the policy of William Morrow and Company, Inc., and its imprints and affiliates, recognizing the importance of preserving what has been written, to print the books we publish on acid-free paper, and we exert our best efforts to that end.

Library of Congress Cataloging-in-Publication Data

Calleo, David P., 1934–
    The bankrupting of America : how the federal budget
is impoverishing the nation / David P. Calleo.
        p.   cm.
    Includes bibliographical references and index.
    ISBN 0-688-05162-6
    1. Budget deficits—United States.   2. Fiscal policy—United
States.   I. Title.
HJ2052.C35   1992
339.5′23′0973—dc20   91-30373
                                                                      CIP

Printed in the United States of America

First Edition

1 2 3 4 5 6 7 8 9 10

BOOK DESIGN BY LISA STOKES

For Robert Skidelsky

Acknowledgments

A book concerning so many subjects needs a great deal of help. Fortunately, I have found it over the past few years in abundance among my graduate students at SAIS (The Paul H. Nitze School of Advanced International Studies, The Johns Hopkins University)—in particular, Hugh Aller, Jörg Boche, Gernot Brodnig, Brian Coleman, Erik Jones, Claudia Morgenstern, Marco Santamaria, Mark Scully, and Andrea Wuerth. Aller and Coleman saw the book through its final drafting and checking and contributed greatly throughout, but in particular to Chapters 7 and 8. Aller produced most of the graphs and tables. Boche was also closely involved throughout and had a major part in the research and argument of Chapters 4 and 7. Morgenstern was particularly helpful with Chapter 7 and also with parts of Chapter 8. Jones developed much of the material in Chapter 3 and in parts of Chapter 7. All of them not only have been tireless researchers but have given good advice and great encouragement. I only hope their education from me has been as rewarding and agreeable as mine from them.

Numerous friends and colleagues have also been generous commentators as the manuscript was being written. My old friend Robert Skidelsky encouraged me from the start and read much of the manuscript as it evolved. Benjamin Rowland

and Harold van Buren Cleveland have read several parts and commented generously. Among my colleagues at SAIS who have done the same are Harold Brown, Isaiah Frank, and Grace Goodell, along with Michael Veseth from the University of Puget Sound. Judy Feder, of the Center for Health Policy Studies, gave generous help with Chapter 4. I am also grateful to the Washington Foundation for European Studies for two lively seminars of experts to discuss the earlier chapters. Among those who attended, and then offered extensive help, I want particularly to thank Edwin Dean, associate commissioner for the Office of Productivity and Technology of the Department of Labor, Jessica Einhorn of the World Bank, and Joseph White of the Brookings Institution.

My thanks to all of you. I have certainly learned a good deal and hope you are not altogether dismayed at the results.

D.P.C.

Washington, D.C.

Contents

1. Introduction: Budget Deficits and National
   Decline 11
2. Fiscal Deficits: Definitions and Consequences 26
3. Federal Spending Since 1950 47
4. United States Fiscal Policy: An International
   Perspective 68
5. Taxes and Incomes in the United States 86
6. Financing the Deficit: The International
   Dimension 102
7. Fiscal Deficits, Public Goods, and the
   Real Economy 122
8. The Future According to Present Trends 142
9. Decline Revisited 160
10. Rebalancing America 173
Tables and Graphs 192
Notes 226
Selected Bibliography 276
Index 285

Chapter 1 *Introduction: Budget Deficits and National Decline*

*T*his is a book about America's budget crisis: how we got into it, what it does to us, and what it tells us about our national character, history, and future. As might be expected, there are no simple explanations, solutions, or lessons. The crisis is very deep and has been gathering for a long time. The deficits that became so startling in the 1980s were not simply the fault of mistakes made in the Reagan or Carter administrations. They go back to fiscal and monetary practices that began three decades ago. Step by step since the 1960s, Presidents and Congresses, cheered on by fashionable economists of the hour, have taken the decisions that have accumulated into today's routine huge imbalances. Unable or unwilling to find the resources to pay the bills for our combined geopolitical and domestic ambitions, American governments have developed a perennial tendency toward fiscal deficits and light-fingered accounting. One financial expedient after another has put off the day of reckoning.

The effects reach very far. The ways we have financed our deficits have undermined our money and thereby severely distorted national and international finance. Chronic macro-economic mismanagement, disrupting capital and currency markets, has subverted the mechanisms for business investment. As real investment has faltered, productivity growth has faltered with it. Our national industry has thus found itself handicapped in the race to adopt new technologies to meet increasingly intense global competition. Volatile interest and exchange rates, together with lagging productivity, have undermined our position in international trade. A large external deficit now matches our large internal deficit, and our dependency on foreign credit has grown endemic.

Fiscal habits of this kind are both the symptoms and the mechanisms of a broad national decline. It is not surprising, therefore, that America's "decline" has become a big public issue during this past decade. A large part of the political and economic establishment has reacted angrily, with what may best be described as a militant complacency. The reasons are understandable. For elites accustomed to wielding global power during this last half century, admitting the implications of the fiscal crisis provokes visions of an unfamiliar and dangerous world. For all Americans, the budget deficit implies a future of diminishing wealth and growing social conflict. A widespread determination to ignore the obvious is not so surprising. Hoping to remain an eagle, the United States has become an ostrich.

American complacency has never lacked vigorous apologists. Complacency about the budget rests on three basic arguments:

1. Deficits don't matter.
2. Deficits could easily be cured by spending less.
3. Deficits could easily be cured by raising taxes.

Most of this book is devoted to refuting these three arguments. In the abstract, each one has some merit to it. In theory and practice, a fiscal deficit can be beneficial rather than harmful. Simple arithmetic indicates that cutting spending or raising taxes could relieve a deficit. A good deal of federal spending is obviously inefficient; serious spending cuts are never inconceivable. American tax rates, moreover, are among the lowest in the developed world. The judgment that all three arguments are wrong under current circumstances depends upon a broader view of the nation's economic and political condition, and of the effects of deficits on that condition.

DEFICITS DON'T MATTER

The first argument—that deficits don't matter—is the most complex. The theory about what defines a fiscal deficit and determines its effects is discussed at length in the next chapter. A few points here can sketch how it proceeds.

Any government's budget is an attempt to synthesize its needs, ambitions, and resources. A significant deficit, year after year, suggests that the needs and ambitions are outrunning the resources. More precisely, however, a deficit only indicates that the government's regular income needs to be supplemented by fresh borrowing. The practice of borrowing is not intrinsically harmful, even in purely economic terms. If the government's borrowing results, overall, in commensurately greater economic growth for the whole economy, then the deficit can be considered an investment in the future. But such deficits, even for the best of purposes, are never cost-free. The question is whether the benefits exceed the costs.

Analysts can always be found, of course, to argue that the federal debt doesn't matter, since it is simply money that the nation owes to itself. But that is a tendentious half-truth. Debt has to be serviced. All other things remaining equal, servicing a bigger debt means less income for public needs in the future. If the debt is owed to foreigners, its servicing may also mean less future income and security for the national economy as a whole. Again, the basic question is how additional debt affects the size of future income. Financially, debt is eminently justifiable for expenditures that yield more than enough to pay the interest and amortize the principal. Throughout the nineteenth century, the United States ran up large debts to Europe, and was much the richer for doing so.

From this perspective, however, the record of recent times is discouraging. America's federal debt has grown much more rapidly than its GNP and federal debt service has grown much more rapidly than federal income. From 1980 to 1990, federal debt climbed from 34.0 percent to 59.3 percent of GNP. Net interest payments grew from 8.9 percent to 14.7 percent of federal income. In the end, relatively fewer resources were available for all federal functions—health, education, transportation, or defense.

The reasons that federal borrowing produced no commensurate growth of national or federal income are not mysterious. While real federal spending for military equipment grew greatly over the 1980s, real federal spending on physical infrastructure, education, and the environment declined markedly. Where the federal government's civil spending did rise rapidly, notably for health care, it seems highly inefficient. A debt run up under such circumstances seems likely to weigh heavily on future income. Heavy borrowing for defense is, of course, justifiable when vital interests are really on the line. No one can blame the British for going heavily into debt to keep themselves from being conquered by Hitler. But despite all the alarms and excursions of the Carter and Reagan years, it is not easy to claim that the United States was fighting for its life. In any event, heavy military outlays are not investments to yield future income.

How a fiscal deficit affects an economy depends greatly not only on how it is spent but also on how it is financed. Basically, government deficits are financed either by borrowing the savings of others—Americans or foreigners—or by expanding credit through an inflation of the money supply. Since the federal government's borrowing needs are relatively high, and the national savings rate comparatively low, purely domestic borrowing to finance large deficits is seldom, by itself, a very satisfactory option. It squeezes out private borrowers and depresses the economy. As a result, the practical alternatives for American policy usually lie between creating credit at home or borrowing abroad. Creating credit means an easy monetary policy, with low real interest rates, while borrowing abroad requires a tight monetary policy, with real interest rates high to attract foreign investors.

Those opposite monetary policies produce quite different consequences for the real economy of investment and jobs. A monetary policy loose enough to accommodate both heavy federal borrowing and the needs of private investment points toward a sinking dollar and a high level of inflation. A monetary policy tight enough to attract foreign savings curbs inflation but also overvalues the dollar, discourages private investment, slows the growth of productivity, and depresses industrial competitiveness. In other words, when government borrowing is heavy, and national savings low, each monetary alternative has its dark side and, sooner or later, results in unacceptable consequences. A government with chronic and severe fiscal deficits thus is forced toward a "stop-go" monetary policy—tightening when inflation threatens to accelerate and loosening when conditions grow too depressed.

An oscillating monetary policy has itself very significant effects on the real economy. It makes the price of money erratic—whether that price is measured in interest rates, exchange rates, or even inflation rates. With money erratic, long-term investment grows risky. Capital markets become casinos for speculation rather than efficient mechanisms for channeling savings into real investment.

Since the American economy is so large and the dollar is still the principal currency for international transactions, the United States has found it comparatively easy to draw on the savings of others or to export to other economies the inflationary consequences of creating excessive credit. Erratic American monetary policies have thus spilled out into the world, producing similarly unstable effects in other economies, unhinging the international monetary system, and promoting protectionism and blocs in reaction. An unstable international climate with a high level of unpredictable risk favors business concentration and price-fixing, as well as government subsidies to investment. To a point, at least, such a climate favors countries like Japan, Germany, and France, who are comparatively well developed in private corporatism or government planning, as opposed to the United States, whose laissez-faire and antitrust traditions leave it more vulnerable to the vagaries of unstable markets. Hence, the growing pressure in recent years for the United States to adopt a comprehensive industrial policy, or to permit more concentration and cartelization among its private firms. Meanwhile, unstable world markets have given the states of Europe an unflagging incentive to press forward with their European Community and European Monetary System.

Whatever damage American policy has done abroad is fully matched by the damage done at home. Monetary instability has greatly weakened America's own financial structure. An alarming pile of junk bonds, speculative investments in real estate, and problematic foreign and domestic loans burdens American banks and insurance companies. The takeover mania has saddled many American corporations with a heavy load of unproductive debt. Thus, alongside the mushrooming public debt is an equally debilitating private debt.

The new decade of the 1990s has also opened with a further big jump in the level of federal borrowing. In 1991, the Bush administration faced an escalating fiscal shortfall reckoned to reach as high as $378 billion.[1] With a severe recession reducing private investment and borrowing, financing the hugely increased federal deficit was, for the moment, surprisingly easy. With private investment depressed, national savings were adequate.[2] Permanent recession, however, was an improbable formula for managing the fiscal crisis. Given the perilous state of many American financial institutions, it could soon grow self-defeating.

Prospects for heavy borrowing abroad, however, seem very different in the 1990s from what they were in the 1980s. The geopolitical revolution resulting from the Soviet withdrawal from central Europe implies radical changes for world investment patterns. German reunification and the opening of Eastern European and Soviet markets create an urgent need for capital, just as America's fiscal needs are once more escalating. Europe's new monetary union, moreover, will very likely limit America's former capacity to preempt foreign savings or export domestic inflation.

In short, the future looks not very encouraging. Present trends point toward national impoverishment and inflation. As the going gets tough, naked political power is likely to grow more and more visible in world economic relations. Certainly, the United States, the European Community, and Japan are colliding more and more brutally in trade negotiations.

Americans are themselves increasingly conscious of foreign economic power in their own economy; the heavy dependency on overseas capital in the 1980s has resulted in an increasingly conspicuous foreign control of our real assets.[3] Complacent analysts have sought to soothe the American reaction with arguments already well-rehearsed abroad, where American corporations have, for a long time, led the trend toward global production. Foreign investments are contributions to national growth and productivity, it is said, and heavy foreign investment reflects the great attractiveness and strength of our economy. American public unease nevertheless continues. With the occasional exception of Great Britain, big advanced countries are seldom happy to see foreign owners controlling their principal industries. Even after three decades in the Common Market, France, Germany, Holland, and Italy remain extremely reluctant to permit foreign takeovers of major national firms.

Many analysts shrink from this national or "mercantilist" way of reckoning because they fear a populist xenophobia that could both turn ugly politically and lead to policies, like protection for decaying firms and uncompetitive labor, that would make the American situation still worse. They are certainly right not to encourage the public to blame America's problems on foreigners. Our present economic predicament may be serious and painful, but it is principally of our own making.

Foreign competitors may be unduly or unfairly aggressive, and should be called to account. But our basic problem is not with our competitors but with ourselves. Economic competition in a liberal world is meant to benefit everyone. But to function properly, a liberal system requires all the players to take sensible views of their own long-term national interest, and discipline themselves to remain in a position to compete vigorously. The free market is often not forgiving to those who fail to rise to the occasion. Under present circumstances, the proper response for a rich and developed country like ours is not crybaby protectionism, but a serious policy of national renewal. National renewal is impossible, however, without fiscal reform. At the root of America's decline is not the connivance of foreigners, but the profligacy and incompetence of our own public sector.

All these arguments, sketched quickly here, are examined at length in the chapters that follow. Experts can differ about one point or another. But the overall weight of evidence and analysis seems quite clear: Over time, America's fiscal deficits do matter a great deal.

CUT SPENDING

If America's fiscal deficits matter so much, why can't they be stopped? Why has it been so difficult either to cut spending or to raise taxes? At the heart of the problem lies a double quarrel. One is over guns and butter. The other is between collective goods and private wealth. Those quarrels exist in every country. But because of America's geopolitical role, they are particularly intractable in the United States.

For a significant part of America's political elites, preserving America's postwar international role is an overriding concern. They feel particularly threatened by any link between national decline and military overspending. Isolationism, they believe, lurks like a dormant virus in the American body politic. Decline will provide a convenient excuse, they fear, for abdicating America's international responsibilities. Their concern may be valid, but does not justify denying the obvious. Year after year, the United States has spent a significantly higher proportion of its GNP on the military than has any of its major economic competitors. Nearly a half century after the end of World War II, defense still takes up roughly a quarter of federal spending.

Cutting military spending, however, is not easy. Cutting forces without commensurate alterations in geopolitical responsibilities can be dangerous and self-defeating. As the cyclical vagaries of postwar military spending illustrated several times during the cold war, "hegemony on the cheap" can be very expensive.[4] At the end of 1989, the retreat and apparent disintegration of Soviet power seemed to offer a remarkable occasion for the United States to enjoy a sizable fiscal windfall. Less than a year later, the explosion of long-simmering disputes in the Persian Gulf illustrated dramatically the ample inducements for American military entanglements, even without the cold war. A more modest geopolitical posture will not be easy for the United States to achieve. Without it, if past experience is any guide, military savings are likely to prove ephemeral.

As defenders of America's traditional world role always observe, since the mid-1950s the federal government's civilian

TABLE 1.1

Federal Outlays for Military Versus Human Resources

AS A PERCENTAGE OF GNP

	1950	1960	1970	1980	1990
National Defense	5.1	9.5	8.9	5.0	5.5
Human Resources	5.3	5.2	7.1	11.7	11.5

AS A PERCENTAGE OF FEDERAL OUTLAYS

	1950	1960	1970	1980	1990
National Defense	32.2	52.2	41.8	22.7	23.9
Human Resources	33.4	28.4	38.5	53.0	49.5

Source: *Budget of the U.S. Government, Fiscal Year 1992*, Historical Tables (Washington, D.C.: U.S. Government Printing Office, 1991), Part Seven: 31–36.

spending has grown far more rapidly than its military spending. Real spending for "human resources"—mostly civilian "entitlements"—has increased by about 500 percent, while real spending for defense has remained constant, and fallen from half to one quarter of federal outlays.

The rapid growth of civilian entitlements is, of course, common to all Western democracies. By Western European standards, the American "welfare state" is, in fact, extremely modest. In every Western European country, government spending is a much higher proportion of national income than in the United States, although military spending is significantly lower. By European standards, American entitlements do not look so large. Instead, comparison raises the question whether American public spending is adequate.

Nothing, moreover, indicates any future easing of American civilian spending. Demographic trends will greatly increase the cost of current provisions for pensions and health care. Neglected infrastructure and environment, or guarantees to troubled financial institutions, all point toward further sharp increases in outlays. In short, overall civilian spending seems even more difficult to cut than long-term military spending.

TABLE 1.2

Government Final Consumption Expenditure, 1988 (As Percent of GDP)

	U.S.	FRANCE[1]	GERMANY[2]
Public Order and Safety	1.3	0.9	1.5
Education	4.5	4.9	3.8
Health	0.9	3.1	6.0
Social Security and Welfare	0.6	1.5	2.1
Housing and Community Amenities	0.4	1.2	0.3

1. 1986
2. 1987
Source: OECD, *National Accounts* (Paris: OECD, 1990) and *Historical Statistics, 1960–1988* (Paris: OECD, 1990).

RAISING TAXES

European governments also have fiscal problems, but in recent years have generally been more successful in containing them, despite their relatively high spending. The obvious reason is that their taxes are much higher than in the United States.

Simple arithmetic indicates that raising United States taxes to European levels could resolve the American fiscal problem. Economic theory, moreover, suggests that higher taxes could eliminate not only the United States' fiscal deficit, but also its related evils: current-account imbalances, rising indebtedness

TABLE 1.3

Government Receipts, 1980 to 1988 (As a Percentage of GDP)

	U.S.	FRANCE	GERMANY	U.K.
1980	30.8	44.5	44.7	40.1
1985	31.2	47.6	45.6	42.3
1988*	31.5	47.1	43.7	40.7

*U.K.: 1987
Source: OECD, *Historical Statistics, 1960–1988* (Paris: OECD, 1990), p. 68.

to foreigners, declining investment and competitiveness, inadequate education, and deterioration of social and physical infrastructure. Adequate taxation could cut private overconsumption at the same time as it ended the government's "dissaving."

Throughout the 1980s, Democratic presidential candidates regularly embraced just such an analysis. They blamed the huge fiscal deficits of the 1980s on President Ronald Reagan's tax cut rather than on his military budget. All Democratic candidates regularly called for tax increases and all of them regularly lost their elections. Few analysts believed that their tax stance strengthened their appeal to the voters.

Why won't Americans pay the same taxes as Europeans? Is aversion to taxes more compelling among Americans than among the French or the Italians? It seems less tendentious to assume that Europeans pay higher taxes because they perceive a greater connection between public spending and their own private and collective self-interest. In Europe, the linkage is very direct. A good part of Europe's public spending is transferred directly to private households. Not only are European levels of public spending substantially higher, but the balance is much more heavily weighted toward civilian than military needs. Not only is United States military spending much heavier per capita, and a bigger share of GNP, but it also occupies a very much larger share of government spending. It therefore crowds out that governmental civilian spending that nourishes Europe's constituency for higher taxes.

Public spending in Europe is also much more directly attuned to the interests of the taxpaying middle classes. Europe's public pensions guarantee far greater benefits to those with high previous incomes. Health care and university education are virtually free. Europe's governments deliver a notably higher standard of public infrastructure, urban safety, and general cultural amenities. European taxes, moreover, fall more heavily on consumption while American taxes weigh more on middle-class salaries and property.

Comparisons also reveal the relative inefficiency of the American political system in providing basic public services. Health care is a particularly egregious illustration. Much more is spent on health care in the American economy than in the

French or German, despite insurance coverage in the United States leaving out a substantial part of the population. It is difficult to attribute the relative difference in the overall cost to a higher quality of care in the United States. General figures on health do not support such a view. It seems more plausible to lay America's higher costs to inefficiency—in particular to a comparatively unsuccessful mix of public and private enterprise in the health field. Inefficiency on this scale squeezes America's public and private budgets alike. It limits what the government can deliver and, as a result, the constituencies for its services.

All things considered, it should not be surprising that middle classes in Europe support higher tax rates than in the United States. By European standards, American federal taxes are very high, considering how little they provide the average taxpayer. To go about creating a comparable constituency for higher taxes in America would require changing the amount and direction of public spending, the incidence of taxation, and the general balance between public and private sectors.

Many analysts and politicians prefer America's current fiscal pattern—a smaller public sector and a higher priority for noncivilian spending than in Europe. But, given that American pattern, it is not reasonable to expect American taxpayers to support their public sector as much as Europeans support theirs. As is observed in Chapter 5, American reluctance to pay higher taxes is all the more understandable, given the stagnant or falling income of most American families over more than a decade. In short, raising taxes is not a simple and self-evident panacea for America's fiscal problem. From a comparative perspective, America's tax problem is less the public's obstinate refusal to pay more taxes than its disenchantment with the capacity of the public sector to deliver public goods.

This incapacity of the American public sector seems rooted in the preferences that emerge from the political system. The federal budget embodies priorities that cannot garner enough public support to pay for them. The political system has nevertheless failed to alter its priorities or to improve its efficiency. A chronic and swelling fiscal deficit is the result.

Many of those who advocate higher taxes also defend the

federal government's traditional priorities—above all its pre-occupation with world hegemony. Most of those political leaders who promote tax cuts or resist tax increases are no less fervent defenders of the traditional world role. In that respect, presidential campaigns in the 1980s offered the voter a rather limited choice of policies. The public reacted not altogether illogically—either by not voting (50.9 percent in 1988), or by favoring leaders who oppose raising taxes and who, whatever they say, do not actually reduce civilian entitlements.[5] So long as financing deficits has seemed easy, nothing has compelled either the public or the political system to behave otherwise. The fiscal deficit is the perennial and now self-generating consequence. Unfortunately, its effects poison public and private finance, disadvantage industry, impoverish labor, and turn relative decline into something more absolute.

SEEING THE WAY OUT

Getting out of this fiscal predicament will not be easy. Nothing less than a major and sustained act of political will can remove the fiscal incubus from the American economy. The first step is to admit how serious things really are. Recognition, however, will bring no facile cures. Present trends are making things worse, not better. Civilian needs are fated to grow larger and more urgent. The inefficiency of the public sector shows no signs of diminishing. There may not even be a "peace dividend." And meanwhile, the deficit in particular and the shortcomings of the public sector in general hinder real growth and handicap the American economy against its competitors.

Lamentations about the lack of leadership can be heard on all sides. But today's problem is less a shortage of skillful leaders than a general deficiency of imagination. To be effective, political will needs to be informed by intelligence. In a constitutional democracy, moreover, leaders cannot make water flow uphill. The body politic will follow an innovative leader only where the general progress of ideas has prepared the way. Building sound public visions to assure a better future should begin with a realistic analysis of the present and of how things came to be the way they are. How and why has the deficit grown to proportions that have turned it into a mechanism for national decline? I hope this book will stimulate a deeper understanding and more serious debate about this complex and fateful question, and our national condition in general.

It may be useful at this point to spell out how the book actually proceeds. The next chapter takes up certain critical theoretical and philosophical issues: How should a deficit be defined and measured? What determines the effects of a fiscal deficit on the economy as a whole? What should determine the responsibilities and boundaries of the public sector?

The following three chapters (3 through 5) explore how the deficit has developed. Chapter 3 discusses how federal money has been spent since the war, how the spending priorities have changed from one administration to the next, and what criteria are best for measuring the magnitude and adequacy of outlays. Chapter 4 helps put America's fiscal profile in perspective by comparing American spending patterns with French and German. Chapter 5 examines the distinctive progress of American taxation.

The next three chapters (6 through 8) survey the consequences of the fiscal deficits. Chapter 6 examines how fiscal shortfalls have been financed: how monetary policy has been manipulated and how the dollar's international role has helped to avoid adjustments at home. Chapter 7 explores the effects of this manipulative financing on the real economy and on the financial sector itself. Chapter 8 projects current fiscal and economic trends, combines them with likely demographic, environmental, and geopolitical developments, and foresees grim consequences. Chapter 9 examines some fashionable theories taking a more optimistic view. Chapter 10 asks what policies, institutions, and economic and political ideas would have to change before our fiscal crisis might begin to be resolved.

If the analysis of this book is correct, the period ahead will not be very comfortable. Every society faces periodic changes that make old policies obsolete and throw national institutions and culture into a crisis. Depending on the reaction, the result can be decay or regeneration. For Americans, this is such a moment. The bipolar world order is crumbling and our domestic affairs clearly need restructuring. Since the challenge is, above all, to our nation's political imagination, it seems a moment when academic scholars have a particularly heavy responsibility to break free from the trammels of old clichés to generate a fresh and productive debate. If we can rise to the occasion, perhaps we can make our "decline" the catalyst for our regeneration.

Chapter 2 *Fiscal Deficits: Definitions and Consequences*

*A*merica's fiscal deficits may be a very serious economic problem, but they have also been a very convenient political solution. Presidents and Congresses, unable to reach a principled consensus on the competing claims of civil and military spending, or of taxes and private income, compromise by having a deficit. That they find it difficult to agree in the first place is hardly surprising. Every political system struggles over its priorities. A fiscal budget is simply the notation of how that struggle has been resolved in any given year.

Fiscal politics revolve around three related issues:

1. How large should the public sector be?
2. How should the public sector spend its money?
3. How should the public sector raise its money?

Issues one and two are obviously closely connected. The size of the public sector is intimately related to what it is expected to do. Some believe it should focus primarily on public order: military and police protection and maintaining the society's rules of the game. Others emphasize further benefits— like education, pensions, and medical care—and believe the state should provide them—at least to some degree. The argument for having the state be the provider has, logically, two distinct parts. The first declares the benefit itself to be in the general or collective interest of the whole society. The second asserts that the state can more reliably or efficiently provide the benefit than can the private sector. The parts of the argument are not only distinct but separable. It is possible, for example, to hold education to be a vital public good—in the sense that no society can be democratically governed or economically viable without it—but also to believe that it can and should be provided by the private sector. Education may thus be considered a public good but one that is, under existing circumstances, better supplied privately. If, under different circumstances, the private sector were unable to provide education adequately, the public authority might logically take over all or part of the task.[1] The relative size of the public sector thus depends on judgments about what are genuine collective or public goods and how important they are—as opposed to private possessions and personal self-fulfillment. It also depends on judgments about the extent to which the private or the public sector should provide these public goods.

Obviously, innumerable combinations of answers are possible. No one advocates a society whose government provides no public goods at all. And no one wants a society that leaves individuals no private resources for their personal goals. In reality, neither public nor private goods can be achieved without the other, nor can either be reliably secured without a complex interaction of public authority and private initiative. But the right proportions are a matter for infinite argument. When there is not enough consensus, a budget deficit often makes a workable compromise. The government is then charged with public responsibilities, but denied the direct public revenues needed to carry them out.

A deficit leads to our third fiscal issue: how the public sector should raise its money. For politicians, borrowing is generally more gratifying than either raising or cutting spending. But a deficit is often more than simply a consensus reached by default. Many distinguished economists—on both left and right—argue that federal deficits do little harm, or even positive good.[2] They generally make two broad arguments:

1. Not all expenditures should be weighed the same. Capital and many other expenditures should be "off-budget," or at least counted differently from current expenditures. When these accounting adjustments are made, a good part of the nominal deficit would disappear, and the "fiscal crisis" with it.

2. Deficits stimulate higher growth, including a disproportionate growth of federal revenue, at least in the long term.

The accounting arguments are complicated and interesting, and have been important in political debates over the deficit. At heart, they all have to do with defining the true extent of the deficit. Briefly, there are at least three main issues: One important group of economists believes that distinguishing between the government's capital and current expenditures not only would be logical and desirable, but might also significantly reduce the size of the deficit. In any event, it would focus the debate more on the comparative value of government versus private spending. The issue is less significant than it seems, since capital budgeting would involve depreciation and the government, if anything, has been disinvesting in recent years.

A second large issue is how the government treats its "trust funds," in particular social security. Here the emphasis is reversed. Senator Daniel Patrick Moynihan and others argue that by pretending to "invest" its annual surplus of social security taxes in the federal debt, the government is misleading the contributors and very significantly understating the size of its real deficit. The heart of the issue has more to do with the equity and transparency of the tax system than with the deficit question itself.

Finally, the recent widespread difficulties in the financial industry have focused attention on a third major issue: how to treat the federal government's huge portfolio of guarantees to various depositors and lenders throughout the economy. By 1989, those accumulated guarantees encumbered the government with roughly $5.7 trillion in potential liabilities.[3] The GNP that year was just over $5.1 trillion. The guarantees can become real drains on the public purse. The collapse of large portions of the savings and loan industry in the late 1980s was estimated to cost roughly $500 billion over the next three decades. Experts debate over how much of this expenditure should be treated merely as a vast transfer of savings.

THE GOVERNMENT'S BOTTOM LINE

These accounting, moral, and political issues involved in how to count capital spending, trust fund interest, or off-budget obligations are obviously complex. Our argument here has to do primarily with the general macroeconomic effects of a fiscal deficit. The most practical gauge of that impact is how much the government actually needs to borrow. It is the borrowing that determines the increased demand for credit, as well as the future interest burden. In that respect, it hardly matters whether the spending is on or off the formal budget.[4] In the long run, of course, it does matter greatly whether what is borrowed is spent for productive or unproductive purposes. But the same is also true of spending financed by taxation. A fiscal deficit merely means that the cost of some government expenditures is the cost of borrowing as opposed to the cost of taxation. Strictly speaking, the deficit issue turns on which course costs the economy more: borrowing or taxing. But logically and practically, that issue has to be considered within the context of the government's further option: It could forgo the expenditure altogether.

With all fiscal questions, the ultimate judgment should be whether the spending produces enough benefits to justify the cost. Many advocate deficit spending because they believe it the only way to ensure an adequate provision for public purposes. Neglecting health, education, transportation, urban development, the arts, the underclass, or America's defense and world geopolitical role may, they believe, cost the country and its economy much more than a bigger federal deficit. They may well be right. But they are not justified in pretending that running a fiscal deficit (or taxing) is itself cost-free. No matter how worthy and productive its purpose, a deficit still has to be financed. Our question here is how to determine the real cost of that financing.

FINANCING A FISCAL DEFICIT

A fiscal deficit can be financed in three ways: [5]

1. Domestic borrowing
2. Foreign borrowing
3. Creating money

The United States has followed all three methods in the postwar era. Chapter 6 discusses the actual mixtures used from one decade to the next. Here, we focus on how, in theory, each way can be expected to affect or cost the economy.

DOMESTIC BORROWING

Domestic borrowing's most obvious cost is the "crowding out" of private borrowers, most easily visualized in the hypothetical case of an economy that is closed to the rest of the world.[6] Such an economy has to rely on its own savings to finance its public and private needs for credit. Usually, the government, with its power to tax, can get first claim on the economy's savings, but higher government borrowing also means higher interest rates. It is those that can "crowd out" the private borrowers who cannot afford them. The extent of the inconvenience depends on the supply of savings. The lower the rate of domestic saving in relation to government and private needs, the higher the interest rate. Higher interest rates tend to lower profit margins for businesses and thereby discourage investment. Higher interest rates, by depreciating all assets, also discourage equity financing.[7] Ultimately, of course, the real cost of this crowding out depends on whether the public purposes it finances are more or less valuable to the society and its economy than the private borrowing that is displaced.

FOREIGN BORROWING

The United States has always been able to draw easily on the capital of the whole world. Borrowing abroad reduces crowding out at home, but has other costs. If prolonged, it creates a dependency with troubling consequences. The interest owed to foreigners takes a larger and larger share of national income. The possibility that foreigners might start repatriating a larger share of their earnings, thereby transferring wealth and potential employment abroad, becomes a greater and greater concern. Keeping foreign capital and earnings from leaving the country requires internationally competitive interest rates. In a serious recession, these higher interest rates may hobble monetary policy and thereby prolong the slump, or precipitate something worse.[8]

Interest rates high enough to encourage an inflow of foreign savings also encourage the national currency to appreciate.[9] A currency buoyed by inflows of foreign savings grows "overvalued." The "favorable" terms of trade that result benefit imports at the expense of domestically produced goods and services. Since goods are generally easier to import than services, an overvalued currency tends to distort the economy's investment balance toward the service sector.[10] In short, heavy foreign borrowing induces a variety of particular microeconomic effects that tend to discourage domestic production in favor of foreign production. Those effects point toward a decline in the borrowing country's external balance. Hence, when a fiscal deficit is accompanied by heavy foreign borrowing, it naturally engenders a "twin" current-account deficit with the rest of the world.[11]

The Twin Deficit

From a macroeconomic perspective, linking the fiscal and current-account deficits is a matter of simple logic. A national economy runs a current-account deficit because it "absorbs" more goods and services than it produces. Absorption is defined as consumption (government plus private) and investment. When national consumption and investment combined are greater than national production, the difference has to be made up from abroad. Hence, there is a current-account deficit.[12]

A second formal macroeconomic relationship exists between investment and savings. To avoid having to import from outside, the national economy must save from its income, i.e., forgo from the consumption of what it produces enough to equal its investment. If investment is greater than that saving, total absorption will rise beyond production and the difference will have to be imported. Foreign money will have to be borrowed (or reserves used) to pay for the imports. Thus, the economy that invests more than it saves (or, which is the same thing, absorbs more than it produces) should have a current-account deficit and a capital-account surplus. If, on the other hand, a national economy saves more than it invests, it will not absorb all that it produces. It will tend to export its unabsorbed production and thus run a current-account surplus. It should also tend to export its excess savings, and thus run a capital-account deficit.

This equation explains how Germany and Japan could run regular current-account surpluses, even when they had substantial fiscal deficits. Despite a heavy fiscal deficit, they still saved more than they invested at home. They thus had a surplus both of production and of capital to export. But in a country like the United States, which saves relatively little, a large fiscal deficit makes a twin fiscal and current-account deficit extremely probable. The macroeconomic logic of overabsorption—the excess of consumption and investment over production—reinforces the microeconomic effects of heavy foreign borrowing—the high interest and exchange rates that disadvantage domestic producers.

In summary, the United States has a twin deficit because it absorbs too much. If it absorbed less—and saved more—it could, like Germany in the 1980s, have substantial fiscal deficits without having to borrow from outside the national economy to finance them. And if it did not have to import foreign savings, because of its government's "dissaving," it would not have to import the corresponding foreign goods needed because of overabsorption.

There is, of course, a whole other approach to this equation. Americans, it may be said, prefer foreign products. They import them, and thus compel inflow of foreign capital to finance their purchases. That inflow raises the dollar and disadvantages domestic producers, at the same time as it permits, and indeed encourages, the federal government to expand its borrowing and the economy's own absorption.

This alternative explanation illustrates a larger point: Showing a necessary relationship in an equation does not establish which element is the cause and which is the effect. The choice is as often as not a matter of ideology and temperament. At the simplest level, it seems that the United States saves too little because it either consumes or invests too much. Since it invests less in proportion to its income than most other industrialized countries, consumption seems the culprit. But whether to blame private or government consumption is, as we shall see, a complex and contentious question. All these models, moreover, are based on the standard liberal assumption of a market flexible and unfettered enough to adjust prices promptly to changes in one element or another of the economy. Analysts with a mercantilist or even Keynesian disposition point out that such assumptions need, at best, very serious qualification. In the conditions of the Depression of the 1930s, for example, Keynes believed that an increase in saving over investment would most likely lead not to an increase in exports but to a fall in domestic output and income. Adjustment would take place neither by an improved current account nor by greater investment, but by a reduced national income and a greater propensity to consume relative to it. Happily, these quarrels needn't be resolved in order to make our general point: In our reasonably liberal system, financing fiscal deficits by foreign borrowing is not cost-free. In addition to the dangers of dependence, there is damage to domestic producers and a chronic tendency toward an external imbalance.

CREATING MONEY

Financing Deficits Through Inflation

A fiscal deficit is monetized—financed by inflation—to the extent that a nation's Treasury or its central bank meets the government's need to borrow by creating new money or credit. This credit inflation not only monetizes the government's new debt, but by depreciating the value of money, reduces the weight of old debts as well. Technically, depreciating the real value of the national debt by inflation improves the government's balance sheet and raises its ratio of income to debt. In certain fashionable economic circles, it is argued that monetization's effects are actually deflationary, and should be offset to prevent a recession—presumably by more monetization.[13] Carried to its logical conclusion, this learned prescription would quickly eliminate the burden of all deficits—past and present.

Remedies like these may seem highly unorthodox, but some elements of the diagnosis behind them are widely accepted. Throughout the postwar era, many economists have advocated stimulating a certain degree of inflation in order to achieve other economic benefits. Inflation can be counted as simply another form of taxation, unusually effective because so indirect. Like any other tax, inflation has particular costs and benefits. By reducing the value of debt, inflation is a tax on the capital of creditors. As a hidden tax, inflation takes resources from inactive savers and redistributes them to active spenders—the borrowing government, entrepreneur, or private consumer. The result may be fuller employment, with more investment and increasing productivity.

Indeed, it was widely accepted in early postwar years that every economy has a certain structural trade-off between more inflation and fuller employment—a "Phillips Curve" that if used properly can induce a higher rate of real growth than otherwise. Internationally, inflation can also be justified as taxing rich and slow-growing creditor countries to the benefit of poorer debtor countries, whose greater potential for growth is otherwise stymied by the high cost of borrowing capital. As is discussed in detail in Chapter 6, inflation can also be used among nations to share the cost of empire.

Inflation Through Tax Cuts

Few politicians openly advocate financing deficits through inflation. Instead, that course is packaged in the guise of a tax cut to stimulate growth—a formula that appeals politically to the Right as well as the Left. The rationale for creating deficits through tax cuts has developed within the intellectual universe set up by John Maynard Keynes's celebrated analysis of the Great Depression of the 1930s. For much of the postwar era, economic policy and discussion has been dominated by Keynes's diagnosis.[14] Keynes blamed the Depression, with its terrible unemployment, on a lack of demand. His cure was to reconstitute demand through government deficits. Deficits could obviously be created by either raising spending or cutting taxes. In the discouraged business conditions of the 1930s, Keynes preferred spending. Years of falling prices had dampened the "animal spirits" of entrepreneurs, and prolonged unemployment had led to widespread misery and despair among the poor. Keynes thought spending money would be more efficacious economically, as well as more desirable socially.

Postwar Keynesian fiscal analysis has evolved into two distinct positions. The first merely holds that no attempt should be made to balance the budget when the economy is in a recession. Under such circumstances, a government deficit helps offset the fall in demand, while raising taxes only makes the recession worse. In a boom, a compensating government surplus can restrain excessive demand that might otherwise turn inflationary. Equilibrium may be said to be maintained over the whole business cycle, rather than annually. By the beginning of the postwar era, this version of Keynesianism had won widespread acceptance in the United States.[15]

In the second position, some economies, because of structural faults, are thought unable to achieve full employment without a permanent budget deficit.[16] The fault may lie with inefficient labor or capital markets, an excess of capital in relation to investment opportunities, political barriers, technological stagnation, or social rigidity. Whatever the cause, the cure is a permanent government deficit. Keynes would probably never have accepted this remedy, but it has appealed to later generations of his followers.

This second Keynesian position was not widely accepted in American fiscal politics until the celebrated Kennedy-Johnson tax cut of 1964, when President John F. Kennedy's "neo-Keynesian" advisers popularized the idea of a "full-employment budget," and transformed it into a justification for tax cuts. Actual budgets, they argued, should anticipate what tax revenues would be if full employment were already achieved. Spending should be commensurate. Only on this basis, they argued, should budgets be considered "balanced." Otherwise, as the economy progresses toward full employment, growing tax revenues—raised disproportionately as higher earnings move taxpayers into higher brackets—push the government toward a surplus—a condition that depresses demand and halts the boom. Kennedy's economic advisers, impatient for more rapid growth to finance the administration's ambitious military and social programs, believed that just such a phantom surplus was already impeding growth.[17]

In effect, the full-employment budget mandates deficits at every stage of the business cycle except the actual moment of full employment. With Kennedy, American policy evolved from the first to the second version of Keynesian analysis. Logically enough, from Kennedy's time to the present, the United States has had only one year (1969) without a fiscal deficit.

Many of the Kennedy administration's neo-Keynesians would have preferred to create a deficit by raising expenditures rather than cutting taxes. But Keynes's rationale—that entrepreneurial energies were at a low ebb—was hardly as convincing in the 1960s as in the 1930s. Kennedy's Keynesians could console themselves that a more rapidly growing and inflating economy would at least give a disproportionate increase to federal revenues.

The 1964 tax cut seemed very successful in the short run. Output, employment, and government revenue rose and deficits at least remained stable. By 1965, however, rising price inflation was already visible. It was spurred thereafter first by the effects of financing the Vietnam War and Lyndon Johnson's Great Society, and later by the oil shocks. As inflation mounted, monetary policy revived to control it. Monetary squeezes contributed to increasingly serious recessions—in 1970, 1975, and again in 1982.[18]

The 1980s saw a flowering of the right-wing possibilities of repackaged Keynesianism, bottled this time as "supply-side economics," or simply "Reaganomics."[19] The tax cut of 1981 was justified by a "Laffer Curve" that purported to show how tax cuts, particularly for the upper brackets, would result in more saving and investment, spur economic growth, and thereby compensate with greater tax revenues. Inflation, meanwhile, was to be kept under control by tight monetary policy.[20]

It is monetary policy, of course, that determines whether tax cuts are financed by inflation or borrowing. If monetary policy does not expand to accommodate the deficit—in other words, if the fiscal deficit is not monetized—it will have to be financed by either our first or second methods—from domestic or foreign savings. In practice, arguments for growth through tax cuts have tended to evolve into arguments for growth through inflation. Faced with the consequences of tight money, advocates of tax cuts in both the Johnson and the Reagan administrations tended to opt for monetary ease.[21]

If the matter were left strictly to governments or economists, financing fiscal deficits through monetization would doubtless have been even more prevalent in postwar America than it has actually been. To choose between real spending cuts or higher tax rates is a dilemma that politicians naturally prefer to avoid. And few among them can be found defending high interest rates that crowd out private borrowers, or even heavy borrowing from foreigners. Economists who offer plausible formulas for growth are therefore guaranteed a sympathetic hearing. What finally lessens the allure of these inflationary formulas is experience with the consequences.

Inflation: Stimulation and Addiction

Inflationary policies set in train reactions that tend to defeat them. As the classic liberal economist, David Hume, noted in the early 1750s, inflation stimulates the economy through the effects of what is now called "money illusion." Hume's basic teaching was that the quantity of money in itself is altogether indifferent.[22] When the supply of money increases, prices of labor and commodities eventually adjust upward in compensation. The principal effect is to disadvantage exporting and encourage importing. But there is an interim effect that does stimulate the economy. A greater money supply increases demand before it raises prices. It is "this interval . . . between the acquisition of money and the rise of prices that . . . is favorable to industry."[23] For it is in this interval, or lag, that there exists a difference between the perceived and the real or long-term value of money.

The difference arises because when the supply of money increases, different producers of goods and services do not react together. Some do not grasp what has happened as rapidly as others. And still others may be in too weak a position to raise their prices. This lag means that some economic actors, asking for insufficiently adjusted prices and wages, take what amounts to a real cut. That naturally stimulates more

demand and production, and eventually more profit and investment—particularly if those who are the initial recipients of
this additional credit are themselves active purchasers or
investors. To this point, increasing the money supply seems a
great boon. Indeed, Hume went on to suggest that state policy
should try to keep the money supply growing, if possible, as a
spur to prosperity, particularly since a declining money supply
has a correspondingly depressing effect on the economy.

Experience suggests, however, that these early beneficial
effects of monetary growth can easily be replaced by the mis-
eries of addiction to inflation and the need for a painful and
uncertain cure. That is because Hume's beneficent interval begins to disappear. The expectations of producers eventually
catch up with increases in the money supply. Merchants push
up prices, workers demand higher wages, and the national
economy gets caught in an inflationary spiral. In an open world
economy, foreign purchasers of the currency also begin to lose
their money illusion. If the currency depreciates, the rising
price of imports adds to the domestic price-wage spiral.

Once the inflationary spiral starts, if the stimulative effect
of money illusion is to be sustained, the monetary dosage has
to be increased. The rate of credit inflation has to advance
more rapidly than price inflation, that is to say, than the imaginations of the average merchant, producer, and worker. People's imaginations grow with exercise and it is the natural
tendency of an inflation rate to accelerate. Everyone tries not
merely to catch up but to anticipate future inflation. Some em-
ployments are in a better position to keep advancing their claims
than others. The increasing resentment and militancy begins
to disturb the social equilibrium.[24]

These effects soon become self-defeating. Since creditors
are not totally inert mentally, they grow conscious, sooner or
later, that the real return on their lending is increasingly lower
than it appears. They mobilize to insist on higher interest rates.
If they cannot get higher rates at home, they begin to invest
abroad. Among other things, such a capital flight helps depreciate the currency. The consequent degeneration in the terms
of trade makes imports more expensive and increases the demand for exports. This helps the trade balance and revives
domestic manufacturing, but also raises domestic prices and

accelerates price inflation at home. Carried to its logical conclusion, the inflationary cycle continues until it results in run-
away "hyperinflation" and a collapse of the currency.[25]

Sooner or later the central bank is compelled to react. But
as the central bank tries to stop the too rapid growth of the
money supply, the frenzied momentum of rising expectations
clashes headlong with the reality of the suddenly slower monetary growth. Real interest rates skyrocket and many debtors
face ruin. The political pressure is often very hard for a democracy or any other government to bear. As a result, anti-
inflation policies are seldom carried out long enough to get
rid of the malady. Characteristically, long periods of monetary
inflation are interrupted by bursts of monetary stringency—as
governments try to prevent inflation from running wild, or
the currency from collapsing. In effect, these "stop-go" policies try to preserve a certain precarious balance between political pressure and economic control. With stop-go, inflation
evolves to "stagflation." Oscillations tend to grow more extreme, as booms grow more manic and recessions deeper.

Prolonged inflation begins to have significant and delete-
rious effects on the whole economic culture. With money con-
stantly depreciating, and prices of goods therefore rising, saving
money seems irrational. Borrowing to spend seems more reasonable. Persistent inflation, particularly when evolving into
stagflation, also discourages long-term investments in the real
economy. When prices of goods are perpetually unstable, with
real interest rates oscillating widely and unpredictably, long-
term investment is likely to seem unpromising. More money is
to be made from anticipating or manipulating short-term
monetary shifts than by illiquid commitments to manufacturing and trade. The speculator replaces the entrepreneur.[26]

Sooner or later, persistent inflation leads to violent reactions. Those who have been hurt begin to revolt. Creditors go
on strike and refuse to lend at what are often negative rates
of interest. Foreigners shun the currency and domestic holders flee to foreign currencies or gold. In summary, inflation,
taxing the relatively inert wealth of creditors to favor enterprising entrepreneurs and a free-spending government, sets
loose a chain of reactions leading to hyperinflation or stagflation. The process may take one or several decades, but, for

the classical economist, it has all the inevitability of a Greek tragedy. David Hume writes about the inflation of public debt: "Either the nation must destroy public credit or public credit will destroy the nation."[27]

Power and Money

Hume's view reflects the austere perspective of the old liberal tradition. "There are no free lunches in economics" encapsulates its mentality. If a government persists in manipulating its money to avoid reducing spending or raising taxes, economic collapse and decline are the natural results. Economics of this sort is not only an empirical science but also a natural religion. It presupposes a certain balanced moral order, a self-regulating equilibrium for the economy, as well as for human affairs in general. Liberal economists in the Anglo-Saxon tradition tend to believe, or hope, that such a natural order will establish itself spontaneously, if only markets are permitted to operate freely. Other liberal traditions, notably the French and German, are less confident about the benevolence of undisciplined market forces, and presuppose an enlightened and active public authority that creates and sustains the political, legal, and administrative order a free market needs.[28] But even if various strands of the classical tradition differ on how much the state must do to frame the market, they have more in common that is generally admitted. None approves of undisciplined private anarchy or of heavy-handed state control. They all place their faith in an underlying balanced moral order, inherent in the society and economy and best realized by individuals pursuing their self-interest within free markets. They therefore respect and defend values of economic efficiency and freedom.

Needless to say, other traditions also inform public policy. Alongside the teachings of Hume and Smith are those of Hobbes or Nietzsche. Another "scientific" view believes that the only natural order is one imposed by power and will. Within this worldview, the rules of liberal economics are always subject to the higher laws of Machiavellian politics. The state should not only frame, regulate, and shape the market; it may, when it chooses, manipulate and defy it.

This mentality inevitably attracts governments faced with

severe difficulties in matching their ambitions to their resources. Power beckons them, for example, to monetize their
deficits, and then to impose controls on wages, prices, trade,
and capital movements in order to deny the natural inflationary consequences. Hitler, pursuing his rapid rearmament but
refusing to curtail the civilian sector, noted that it was easy
enough to control inflation with concentration camps. So long
as the political power is available to dominate the domestic
economy, as, for example, it is to nearly every government in
wartime, there is an almost irresistible inclination to use
that power.[29]

Power can obviously also be used internationally—to force
dependent allies to put up capital, or to accept "voluntary
agreements" to limit their trading advantages. Paul Kennedy's
writings remind us that these "uneconomic" policies imposed
by power are often self-defeating. They sap the economy of
its vitality and ultimately result in the loss of power itself. But
as Keynes used to observe, in the long run we all are dead.
Nowadays, the time frame of political consciousness seems much
shorter than it used to be. The profligate Louis XIV reigned
long enough to endure personally the humiliations of a pe-
nurious old age. His successors were his own grandchildren,
and they could recall his extravagance with envy and regret.
Today's democratic governments have much shorter memo-
ries. Bad long-term policies with good short-term results do
well enough for a single administration. And even from Professor Kennedy's long historical perspective, great powers have
generally had a good long run before having to pay for flaunt-
ing their power.

By now, the United States has itself had quite a run as a
superpower. American power has increasingly manipulated and
defied the international marketplace. To succeed over a long
period, such a policy presumably requires a capacity to make
and enforce a long-range economic strategy—not normally
thought to be a strong point of the American political system.
Power has nevertheless eased the American fiscal predicament, but the costs have also been accumulating.

FISCAL DEFICITS IN THEORY

The rest of the book focuses on the history of those accumulating consequences. This chapter has tried to set a certain theoretical framework for that analysis and it may be well to summarize it before going on.

Every government budget has to confront three issues:

1. How large should the public sector be?
2. How should the public sector spend its money?
3. How should the public sector be financed?

Since this is a book about the deficit, most of the chapter has focused on the third issue, and within that issue the consequences of running a deficit rather than of raising taxes or cutting outlays. Three major alternatives for financing such a deficit are hypothetically available. Each has its own costs.

Borrowing from the country's domestic savings crowds out private investment.

Borrowing from foreign savings risks creating a dependency on foreign creditors and their priorities, requires comparatively high interest rates, and promotes a correspondingly high exchange rate. These discourage and distort domestic investment, hobble countercyclical policy in a recession, and reinforce what becomes a chronic tendency to overabsorption and external deficit.

Monetization is the third course and often seems the easiest politically. It leads to price inflation, but many economists have advocated using inflation as a tool for broader public purposes. As a form of taxation, inflation not only can provide the resources for a current government deficit, but can reduce the real value of all the deficits accumulated in the past. As a stimulus to the economy, inflation can take wealth away from relatively inert capital and labor and give it to entrepreneurial borrowers and all others in a relatively strong position to raise their incomes.

But these benefits, coming as they do from "money illusion," set in train a series of reactions that logically require an ever accelerating rate of inflation, if the benefits are to continue. The need to control that accelerating inflation makes periodic bouts of tight monetary policy endemic. Inflation thus generally evolves into stagflation. The oscillations tend to grow ever more extreme and are, in themselves, harmful to real economic growth. Rooting out inflation, however, is economically and politically painful. For many segments of society, the cure may easily seem worse than the disease.

Some countries, particularly a relatively autarchic "superpower" like the United States, may be able to exploit their international position to import savings or export inflation. In the past, however, using power to defy economics has often proved self-destructive over the long run.

The rest of the book looks at how these theoretical issues have played themselves out in postwar American fiscal history. The next three chapters examine how the United States has been spending and raising its money, and why, therefore, it has developed large fiscal deficits. The three chapters that follow discuss the consequences.

APPENDIX FOR CHAPTER 2: FURTHER THOUGHTS ON DEFINING A DEFICIT

COUNTING THE FISCAL DEFICIT: CAPITAL VERSUS CURRENT EXPENDITURES

Why shouldn't federal accounts, like those of private corporations or households, distinguish between current and capital spending?[30] Most private businesses, after all, would also be perpetually in deficit if they wrote off capital expenditures entirely in the same year as they made them.[31]

The point is neither as simple nor as significant as it seems. The financial parallel between public and private investments is questionable. Private investments yield an annual income over their lifetimes that is expected to exceed the interest rate plus the amortization of the capital. But many public investments, even if essential to the society and its economy, do not yield commensurate direct income to the state. An educated and disciplined work force is essential to any developed economy, but schools and universities generally have to be subsidized heavily. Spending for national defense yields very little income at all. Public investments in libraries, theaters, symphony orchestras, ballet companies, or the opera are similar. Yielding

little direct income does not necessarily make them less valuable to the society, or its economy. But should their capital
costs be spread out on the grounds that they are yielding a
profitable return?

Presumably, their costs should at least be amortized over
their lifetimes. But this would cut the annual deficit very little,
if at all. Not counting a capital investment all in one year logically means counting its depreciation over several years. Annual charges would thus reflect past capital spending. Our
federal government, however, has probably been running down
investments in the civilian sector at least since the 1980s. Am-
ortizing capital expenses might well increase annual deficit
figures.[32]

OFF-BUDGET SPENDING: THE TRUST FUNDS

How to count the huge portion of federal spending that
is already "off-budget" seems a more urgent issue than capital
budgeting. Social security taxes and payments, for example,
have traditionally been off-budget—in a "trust fund" to ensure that the system remains secure and self-financing. In 1983,
the payroll taxes that fund the system increased significantly.
Demographic trends indicated a heavy increase in future pay-
outs. With the higher taxes, the system began accumulating a
sizable surplus, which was stored in its trust fund and earned
substantial interest. The assets in the trust fund, of course,
were federal obligations and the Treasury paid the interest.
Since the federal government was heavily in deficit, the social
security surplus was, in effect, financing other federal outlays.

The government was simply borrowing the social security
surplus to cover its other spending and was even counting the
self-paid interest as part of its own regular income. In addition to social security, there are several other off-budget trust
funds, like Medicare, highway trust funds, or pension plans
for government employees. By 1989, the self-paid interest from
these funds reached over $61 billion, while the "assets" were
over $676 billion.[33] The future capacity of these funds to meet
their contractual obligations depends on the federal government's future income, which would be the case whether these
imaginary off-budget trust funds existed or not.

Leaving aside the issue of the regressive character of many

of these dedicated taxes, whether there is any great harm in the financial charade of the trust funds depends on their future needs.[34] Social security depends on demographic trends. If the trends are in balance, the taxes of future workers can reasonably be expected to cover the pensions of those working now. The trust fund surplus will never be needed. But since the future will see fewer and fewer workers supporting more and more pensioners, the system is facing a crisis that the trust funds cannot resolve. The money supposedly in the trust funds will not be there. It will have to come from current revenue. In other words, the future young may have to devote more and more of their labor to support the future old, not a promising situation politically or socially.[35] Since social security's phantom assets will already have been spent on other government programs that the older generation endorsed and enjoyed but for which they refused to pay adequate taxes while they were working, even the moral claim to the younger generation's income will be shaky.

The problem is not simply fiscal legerdemain. How, in fact, can a whole generation "save" effectively for its old age in such a demographic situation? Where can the savings be invested to be available to spend later?[36]

The best solution lies in building the nation's productivity at home. If an economy is sufficiently productive a generation hence, taking care of its more numerous old will not impoverish its less numerous young. If, therefore, a generation wants to contribute effectively to its own retirement income, it should put its savings into investments that will add to future productivity. Logically, the money accumulated in the social security trust funds should be invested in enhancing America's capital assets, including its educational system. But given the federal government's general low rate of investment in civilian infrastructure, investing the social security surplus in the fiscal deficit does not seem a very effective way to enhance productivity.[37]

OFF-BUDGET SPENDING: SPECIAL EXPENDITURES

The federal budget has another whole category of off-budget items. These are those special costs that could not have been anticipated and are therefore funded by borrowing and not counted as part of the fiscal deficit.

The savings and loan crisis that exploded in the late 1980s illustrated all too well the issues involved in such practices. By 1990, estimates for the cost of meeting federal obligations to S and L investors commonly ran from $200 billion over a decade to $500 billion over four decades.[38]

The S and L mess focused attention on the large number of other federal guarantees. By 1989, all its accumulated guarantees encumbered the government with an estimated $5.7 *trillion* in potential liabilities. The GNP for 1989 was just over $5.1 trillion. In many cases, the guarantees are given because the risks of default are sufficient to require otherwise a notably higher interest rate, or to deny credit entirely. In effect, the government lowers particular interest rates for worthy purposes by assuming risk. As the S and L crisis illustrated, such risks can be more than merely potential. When they grow real, government can realistically only cover the defaults by borrowing on a grand scale.

The propriety of placing such payments and borrowings off-budget depends partly on whether the putative emergency is really a random act of God as opposed to something that should have been anticipated—an earthquake as opposed to fixing the roof. And it also depends on whether the sums borrowed to cover defaults should be treated as an expenditure or merely as a transfer, via the government, of funds from one group of savers to another.[39]

Chapter 3 *Federal Spending Since 1950*

*F*or obvious reasons, patterns of government spending and taxation reflect all sorts of vested interests and expectations and are not easy to change quickly—even when a budget is seriously out of balance. The next three chapters examine the evolution of American patterns since 1950. This chapter focuses on federal spending.

In the four decades from 1950 through 1990, the federal government spent a total of $15.3 trillion.[1] In nominal terms, roughly half the spending took place in the 1980s alone. Inflation, of course, greatly exaggerates figures for recent years. Inflation's hyperbole notwithstanding, real federal outlays have increased sharply from one decade to the next. In inflation-adjusted, or *constant,* dollars, the total spent in the 1960s was 35 percent higher than in the 1950s. The total in the 1970s was 36 percent higher than in the 1960s, and in the 1980s was 41 percent more than in the 1970s. Even discounting inflation, roughly 40 percent of all federal spending from 1950 to 1990 occurred from 1980 to 1990.[2]

While government spending has increased sharply, so has the nation's income. From 1950 to 1990, the American gross national product increased by 268 percent in constant dollars.[3] But real federal spending increased 328 percent. In 1950, the government share of national spending was 16 percent. By 1990, it was 23 percent.

Throughout that forty-year period, revenues have generally lagged behind outlays.[4] As a result, the federal debt increased from $257 billion in 1950 to $3.2 trillion in 1990, in constant dollars an increase of 84 percent.[5] As the debt has grown, so have the costs of servicing it.[6] By 1990, net interest payments alone, in constant dollars, were equal to rather more than half the entire budget in 1951.

Where has the money gone over the years?

SPENDING TRENDS

Federal expenditures divide up into five general categories or "superfunctions":

- Defense
- Human resources
- Physical resources
- Net interest
- Other functions

As the tables below indicate, defense, human resources, and net interest together generally comprise around 90 percent of the federal budget.

Since the early 1950s, the relative share of some functions has shifted very substantially. Human resources, for example,

TABLE 3.1

**Federal Expenditures on Superfunctions
(In Current Billions)**

	1950	1960	1970	1980	1990
Defense	13.7	48.1	81.7	134.0	299.3
Human Resources	14.2	26.2	75.3	313.4	619.3
Physical Resources	3.7	8.0	15.6	66.0	124.6
Net Interest	4.8	6.9	14.4	52.5	184.2
Other Functions	8.0	7.8	17.3	45.0	60.9

Source: *Budget of the U.S. Government, Fiscal Year 1992* (Washington, D.C.: U.S. Government Printing Office, 1991), Table 3.1, Part Seven: 31–36.

has grown from a quarter to a half of all outlays, while defense has shrunk correspondingly, from more than half to around a quarter.

What do figures like these actually tell us? Do bigger outlays mean more purchasing power? Does changing budget share indicate shifting federal priorities? Such questions are more elusive and contentious than they might seem.

There are at least four different ways of measuring federal expenditures:

in *current* dollars
in *constant* dollars
as a percentage of total federal outlays
as a percentage of gross national product (GNP) or gross
    domestic product (GDP)[7]

Confusing the significance of these quite different measurements causes a great deal of fruitless controversy.

CURRENT VERSUS CONSTANT DOLLARS

For obvious reasons, annual budgets use current dollars. But, inflation means that current dollars are not equivalent to earlier dollars. Since 1950, prices have inflated by 450 percent. This means that a newly printed dollar locked in a drawer in 1950 was worth, by 1990, only eighteen cents of its initial value. Since 1970, the same dollar would have lost 70 percent of its

TABLE 3.2

**Federal Expenditures on Superfunctions
(As Percent of Total Outlays)**

	1950	1960	1970	1980	1990
Defense	32.2	52.2	41.8	22.7	23.9
Human Resources	33.4	28.4	38.5	53.0	49.5
Physical Resources	8.6	8.7	8.0	11.2	10.0
Net Interest	11.3	7.5	7.3	8.9	14.7
Other Functions	18.7	8.4	8.8	7.6	4.9

Source: *Budget of the U.S. Government, Fiscal Year 1992* (Washington, D.C.: U.S. Government Printing Office, 1991), Table 3.1, Part Seven: 31–36.

TABLE 3.3

Federal Spending, Percentage Increase, 1950–1990

	CURRENT	REAL[8]
Human Resources	4255%	542%
Physical Resources	3297%	400%
Net Interest	3728%	464% (126% in 1980s alone)
Defense	2081%	221% (highest in 1953)[9]
Other Functions	665%	13% (107% since 1952)

Source: *Budget of the U.S. Government, Fiscal Year 1992* (Washington, D.C.: U.S. Government Printing Office, 1991), Table 1.3, and Table 3.1, Part Seven: 17, 31–36.

value.[10] To discount inflation from one year to another, economists use a *GNP deflator,* calculated from a sampling of prices for products and services. The calculation rests on the assumption that the products or services remain equivalent and that only their prices change. In fact, the assumption is shaky, since products are always changing. Television sets or cars may have cost more in 1980 than in 1950 but were vastly improved in quality. How much of their price increase was inflation? Measuring inflation in services or labor poses a similar problem. Costs may be higher but the quality of the service or the productivity of the labor may also be higher. How much do higher wages, in such circumstances, reflect inflation and how much a better endowed and more productive work force?[11]

Trying to compare the relative outlays for different budget categories raises a further complication. Prices for goods and services inflate at different rates in different sectors of the

TABLE 3.4

Percent of Federal Budget, 1950–1990

Human Resources	33.4% to 49.5%
Physical Resources	8.6% to 10.0%
Net Interest	11.3% to 14.7%
Defense[12]	32.2% to 23.9%
Other Functions	18.7% to 4.9%

Source: *Budget of the U.S. Government, Fiscal Year 1992* (Washington, D.C.: U.S. Government Printing Office, 1991), Table 1.3, and Table 3.1, Part Seven: 17, 31–36.

economy. And since each budget function purchases a different mix of goods and services, adjusting outlays for the overall
inflation rate gives only a rough view of the changes in real
purchasing power within each function. This complication is
particularly relevant to functions that purchase highly distinctive products and services. Defense is a good illustration.

MEASURING BY BUDGET OR GNP SHARES

Budget shares reveal a government's priorities, but only
at its current level of income.[13] When a government has more
(or less) to spend, nothing in logic requires it to go on giving
each budgetary function the same share. If a government de-
cides that spending $200 billion on the military is essential to
national security, it may well give that requirement its highest
priority and, if necessary, be prepared to restrict other functions severely. Under such circumstances, defense could represent half or more of federal spending, as was true during
most of the 1950s. But if real government revenues go up
significantly, and the needs of defense have been met with $200
billion, spending the extra billions on environmental protection, urban amenities, or aid to the indigent may seem to yield
more general benefit than adding these revenues to defense.
By the same logic, if the government were suddenly to grow
much poorer, defense's priority over other functions should
logically reassert itself in the form of a higher share of the
reduced budget.

What is true for defense is broadly true for all other budget functions. Any claim for more public resources should logically depend not on a presumed entitlement to some fixed
share of the nation's budget, but on such questions as how
adequately the function is being fulfilled already, how much
its costs are increasing, or how much general welfare will be
added and how much sacrificed by increasing outlays for one
function as opposed to another. The same analysis obviously
applies when a budget function is measured by its share of
GNP. Here its claims to provide for the general welfare compete not only with those of other budget functions but also
with those of the private sector.

THE POLITICAL MARKETPLACE

Reckoning optimal budget shares in terms of some idea of the general welfare is not unlike the decisions that a private consumer faces with a personal budget. Advertising stimulates his various needs and appetites, and purchases register his priorities. In a democracy, public choices are made in what is, in effect, a political marketplace. Interest groups of all sorts hawk their particular versions of the public good in order to arouse and mobilize the preferences of the body politic. Political choice can be viewed as the process by which the strongest, best-mobilized passions prevail.

This is a somewhat impoverished view of politics, however, because it ignores the moral dimension to public choices. Even private market choices are meant to embody more than random impulse. Sensible buyers are supposed to reflect and calculate before they act. Their deliberations are conditioned, consciously or not, by an inner ranking of values. Those inner preferences may not correspond objectively to the individual's real welfare, but it is desirable that they should. Similarly, public spending reflects not only the mechanical balance reached among competing interest groups but also prevailing notions about the public interest. In principle, democratic politics is not meant to be merely a struggle of special interests, in which the general interest is served only by accident. Prevailing notions about the objective public interest may be wrong, but some reasonable correspondence is highly desirable. A fit seems more likely when the public choice is informed by objective information, reasoned reflection, and free discussion.

Inevitably, habit plays a large part in both private and public decision. Nobody can consciously reformulate his whole strategy of life every time he faces a practical choice about what to buy. The same is obviously true about the body politic's conceptions of the general interest. With a crowded agenda of choices, what has been done before often seems the natural guide for what to do now. Thus, in the ongoing struggle of interests within the political marketplace, previous budget share easily seems a legitimate standard of adequacy, particularly for programs whose structures take time to build and whose aims and commitments cannot be fulfilled within an annual budget cycle. Nevertheless, past budget or GNP share cannot be a definitive standard for determining how adequately public functions are being fulfilled. No function, however vital, is entitled to a fixed share of the public purse, or of the nation's wealth.

GENUINE CRITERIA

What are the appropriate criteria for comparing and assessing spending trends among budget functions? They may be reduced to three:

Cost trends
Changes in efficiency
Changes in need

The criterion of cost refers to whether the prices of the goods and services in one particular budgetary function have increased more or less rapidly than prices in the economy as a whole. In other words, to what extent are dollars adjusted for general inflation an appropriate standard for comparing budgetary outlays from one period to another? For some functions, unemployment benefits for example, they are obviously appropriate. For others, like health or defense, they are less so because the prices in these functions have risen much more rapidly than most other prices.

The criterion of efficiency requires assessing how appropriately government is spending its resources in order to meet the needs of a particular budgetary function. Inefficient bureaucracy or legislation may cause too much of the purchasing power of outlays to be wasted, or an inappropriate military strategy may cause huge sums to go to the wrong weapons. The cure is not larger outlays, but changes in strategy and organization. Significant changes in the level of efficiency imply corresponding changes in the level of outlays.

Finally, the criterion of need requires determining whether changing objective conditions in the nation or the world should require a greater or lesser real outlay for a particular function. A world moving toward war, for example, greatly reinforces the need for military spending. And demographic change greatly affects the need for spending on human resources.

With these three criteria in mind, how should we assess the shifting patterns of federal outlays for the superfunctions?

DEFENSE

In many respects, defense has always been the most controversial and volatile part of the postwar federal budget. To survive in wartime, a nation may spend all its present resources and mortgage its future. But for a successful longer-term strategy, military outlays have to be reconciled with a healthy civil economy. Without its military white corpuscles, the body politic will be defenseless before outside enemies. But if the military white corpuscles begin devouring the red corpuscles of the civil economy, the body politic will sicken and wither. Over the years, the United States has had great trouble in reaching a consensus on the right balance. As a result, defense outlays have been highly volatile.

The defense budget has four major components:[14]

Procurement
Military personnel
Operation and maintenance (O and M)
Research, development, testing, and evaluation (R and D)

Over time, the spending ratios among the four have shifted markedly. Procurement was the major component between 1953 and 1964, between 1968 and 1969, and again in the mid-1980s. The rest of the time, either personnel or O and M was larger.[15]

Assessing cost trends or changes in efficiency and need among these four components of the defense budget poses numerous interlocking difficulties. Costs for weapons procurement usually rise more rapidly than general prices, for reasons that bear closely on efficiency. Defense prices are not subject to the same market forces that help keep down prices in other sectors. The Pentagon often prefers to design its own weapons rather than to buy existing products. In any event, there are very few domestic or foreign producers of bombers or aircraft carriers. The capital investments needed for new weapons systems are often colossal and getting the systems designed and produced requires collaborating with and subsidizing the suppliers. If a major American weapons builder fails, the Pentagon loses something of its capacity to develop and acquire advanced weapons in the future. "Cost-plus" contracts are the norm and competition from foreign producers is highly restricted. Neither condition encourages private contractors to economize. Some countries, France for example, try to regulate costs by having the state own or control directly a large part of the defense industry.[16] The American economic culture would not easily accept this degree of tutelage and the American bureaucracy probably lacks the requisite technical and managerial skills, let alone the political prestige. Instead, the Pentagon tries to hold down costs through a complex array of legalistic pricing and reporting regulations, along with ostensibly competitive and open bidding procedures.

Trying to combine legalistic oversight with collaborative support often doesn't work very well. The additional layers of bureaucracy add to costs and discourage coherent policies or strong and responsible direction. Alongside the Pentagon's excessive but inefficient supervision, Congress, with its own expert staffs, also tries to control procurement. Since military contractors must be vigorous lobbyists, and are often major regional employers and political contributors, questionable practices are endemic. Civilian Pentagon officials and the military themselves are often placed in positions that are inherently compromising. With military careers that permit relatively early retirement, many move on to lucrative posts as employees of their old suppliers. With this sort of structure for controlling procurement, it is not altogether surprising that costs in defense spending rise more rapidly than throughout the economy as a whole, where foreign as well as domestic competition weighs more heavily.

Successive administrations have launched major campaigns to reform the Pentagon's procurement procedures and streamline its management. Matters might well be much worse otherwise. But any basic improvement in management efficiency seems unlikely without more fundamental reforms, including altering the role of Congress in appropriations and surveillance. As it is, the Pentagon's inefficiency reflects the nature of America's great sprawling federal democracy. Trying to separate the system's managerial shortcomings from its political virtues becomes a tricky business.

Military cost and efficiency are determined not by management alone, but also by strategy. As the world's strongest technological power, the United States has tended to see its military advantage in sophisticated weaponry rather than abundant manpower. The United States has set the technological pace that the Soviet Union and other major states have felt constrained to follow. The result has been a constant stream of new and more complex weapons that cost much more. The trend may well continue. Even if the bipolar arms race should abate in the 1990s, the increasingly powerful military establishments in the third world will probably mean that the United States should continue to look for comparative advantage from advanced weaponry rather than manpower. The experience of the Gulf war in 1991 is likely to reinforce that tendency.

A strategic preference for advanced weapons obviously determines the shape of the military budget and its costs and benefits to the rest of the economy. It favors, for example, heavy spending on research and development. Thanks to its strategic preferences, the United States has regularly devoted somewhat more to basic scientific and technological research, relative to GNP, and much more absolutely, than any other major country.[17] A large and well-trained scientific establishment is the result and some of its research undoubtedly benefits the civilian economy. But orienting so large a part of scientific and engineering talent to military rather than commercial products may also be a heavy indirect cost. So, perhaps, is entrammeling a good part of American management in the rather special business culture that grows up around the Pentagon.[18]

The preference for weapons over manpower also affects personnel costs, the predominant defense outlay. In 1974, the United States abandoned conscription and opted for an all-volunteer armed forces hired at market rates. While the public's disenchantment with the Vietnam War might well have forced an end to the draft in any event, the military argued that a volunteer force is anyway more cost-effective. Long-term enlistments seemed preferable since complex weapons require elaborate training. Thereafter, the numbers of military manpower dropped sharply, while overall personnel costs declined moderately.

Such radical changes in cost per soldier make it hard to compare the purchasing power of military dollars in a year with a predominantly draft army as opposed to a year with an entirely professional army. It is also difficult to compare military spending and efficiency in America, with its volunteer army, with military spending in countries like Germany, with large conscript armies.

Measuring military manpower costs is complex in any event. Many costs of a draft army are indirect. There may also be indirect benefits. Military training may improve the socialization and skill of the young work force, and thus its future productivity. It may also provide employment and training to young workers who might otherwise be unemployed.

Shifts among the military budget's four components interact with changes in geopolitical strategy. Rapidly rising manpower and weapons costs undermine commitments to regions, like Western Europe, that require large standing forces. Thus, whether a professional army is more cost-efficient is also a geopolitical question. In other words, military efficiency cannot be determined in a geopolitical vacuum.

DEFINING AMERICAN SECURITY: THE GEOPOLITICAL DIMENSION

Throughout the more than four decades of the cold war, the Soviet Union seemed the greatest threat to the United States. America's security policy has been "containment" of that threat. The resulting military strategy has had two interdependent elements—strategic nuclear deterrence and a Eurasian balance of power. Each element has been deeply embedded in the budget for defense. The nuclear deterrent has consumed roughly one tenth to one quarter of military outlays.[19] Eurasian commitments consumed a good part of the rest.[20]

The Eurasian commitments have been principally to Western Europe, Japan, and South Korea. Of these, NATO has been incontestably the most expensive. Costs attributed to NATO regularly constituted from 40 percent to 60 percent of the defense budget. But the commitments to Japan and South Korea have also absorbed substantial ground forces and very large air and especially naval forces.[21]

These Eurasian commitments secured for the United States a hegemonic military relationship with Western Europe and

Japan, the noncommunist world's two other great centers of industrial and financial power. The military relationship, in turn, helped sustain close political and economic interdependence. This trilateral entente contained the Soviet Union on its own home ground in Eurasia, while providing an overwhelming predominance for the United States and its allies in the world at large. A global Pax Americana has been the result.

America's geopolitical commitments behind this trilateral entente have remained remarkably stable since the early 1950s. But the actual military costs and forces have oscillated sharply. Since 1950, there have been three major cycles of military spending. From the top to the bottom of such cycles, real budgetary outlays have sometimes changed by over 60 percent.[22]

The case for less hectic budgeting in defense is self-evident. Since weapons systems take many years to develop and put into production, feast-or-famine budgeting involves great waste. Spending nevertheless oscillates because successive administrations and Congresses cannot reach a stable consensus on what is adequate.

Throughout the cold war, budgetary cycles reflected volatile assessments of Soviet capabilities and intentions. Shortly after World War II, with civil claims reasserting themselves vigorously, the emerging Soviet threat sparked an intense debate over the need for a massive rearmament. The famous National Security Council paper *NSC-68* became the rearmers' manifesto.[23] It saw the United States locked in an implacable global competition with the Soviet Union and its Red Chinese ally. War might be avoided, it argued, if the United States committed adequate military forces to contain the Soviets. Nuclear armaments would not be enough; a major conventional rearmament was required. President Truman was initially skeptical about finding the resources, but *NSC-68* offered a solution, drafted by the neo-Keynesian economist, Leon Keyserling. Since the United States had a large potential for growth, high government spending would expand the economy and augment government revenue. North Korea's attack in June 1950 overcame presidential and congressional hesitations. America rearmed and both solidified and expanded its external commitments. NATO took a form that put the United States firmly in charge of Europe's territorial defense and an American military protectorate was formalized for Japan.[24]

As *NSC-68* had predicted, rearmament did provoke an economic upturn. But as Truman had feared, it also meant higher tax rates,[25] and required wage and price controls to suppress inflation. When Eisenhower became President in 1953, he was determined to end wartime taxes and controls. But he was also unwilling to relinquish *NSC-68*'s basic European and Asian commitments.[26] His solution was a strategy that emphasized nuclear retaliation, much cheaper than balancing Soviet conventional forces directly. The new strategy took comparative advantage from America's great qualitative lead in nuclear forces and virtual invulnerability to nuclear attack.

As strategic conditions changed after *Sputnik,* old and new partisans of *NSC-68* rallied the country to rearm against the "missile gap." Since Eisenhower's time, the nation has gone through two additional cycles of rearmament and relative disarmament.[27] By 1990, the disarray of the Soviet Union at home and the gradual withdrawal of its Eastern European forces were undermining the rationale for sustaining the Eurasian protectorates. A "peace dividend" for the budget was widely anticipated. While unsettled Soviet political conditions prompted caution, major reductions in United States forces were being planned and announced.[28]

Iraq's invasion of Kuwait in 1990 indicated, however, that a nonbipolar world had its own threats. The American response suggested a new round of commitments, indeed a geopolitical self-definition as the world's peacekeeper that was, if anything, even more ambitious militarily than containing the Soviets. At the same time, the spectacle of the secretaries of state, defense, and the treasury traveling around the world to collect funds for the Persian Gulf expedition suggested growing financial limits to America's military power.[29]

The clash between geopolitical ambition and fiscal pressure pointed American politics toward a major reconsideration of the nation's world role and military budget. As federal resources grew more straitened, the civilian claims more urgent, the assessment of America's military needs was being pushed to a crisis not seen since the time of *NSC-68*. But it remains to be seen whether a durable peace dividend will emerge or whether the United States is merely going through another cycle. Much will depend not only on what happens in the world, but also on whether foreign policy, military strategy, and defense spending are working together or at cross-purposes.

ASSESSING THE CIVIL BUDGET

HUMAN RESOURCES

Civil spending falls into two major superfunctions: human resources and physical resources. Human resources has grown tremendously. Physical resources, until recently, has grown relatively little.[30]

Human resources is a grab bag of programs with six subdivisions:

Education, training, employment, and social services
Health
Medicare
Income security
Social security
Veterans benefits

Of these six, social security absorbs roughly 40 percent.

In the 1980s, partisans of increased spending for defense could note how real military outlays had remained stagnant since 1955 while real spending for human resources had increased more than five times. Measured in constant dollars, spending on human resources has risen steadily almost every year since 1954.[31] By the early 1970s, it was absorbing half or more of the federal budget. By 1980, the share was nearly 55 percent but was back to roughly 50 percent in 1989. Despite the lower budget share, real outlays were 22 percent higher at the end of the decade than at the beginning.[32] Important shifts occurred among the component functions. Health and especially Medicare grew rapidly; social security payments held a stable budget share; income security and veterans benefits declined relatively; and education actually suffered a sharp drop in real spending.[33]

How do the criteria of cost, efficiency, and need apply to human resources? Costs presumably follow the economy's general inflation rate more closely than military prices. Broadly speaking, increases beyond the general inflation rate represent real gains. But health and Medicare prices are a major exception and have, in turn, an inordinate effect on the budgets and real incomes of aged or infirm social security recipients. Inefficient government structures and policies are a major cause of these high costs of medical care, where the market suffers from several of the imperfections familiar to the military sector, a topic taken up in the next chapter.

Still more important are the changes in the society's need for welfare. The Soviet geopolitical threat has been the benchmark for military needs; shifting demographic patterns are the equivalent index for human resources. The demographic changes have been dramatic. From 1950 to 1990, overall population jumped from 152 million to 251 million—an increase of nearly 66 percent. Thus, the fivefold increase in real outlays was only threefold, per capita.[34] Changes in the population's age distribution obviously also affect the need for human resources, most directly for social security, which regularly absorbs roughly 40 percent of the outlays.

Social Security

From 1950 to 1989, the age group of sixty-five years and older climbed from 12.4 million to 31.0 million, a rate of increase 134 percent greater than for the overall population. During that period, total real outlays for social security jumped almost forty-five times, but for every person sixty-five or older, they increased just over seventeen times.[35] While the 1950s did see dramatic real increases in individual benefits, after 1960, the ratio between demographic change and outlays grew much closer. For every person sixty-five or older, average outlays in 1982 dollars were $2,569 in 1960 and $5,967 in 1989—only 2.3 times greater.[36] Since real GNP per capita approximately doubled over the 1960–89 period, increases in income to beneficiaries of social security was only slightly ahead of the general increase in national wealth. Logic, of course, does not require that the income of the aged has to rise in tandem with that of the population as a whole. But the case for giving the aged a constant per capita share of growing real national income probably strikes most of the electorate as more reasonable than a comparable claim for the defense budget. In any event, that is what has happened since 1960. Social security's increased share of GNP can be explained almost entirely by demographic need.

To say that social security pensions have kept their per capita share of national income since 1960 is not to say, of course, that the level was adequate—either in 1960 or in 1990. By comparison with wealthy Western European states, income for social security pensioners in the United States has stabilized at a comparatively low level. This is not necessarily because Americans have lower pensions, but because a much larger share of America's middle- and upper-class pensions are administered in the private rather than the public sector. Whether America's is the most efficient or equitable arrangement is obviously a complex and uncertain issue. What is not contestable is that benefits from social security are much lower in the United States than in European countries.[37]

Medical Care

Health and Medicare expenditures have mushroomed over the past two decades. By 1990, they absorbed roughly 25 percent of the budget for human resources. The rise in federal spending parallels a very large increase in private and public budgets alike. Like military spending, medical spending greatly reflects changing technology and rapidly rising costs.[38] It also reflects an exceptionally inefficient national policy—topics explored further in the next two chapters. But medical spending also reflects the country's shifting demography. There are more older people; the proportion of the very old is growing among them; the care required is more extensive and, for this reason alone, more costly. Medicare reimbursements, in constant 1982 dollars, were $22.7 billion in 1975 and $74.5 billion in 1990, a rise of 228 percent.[39] The number of people served nearly doubled; the ratio of those served to those enrolled increased by nearly one half; average real outlays per patient served grew by a half.

Education

Demographic change obviously affects the need for education outlays.[40] America's school-age population (five to fifteen) peaked in 1969, had dropped nearly 16 percent by 1983, and stabilized thereafter. Real federal outlays for the education, training, employment, and social services function of human resources grew by 76 percent during the 1970s but fell by 20 percent during the 1980s. The federal role in financing education is, however, minor compared to that of the state and local governments. In 1980, the federal contribution to education stood at 0.33 percent of the GDP, while state and local shares were 3.29 percent. By 1985, the respective figures were 0.25 percent and 3.57 percent. In other words, the federal share fell sharply.[41]

In themselves, figures for government spending tell us little about the cost or adequacy of American education, since the private sector in America carries a large part of the expense. Thus, international comparisons rank United States public spending on education, relative to GDP, fourteenth among the sixteen leading industrial countries.[42] The same study, however, ranks overall United States spending—public and private in proportion to enrollment—near the top. The study also shows a remarkable lopsidedness in American allocations. Overall spending on kindergarten through twelfth grade ranks at the bottom, whereas spending on higher education ranks near the top. So eccentric a distribution complicates any assessment of adequacy, and raises fundamental questions about the efficiency of the national system as a whole.

Human Resources in Perspective

Comparisons of real outlays, budget shares, or GNP shares are bound to be misleading, unless demographic changes are also taken into account. When adjusted for demographic changes, real outlays for human resources still show substantial postwar increases in most functions. When also adjusted for the growth in GNP, however, increases for social security are very modest since 1960. Escalating health care costs are another matter. Demography, technology, and systemic inefficiency all seem to play a major part in escalating both public and private sector burdens. Quite apart from these issues in reckoning the size and adequacy of outlays, serious questions arise about the efficiency of American arrangements for providing social goods. Education's eccentric distribution of resources seems noteworthy in this respect. So, obviously, do health care's rapidly rising costs, which, as Chapters 4 and 5 will observe, have had major macroeconomic effects.

PHYSICAL RESOURCES

Physical resources breaks down into five functions:

Energy
Natural resources and environment
Commerce and housing credit
Community and regional development
Transportation

Over the years, these together have rarely absorbed as much as 10 percent of federal spending. Real outlays have fluctuated widely but remained very roughly equal to the growth of federal spending as a whole. Outlays have thus been two times the growth of the GNP as opposed to five times for human resources.[43] Needs presumably reflect the physical infrastructure required for a larger and less rural population, rapidly expanding technology, greater concern for the environment or greater cumulative damage to it. The federal role is complicated, as always, by America's complex division of public labor and shifting boundaries between public and private sectors.

"OTHER FUNCTIONS"

This superfunction comprises both the federal government's housekeeping and some of its major discretionary enthusiasms. Its functions are:

General government
Administration of justice
International affairs
Agriculture
Science, space, and technology

In 1950, outlays, vastly swollen by the Marshall Plan, were almost 19 percent of the federal budget, but had fallen to less than 5 percent by 1990.[44] Despite its small share, several of its categories—like agriculture or international affairs—remain deeply fixed in the public mind as major sources of public overspending.

NET INTEREST

The rapid growth of the last superfunction, net interest, is the most direct evidence of the fiscal crisis. From 1952 until the mid-1970s, net interest absorbed around 7 percent of federal outlays and 1.5 percent of GNP. By 1980, the figures were close to 9 percent and 2 percent, respectively. By 1990, net interest was close to 15 percent of outlays and 3.5 percent of GNP. Real outlays grew 40 percent in the second half of the 1970s and more than 100 percent in the 1980s. The net interest bill for 1990 was over 60 percent of the outlays for defense and nearly three quarters of those for social security. In other words, by the 1990s the American fiscal deficit had begun to acquire a self-generating character. Escalating interest payments were themselves a major factor in causing and perpetuating the annual deficits. Hence the gathering fiscal crisis of the 1990s.

FISCAL SPENDING AND FISCAL DEFICITS

Broadly speaking, what can the spending patterns that emerge from the past four decades tell about the deficits of the 1990s? The patterns seem clear enough. From 1950 through 1990, real federal spending grew 333 percent, whereas the nation's real income merely doubled.[45] Among the superfunctions, real spending went up 542 percent for human resources and 400 percent for physical resources. Real outlays for net interest increased 464 percent, and 126 percent during the 1980s alone. Real outlays for defense more than doubled from 1950 but remained roughly the same after 1955.

In themselves, historical spending patterns cannot give a definitive judgment about the appropriateness of current outlays. To note that the federal government spent, in real dollars, 542 percent more on human resources in 1990 than in 1950 does not signify, in itself, whether or not the outlays in either period were adequate. To begin with, adequacy is always in the eye of the beholder. A society can be organized in innumerable ways. What seems appropriate to a modern

Western democracy, with deeply rooted notions of universal human rights and dignity, would have seemed strange to Plato or Aristotle, living in a more straitened world where the progress of the few was based on the slavery of the many. Notions of appropriate standards for public goods in American society have undoubtedly grown more generous since 1950, as they have in every other Western society. But how much the standard has actually improved, or the public provision to provide it really increased, depends on the factors that have been discussed—the changes in real costs and in demography, as well as the general rise in the standard of living.

The purely moral and cultural criteria of appropriateness cannot stray too far from the practical consequences. The standard should be not only what appeals to the moral sensibilities of a national community, but also what keeps that community vigorous and united politically and socially, secure militarily and prosperous and competitive economically. Happily, the moral and the practical dimensions can often reinforce each other. Excellent public education for all is a good in itself, and a high priority for a healthy democracy. It may also be a fundamental requirement for an advanced economy that hopes to remain competitive, or wealthy enough to fulfill its own notions of a good society. Advancing technology may require a better-educated work force, and more investment in education may yield a disproportionate growth in national income. Less spending may retard economic growth and make fiscal deficits worse.

In short, underspending on public goods may impoverish a country as much as overspending. Foreign observers often blame America's lagging economic performance on its comparatively large, uneducated, unhealthy, and unemployable underclass.[46] Thus, while a chronic fiscal deficit may be counted as a sign of not adapting successfully to changing conditions, the cause may be spending too little rather than too much. Obviously, the problem is compounded by spending inefficiently in ways that do not promote long-term productivity and economic growth. While we can hope that a good society will also be more competitive, there is a gloomier view. The rapid diffusion of technology and globalization of industry put advanced rich societies under increasing competitive strain.

Earning enough to support high Western standards of living and welfare will grow more and more challenging. The margin for national inefficiency and self-indulgence will probably keep shrinking. The temptation to use military and political power to compensate for economic weakness will probably grow, and become increasingly dangerous. Those who believe in a good and rational world will have to work very hard. Above all, they will have to make sure that their own national house is in order.

In the end, a political system has to set its own public priorities, based on its own cultural values and practical expectations. Only time can tell the consequences. History indicates, however, that not all choices prove equally good. Nations decline as well as grow. In an interdependent world, the standards for national success are never purely domestic. National societies are always in at least implicit competition with each other—for self-esteem as well as for military or economic position. Standards of adequacy are thus comparative as well as historical.

Trying to decide whether America's public spending is appropriate for today's world requires looking not only at ourselves and our own history, but at those rivals whose societies are most like our own. The next chapter looks at France and Germany, two rivals with whom we share many values and institutions, but who have achieved rather different results.

Chapter 4 *United States Fiscal Policy: An International Perspective*

COMPARING COUNTRIES

What do international comparisons reveal about the causes of America's fiscal troubles? Are America's outlays, taxes, or ratios of public and private spending radically different from those of other rich, democratic Western countries?

Every country has its own fiscal profile, and international comparisons are notoriously tricky. To yield serious insight, comparisons should be of like with like. But national accounting categories differ and governments can spend in ways that do not show up in their normal accounting. Several large international agencies are preoccupied with comparing national statistics, but their findings sometimes differ sharply. Indeed, the same series from the same agency can occasionally show abrupt discontinuities.[1]

Even when the different national outlays can be measured properly, assessing their significance remains a formidable task. Similar budgetary outlays for pensions, education, or family support can have quite different effects according to a country's demography, income distribution, or division of labor between public and private sectors. In Japan, for example, pensions are mostly a private concern. In Germany, by contrast, they are mostly public. Japan's public sector thus appears much smaller than Germany's, which does not automatically mean, however, that Japanese are less well provided with pensions.

For the period of the 1980s, France and the Federal Republic of Germany are perhaps the most suitable countries to compare with the United States.[2] While neither France nor Germany has a population or GNP on the American scale, each is a large economy, with a national income, per capita, roughly equal to the American. Both are also Western-style democracies with capitalist, market-oriented economies, albeit with distinctive national economic cultures. Both are in the forefront of international scientific and technological innovation. If not military superpowers on the American scale, both are formidably armed, have important strategic commitments, and devote a significant proportion of GNP to military spending.

There are, of course, important differences. Both France and Germany are European "welfare states" that provide their citizens with benefits well beyond anything developed in the United States. Their versions of capitalism are also different from the American and also from each other's. In France, the state unashamedly intervenes to guide and condition private enterprise. Liberal Germany's "social market economy" enfolds private ownership, competition, and collective bargaining within a complex corporatist structure, where government—state as well as federal—is an active partner but less of an overseer than in France. Government structures are also different. France is highly centralized, while in Germany regional governments play almost as large a role in providing public services as in the United States.[3] Germany's central bank is also more independent. Furthermore, the three countries differ in their basic demography. Germany has the lowest birth rate and the highest proportion of people over sixty-five. The United States has the highest proportion of people under twenty-five. Income distribution is also different. Before unification, Germany had only a relatively small proportion of its population below the poverty level (3 percent). France had the highest (16 percent), but the United States was not far behind (13 percent).[4]

COMPARING FISCAL DEFICITS

All three countries have had serious fiscal problems. If deficits for all levels of government are compared, the United States is no worse than the others. But if central government deficits only are compared, the United States is much the worst. The difference is even sharper when the social security surplus is excluded, as it should be.

Which deficits are more significant—general government or central government? As has been observed in Chapter 2, the effects of a deficit depend upon how it is financed. A big deficit can affect the demand for credit—by crowding out private borrowing—or it can affect the supply of credit—by inducing the central bank to increase the money supply. To assess crowding out, the deficit for government at all levels is obviously more relevant. But to assess the consequences for monetary policy, the deficit of the central government is more

TABLE 4.1a

General Government Financial Balances (As a Percentage of Nominal GNP/GDP)

	1985	1986	1987	1988	1989
United States	−3.3	−3.4	−2.4	−2.0	−1.7
Germany	−1.1	−1.3	−1.9	−2.1	+0.2
France	−2.9	−2.7	−1.9	−1.8	−1.5

TABLE 4.1b

Central Government Financial Balances (As a Percentage of Nominal GNP/GDP)

	1985	1986	1987	1988	1989	1990
United States	−4.9	−4.9	−3.5	−2.9	−2.6	−3.1
United States Excluding Social Security	−5.2	−5.3	−4.0	−3.8	−3.6	−4.2
Germany	−1.2	−1.2	−1.4	−1.7	−0.4	−2.8
France	−2.9	−2.2	−1.9	−1.7	−1.5	−1.2

Source: OECD, *Economic Outlook, 48* (Paris: OECD, December 1990), pp. 115, 188.

relevant. Since the central government weighs more heavily on the central bank than regional governments, a central government deficit is more likely to be monetized, and thus to generate an inflationary monetary policy. Some central banks, of course, resist government pressure better than others. The Federal Republic's powerful Bundesbank was able to keep Germany's monetary policy comparatively tight and inflation comparatively low throughout the 1970s and 1980s, despite sometimes heavy federal and state deficits.[5] In France, the central government has traditionally dominated the Bank of France, and, until recently, France has been more prone to inflation than Germany. The most effective check on expansive French monetary policy has been the fear that the franc would depreciate rapidly in international currency markets.[6]

In the United States, states have little influence over monetary policy, but the Federal Reserve has traditionally been inclined to accommodate federal deficits. Nor has there normally been any great external constraint. Thanks to the dollar's international role, and the size and relative autonomy of the national economy, American monetary policy has generally been able to proceed with relative indifference to reactions in currency markets.

COMPARING PUBLIC SPENDING

In proportion to national income, overall public budgets are much larger in Europe than in the United States. But European taxes are also proportionally much higher.

European governments, moreover, spend a far greater

TABLE 4.2

Total Outlays and Receipts of Government, 1967 to 1988 (As percent of GDP)

	1967		1977		1988	
	OUTLAYS	RECEIPTS	OUTLAYS	RECEIPTS	OUTLAYS	RECEIPTS
U.S.	30.5	27.1	31.6	29.9	36.3	31.5
Germany	38.6	36.7	47.8	44.7	46.6	43.7
France	39.0	38.2	44.6	41.1	50.3	47.1

Source: OECD, *Economic Outlook, 48* (Paris: OECD, December 1990), pp. 189–90.

proportion of their income for civil as opposed to military purposes. A good part of Europe's larger government outlays are in the form of direct social security and welfare transfers to private households. This reflects state pension schemes and income support more generous than anything known in the United States.

Such big differences in the level of direct transfers and civil spending generally help to explain the European public's willingness to accept much higher tax levels. Any attempt to measure the taxpayer's tolerance for higher government spending and taxation must logically take into account direct transfers and other government outlays for welfare goods and services. Table 4.4 reports the results of a broad comparison among American, West German, and French public spending and household taxation. The first two columns show how netting out current transfers (mostly social security benefits and social assistance grants) from household taxes and government spending reduces the gap between European and American spending and taxation levels. The fourth column indicates that if both transfers and government consumption expenditures for welfare goods and services are subtracted from household taxes, American households bear a higher residual tax burden than their French and West German counterparts. The fifth column shows that United States government disbursements, net of welfare, are higher.

In summary, America's fiscal profile is very different from that of either France or Germany. In proportion to national

TABLE 4.3

Distribution of Central Government Spending, 1985 (Percent of Total Spending)

	DEFENSE	INTEREST	SOCIAL SECURITY AND WELFARE
U.S.	24.9	15.4	29.0
France	6.3	4.4	37.5
Germany	9.0	5.2	49.1

Source: IMF, *Government Finance Statistics Yearbook, 1989* (Washington, D.C.: International Monetary Fund, 1990), pp. 58, 74.

TABLE 4.4

Government Spending and Household Taxes, 1986
(As Percentage of GDP)

	1. NET HOUSEHOLD TAXES[1]	2. NET GOVERNMENT DISBURSEMENTS[2]	3. GOVERNMENT CONSUMPTION FOR WELFARE GOODS AND SERVICES[3]	4. HOUSEHOLD TAXES LESS WELFARE (1 MINUS 3)	5. GOVERNMENT DISBURSEMENTS LESS WELFARE (2 MINUS 3)
US	14.7	20.0	9.0	5.7	11.0
FRG	20.4	26.6	16.3	4.1	10.3
France	16.4	24.8	13.9	2.5	10.9

1. Direct taxes and social security contributions paid by households plus government receipts from indirect taxes *minus* current transfers by government.
2. Total government disbursements *minus* current transfers.
3. Government consumption expenditure for general public services, public order and safety, education, health, social security and welfare, housing and community amenities, and recreational, cultural and religious affairs.
Source: United Nations, *National Accounts Statistics: Main Aggregates and Detailed Tables, 1987* (New York: United Nations, 1990). Detailed Tables for France, pp. 474–511; for West Germany, pp. 525–74; and for the United States, pp. 1586–639. French government consumption figures are for 1985.

income, both European countries have markedly higher over-all expenditures and taxes. Their budgets give much more proportionally to civil spending and include much more for transfers to private households. Their accumulated public debt in proportion to national income is only marginally lower, but it grew less rapidly through the 1980s. Debt service has re-mained a much smaller proportion of their budgets. Both Eu-ropean governments, moreover, seem to have greater structural impediments to monetizing deficits.

When central governments alone are compared, most of these transatlantic fiscal differences grow more striking. In particular, the United States federal government has had a much faster rate of indebtedness, a much higher ratio of debt and debt service to income, and a much higher ratio of mili-tary to civil expenditures.

OVERCONSUMPTION AND EXTERNAL IMBALANCES

In the 1980s, the American economy's exploding fiscal deficit was matched by an equally egregious rise in its trade deficit with the rest of the world economy. Many analysts be-lieve the parallel was more than coincidental. As was noted in Chapter 2, such an external imbalance means that a nation's economy "absorbs" more goods and services than it produces, with the difference imported from abroad. In other words,

TABLE 4.5

**Absorption: Five Year Averages, 1983 to 1987
(As Percentage of GDP)**

	UNITED STATES	FRANCE	GERMANY
Government Consumption	18.4	19.4	19.9
Private Consumption	66.1	60.7	56.4
Investment	18.4	19.4	20.1
Total Absorption	102.8	99.4	96.4

Source: United Nations, *National Accounts Statistics: Main Aggregates and Detailed Tables, 1987* (New York: United Nations, 1990). Detailed Tables for France, pp. 474–511; for West Germany, pp. 525–74; and for the United States, pp. 1586–639.

consumption and investment, added together, are greater than domestic production—or GDP. In that respect, the United States differed sharply in the 1980s both from France, which was in rough equilibrium, and from Germany, which was in surplus (see Table 4.5).

What has been responsible for America's excess absorption? Absorption is the sum of three elements: government consumption, private consumption, and domestic investment (public and private). If comparative measurements are any indication, it is not America's investment that is excessive. In the 1970s and 1980s, United States investment, or "gross fixed capital formation," fell in relation to GDP and was a lower proportion to begin with than in either France or Germany. Government consumption was also lower in the United States. Private consumption, however, was very much higher. During the 1983–87 period, American private consumption, as a percentage of GDP, was 8.9 percent higher than in France and a stunning 17.2 percent higher than in the Federal Republic of Germany.

AMERICA'S OVERCONSUMPTION: PUBLIC OR PRIVATE?

While at first glance, America's private consumption seems out of line, a deeper look suggests quite different conclusions. Every country has a distinctive division of labor between public and private sectors. European governments, for example, pay a much larger proportion of their economy's overall health and education expenses. These differences in a political economy's division of labor logically affect any assessment of the relative size of its public and private consumption spending. Not counting health care and education, America's private consumption, measured as a share of GDP, is about the same as that of France, and not much more than that of West Germany, while America's public consumption ranges 10 to 20 percent higher than France's and nearly a third higher than Germany's:

TABLE 4.6a

Private Final Consumption Expenditure With (and Without) Health and Education, 1970 to 1987 (As Percentage of GDP)

YEAR	GERMANY	FRANCE	U.S.
1970	54.6 (53.2)	57.9 (53.5)	63.0 (55.8)
1975	57.0 (55.4)	58.7 (53.9)	63.5 (55.4)
1980	56.9 (55.1)	58.9 (54.1)	64.0 (55.1)
1985	56.7 (54.9)	61.1 (55.6)	65.9 (55.5)
1987	55.3 (53.6)	60.9 (55.3)	66.7 (55.4)

TABLE 4.6b

Government Final Consumption Expenditure With (and Without) Health and Education, 1983 to 1985 (As Percentage of GDP)

YEAR	GERMANY	FRANCE	U.S.
1983	20.1 (10.2)	19.5 (11.2)	18.4 (12.9)
1984	19.9 (10.0)	19.6 (11.2)	18.0 (12.7)
1985	20.0 (10.0)	19.4 (11.2)	18.3 (13.1)

Source: United Nations, *National Accounts Statistics: Main Aggregates and Detailed Tables, 1987* (New York: United Nations, 1990). Detailed tables for France, pp. 470–511; for West Germany, pp. 525–74; and for the United States, pp. 1586–639.

In short, considering how relatively little it provides in welfare goods, American government consumption seems relatively high, thanks to substantially greater United States military spending. The welfare burdens not borne by the public sector in America fall on the private sector. Considering what it bears, private consumption in America is not notably greater than in the two European countries. International comparisons thus do not support the common view that private consumption in the United States is excessive.

COMPARATIVE COSTS

International comparisons highlight not only different national divisions of labor between public and private sectors, but also the exceptional size of America's overall outlays for defense and health care. Both significantly exceed European levels of GDP. In 1987, for example, United States expenditures for defense exceeded 6 percent of GDP, while West Germany spent 3.2 percent and France 4 percent.[7] Similarly, the United States spent 11.2 percent of its GDP for health care in 1987, Germany 8.2 percent, and France 8.6 percent.[8] Among our three countries, medical outlays have also risen substantially in France, but only in the United States have medical costs inflated well beyond the rest of the economy's inflation rate:

TABLE 4.7

Inflation for Health Care and GDP Price Deflator, 1975 to 1987 (Average Annual Percentage Rates)

	FRANCE	GERMANY	U.S.
Health Price Deflator	7.6	3.9	8.1
GDP Price Deflator	8.8	3.4	5.8

Source: OECD, *Health Care Systems in Transition* (Paris: OECD, 1990), p. 14.

It seems difficult to overestimate the significance of these outsized military and health expenditures on both the fiscal and the external deficits of the United States. Between 1977 and 1986, total United States government consumption expenditure as a share of GDP rose from 17.6 percent to 18.6

percent. Excluding defense, it fell slightly from 12.4 percent to 12.0 percent. Defense consumption expenditure itself rose from 5.1 to 6.6 percent of GDP.[9] More striking still, between 1970 and 1987, the rise in private consumption for health care, in dollar terms, exceeded the entire increase in America's absorption.[10]

In effect, American outlays for defense and medical care were fast-growing cancers pressing on public and private budgets. As they grew, other functions resisted being crowded out. Both government and private consumption thus ballooned and pushed overall absorption to the limit of the economy's resources and beyond. Since the American economy could easily finance a trade deficit by borrowing abroad, it did so rather than cut its excessive consumption. At the same time, with household spending bloated by medical costs, as well as the rapidly rising costs of education, the public was deaf to pleas for higher taxes. In short, if defense caused the government's fiscal deficit, medicine prevented its cure.

How can America's internationally outsized outlays for defense and medical care be explained? Logically, there would seem to be three possible explanations:

1. In the United States, politicians and the public prefer a relatively higher level of these functions.
2. Objective factors, like respective geopolitical roles, demography, or cultural diversity, make these functions inherently more expensive in the United States.
3. These functions cost more because American institutions provide them less efficiently.

The first interpretation attributes America's outsized outlays to higher preferences, the second to greater needs, and the third to a less efficient way of supplying them. How do these explanations fit each case?

DEFENSE

The discussion of military spending in Chapter 3 suggests that all three explanations apply. Since the end of World War II, the United States has spent more relatively on defense because, among other things, it has assumed a more ambitious geopolitical role than either France or Germany. Europe's ruin and Russia's rise after World War II made such an American role almost inevitable. The objective demands of that role have made United States military costs relatively high. Extending nuclear deterrence to Western Europe has meant not only heavier strategic forces but a large transatlantic commitment of conventional forces, whose cost has taken up roughly half of America's defense budget for several decades. Geography alone would thus explain why American military costs have been relatively higher than French or German.[11] At the same time, America's way of running its huge military-industrial complex, with its particular mix of public demand and private supply, also seems comparatively inefficient.[12]

HEALTH CARE

Higher American outlays for defense are easy to understand. But what about higher American outlays for health care? Do Americans demand or need more care? Do they actually get more or are they simply less efficient in supplying what they get?

It would be comforting to lay America's higher costs to a superior level of care. But claims for superiority are difficult to substantiate. Deciding whether anybody's health care is better is obviously an uncertain and disputatious exercise. It presumes common preferences and perceptions that may not, in fact, be shared. Some societies may prefer a relatively low level of health care for everyone, as opposed to a much higher level for fewer. There are anyway uncertain relationships between the price, volume, and quality of medical care. Benchmarks for quality are hardly uncontroversial. Heated arguments over various treatments and procedures or the right trade-offs between more technology or longer care are commonplace inside national systems, let alone among them. Comparisons also presume similar needs. But some societies may be intrinsically healthier than others—for demographic, environmental, dietary, social, cultural, or even genetic reasons. An exhaustive comparison of such high-level systems as the American, French, and German would be a major work in itself.

General statistics, however, do not grant the American system the clear superiority that its outsized cost implies. Infant mortality, for example, is supposed to indicate the availability and effectiveness of health care, as well as general socioeconomic conditions.[13] In 1960, the United States had the lowest rate of infant mortality among the three countries. Since then, the American rate has fallen very significantly. Nevertheless, it is now much the highest:

TABLE 4.8

Infant Mortality Rates, 1960 to 1987
(As Percentage of Live Births)

	FRANCE	GERMANY	U.S.
1960	2.74	3.38	2.60
1965	2.19	2.38	2.47
1975	1.36	1.97	1.61
1985	0.81	0.89	1.06
1987	0.76	0.83	1.00

Source: OECD, *Health Care Systems in Transition* (Paris: OECD, 1990), p. 193.

Other general indicators do not support any American claim to superior medical services either, at least not in any obvious quantitative sense:

TABLE 4.9

Indicators of Health Care Resources and Utilization

	AVERAGE PATIENT: DAYS PER ADMISSION (1983)	CITIZENS PER HOSPITAL BED (1986)	CITIZENS PER PRACTICING PHYSICIAN (1986)
France	14.2	93.5	419
Germany	18.6	90.6	370
U.S.	9.6	187.6	441

Source: OECD, *Health Care Systems in Transition* (Paris: OECD, 1990), pp. 121–94.

Again, such figures are far from definitive, since they raise familiar issues about trade-offs. Less technology, for example, may mean longer hospital stays and require more beds per capita. With the best will in the world, opinions will differ about the ideal ratio between beds and machines, or preventive medicine and "interventions," or the numbers of doctors and the length, elaborateness, and cost of their training. All these issues notwithstanding, the fact remains that United States costs are proportionally much higher, and inflating faster, while American care does not show anything like a commensurate superiority (see Table 4.7).

Are costs in America higher because needs are greater? Broadly speaking, it is not easy to see why. Demographic factors favor the Americans. The United States has a younger population than France and much younger than Germany (see "Tables & Graphs," Table 3). No obvious economic factors suggest why Americans should be comparatively less healthy or more expensive to care for. Per capita income is highest in the United States, although the United States did have proportionately more poor people than the Federal Republic before reunification, but not more than France.

In one critical respect, coverage, the American system is intrinsically cheaper than either European system. French and German systems give complete coverage for medical costs to virtually everyone. In the United States, a recent study estimated some thirty-five million people—17.5 percent of the entire population under sixty-five—to be without any public or private coverage at all.[14] Millions more have inadequate coverage that leaves them and their families exposed to the risks and humiliations of impoverishment or the sufferings of inadequate care.[15] It is hard to know which is more shocking

TABLE 4.10

Percent of Population Covered by Public Health Insurance, 1987

	HOSPITAL CARE	AMBULATORY CARE
France	99	98
Germany	92	92
U.S.	40	25

Source: OECD, *Health Care Systems in Transition* (Paris: OECD, 1990), p. 88.

about the American system—its limited coverage or its high cost, despite the limited coverage.

In some respects, the United States has the worst of all possible arrangements for health care, with neither enough state control nor enough private competition to keep down costs. Competition is inherently ineffective because patients with adequate insurance are not constrained to be cost-conscious about their own care. In any event, the seriously ill patient is hardly able or inclined to shop around and bargain for treatment. Competition among insurers takes the perverse form of using cheaper rates to lure the healthy, and making up for it by avoiding commitments to the aged or chronically ill. Insofar as this strategy succeeds, it gives insurance only to the healthy, while the poor, old, and chronically ill are left uninsured, and have to be covered by charity from public hospitals at general public expense. Meanwhile, no one seems in a position to control the actual costs of medical treatment itself— by deciding, for example, on a less expensive trade-off between technology and cost. Insurers certainly have never been effective in playing this role. Thus a system that provides no coverage at all to roughly one fifth of America's working population can still manage to cost more than high-quality European systems that cover the entire population.[16]

If American health care is not demonstrably better, serves relatively fewer people whose needs are no greater, and also costs the economy relatively more, there seems a strong case for believing it to be relatively inefficient. Searching for the reasons opens a vast series of specialized and controversial issues, which we obviously cannot pursue here. A more general point, however, seems worth making.

As a matter of principle, American health care has prided itself on being more market-oriented than European. The trend in the 1980s was to strengthen that orientation. More "competition" was widely seen as the best way to maximize the patient's choices, while preserving quality and constraining cost.[17] The results, however, suggest that this whole bias, and the broad thinking that lies behind it, is seriously dysfunctional. At heart, the market is not a particularly appropriate mechanism either for delivering health care or for allocating resources to it. Many people who tout the virtues of the market have a rather unclear notion of what they mean by it. A market system, after all, implies more than consumer choice; it is also driven by whatever arrangements yield maximum profits for producers. Using the market as the prime regulator for health care raises rather obvious ethical questions. Should profit regulate the medical profession, or be the primary goal for medical institutions? The ethical confusion and declining prestige of the profession in recent years suggest otherwise, not to mention the increasing tendency of patients to sue their doctors and hospitals.

There are also obvious economic difficulties with using the market to allocate medical resources. The capital needed for the big modern hospital is enormous. In what sense is it economically efficient for such hospitals to compete with each other? Duplicating expensive equipment within the same region seems a misallocation of resources that greatly boosts hospital prices in the name of a largely illusory consumer choice.

European nations take for granted that the market for health care is imperfect. Inevitably, they believe, suppliers enjoy significant monopoly rents while the "shoppers" lack the necessary information or market power to provide the necessary countervailing pressure. Nor do they expect unstructured competition among insurers to control costs. The European state is thus less reluctant to step in between the payers and the providers. In some countries, notably Great Britain and Scandinavia, the state controls costs by itself managing the flow of funds to the suppliers. In others, Germany for example, regional associations of private insurers, enjoying quasi-governmental power, negotiate contracts with corresponding regional associations of private suppliers.[18] The criteria for setting prices are not only the region's overall budgetary constraints, but include studies monitoring the actual use of various facilities and services. In both cases, the state organizes the demand side to counterbalance the inherently stronger position of the suppliers.

The American system offers no comparable strengthening of market power on the demand side. Instead, a very heterogeneous and dispersed collection of agencies, firms, unions, and insurers try to confront the suppliers. Efforts at reform have concentrated on either converting the patient into a more knowledgeable and agile consumer, or encouraging greater competition among insurers. Neither creates effective bargaining power. As a recent OECD study observes about the patient/consumer: "The belief that overall health care expenditures can be effectively controlled by these sick human beings . . . seems to be uniquely American and, even within the United States, uniquely incident upon the economics profession, whence the idea originated."[19] Competition among insurers, on the other hand, tends to benefit the healthy by denying care to the sick—surely the reverse of what a national system should seek to achieve.

Furthermore, the heterogeneous American system, although it provides little control over monopolistic suppliers, is extremely burdensome to administer. Bureaucratic costs are reckoned at about 8 percent of the whole—higher than in European systems—despite their greater degree of regulation.[20]

In short, trying to use market allocation for public purposes for which it is not suited seems a recipe not for liberty and efficiency, but for social discord and fiscal impoverishment. In the 1980s, "deregulation" to impose market efficiency became the American panacea for the complex needs of a modern society. But in health care at least, deregulation has promoted manifest inefficiency and ethical disarray. Ironically, among the three health systems, the American, with its misbegotten market, is the one where costs seem the most out of control. Meanwhile, our medical care seems no better and its distribution is shockingly incomplete and regressive.

INEFFICIENCY

Comparing American with French and German fiscal practices results in some illuminating insights. Taking the 1980s as a whole, overall American fiscal deficits were relatively larger and growing more rapidly than in France or Germany. Measuring the deficits of the three central governments alone accentuated America's higher deficits still further. The United States also had the highest increase of debt relative to GDP. The rising cost of debt service was, in itself, a major cause of our federal deficits.

Should America's fiscal deficits be blamed on excessive public spending or inadequate taxes? Comparison seems to support neither proposition. Defense is the only broad category in which American public outlays are relatively higher than in France or Germany. American spending for welfare goods and services is notably lower. Certainly European comparisons furnish little support for the proposition that American civil transfers are excessive. American taxes do seem comparatively low. But when direct transfers are netted out, American household taxes are roughly comparable to European. And if all state-provided welfare goods and services are taken into account, American taxes are substantially higher in relation to what they purchase (see Table 4.4). In other words, international comparisons do not bear out the proposition that American civil spending is too high, or taxes too low. Quite the contrary.

Perhaps the most telling revelation from international comparisons is that the American way of dividing functions between public and private sectors seems to cost more in relation to what it provides than elsewhere. Higher American military spending may reflect not only a more ambitious and extended geopolitical role, but also less efficient procurement. Inefficiency certainly is marked in the way the American system supplies health care, which takes a substantially bigger proportion of overall national income in the United States—public and private sectors combined—than in France or Germany. Without clear evidence that the more expensive American arrangements provide correspondingly superior services, it seems logical to assume that America's way of supplying certain public goods and services is less efficient. In these cases, higher American outlays seem to reflect not more ambitious standards so much as an inability to provide comparable public goods and services as cheaply as the French and Germans do. This inefficiency, in turn, pushes up the level of American spending on consumption, but without providing any corresponding increase in the real level of goods and services.

Inefficiency in providing public goods has direct consequences for America's "twin deficit" or absorption crisis. In the 1980s, the American balance between production and absorption (consumption plus investment) deteriorated dramatically. Logically enough, this brought a radical rise in the economy's trade and current-account deficits with the rest of the world. Much of the blame lay with a sharp rise in consumption, especially private consumption. Between 1970 and 1987, the overall rise of private consumption in the United States was less than the increase in private consumption outlays for health care alone. Inefficiency on such a scale obviously impoverishes both the government and private households. Government is not only less willing but also less able to provide greater public goods to the civil sector. And private households are not only less disposed but also less able to cede income to the public sector. As a result, both are poorer. With this insight in mind, it is time to take a deeper look at American taxes.

Chapter 5 *Taxes and Incomes in the United States*

*T*hroughout the 1980s, American fiscal politics turned on the question of whether to cut federal spending or to increase federal taxes. Republican presidential candidates advocated tax cuts and Democratic candidates tax increases. While Ronald Reagan and George Bush won the elections, many economic analysts have thought that Walter Mondale and Michael Dukakis had the better arguments. America's taxes are the lowest of any major Western country.[1] Not confronting the record fiscal deficits by raising those taxes is widely seen as a major historical failure of America's political system.

Some federal taxes did increase in the 1980s—most prominently payroll taxes for social security. But rates for most other federal taxes fell and revenue, which remained roughly constant as a percentage of GDP, did not grow sufficiently to keep pace with expenditures.[2] The decline in the federal deficit that did occur in the fiscal years 1987–89 resulted mostly from cyclical improvements in business conditions.

As the long boom began to wind down at the beginning of the 1990s, and the nation's financial disorder sharply increased federal outlays, the federal deficit began to soar once again. Even a Republican President admitted it was time for a tax increase, but was resisted by a large segment of his own party in Congress. The huge political struggle needed to pass a modest package of tax increases and spending controls in October of 1990 suggested that tax policy would remain a major bone of contention for the foreseeable future.[3] That would be nothing new.

In recent decades, taxes have been a much more central and volatile political issue in the United States than in most European countries. Since the early 1950s, several major "reforms" have altered tax arrangements in quite significant ways. Nearly every reform, however, has reduced the revenue base.[4] Why has it proved impossible to arrive at a stable consensus on tax policy? And why, in the face of record fiscal deficits, has it been so difficult to raise taxes that are so much lower than in other Western countries?

The most common explanations are political and cultural, even anthropological. The United States was, after all, launched by a tax revolt. "No taxation without representation" was America's revolutionary slogan, its equivalent to the "liberty, equality, and fraternity" of the French. A political culture formed around the promise of unlimited abundance does not easily adapt when needs finally begin to catch up with potential. Certainly America's constitutional arrangements allow governments to evade responsibility to an unusual degree. In few other Western political systems could the executive and the legislature both so plausibly blame each other for a fiscal situation that each, with increasing conviction, admits is deplorable.

America also has a unique capacity for getting away with its improvidence. The huge size of the national economy, the special role of the dollar in world finance, and the country's unique geopolitical position have long shielded the United States from the international retribution usually visited upon countries that indulge in sustained periods of irrational behavior. Possibly, too, the economics profession in America has itself been unusually accommodating to those arguments linking tax cuts to economic growth.

Whatever the weight of these cultural, constitutional, and geopolitical factors, there are perfectly rational economic reasons to explain why the American public is unwilling to pay the same taxes as its counterparts in Western Europe. These may be grouped under four headings:

1. The inadequacy of American public spending
2. The skewed incidence of American taxes
3. The historical decline of the American middle class
4. The inefficiency with which the American system provides critical goods and services

INADEQUATE SPENDING AND LOW TAXES

There is an obvious link between the American government's low rate of civil spending and its low rate of taxation. If taxpayers are consumers buying a package of public goods provided by the state, and taxes are the price they pay, America's lower tax rates do not seem out of line with those in Europe. Indeed, as the last chapter indicates, when the quality and extent of American public goods are compared with what is provided publicly in Europe, Americans seem to be paying rather a lot for what they get. Government spending in America is a significantly smaller part of GDP than in almost any other Western country. And while military spending is proportionally much higher in America, government civil spending is significantly lower. Granted, Americans do get—among their public goods—the security and benefits of their country's being a military superpower. But Europeans, thanks to NATO, can be "free-riders" on these same benefits.[5] In addition, they receive significantly higher direct and indirect civil benefits from their governments. A large part of government spending in most European countries consists of direct transfers to private households. As we have seen, taking out all such direct transfer brings American public spending and taxation much closer to European levels.[6] But even without transfers, European spending remains significantly more oriented to civil than to military spending. Europe and America have a very different distribution of functions between public and private sectors. Middle-class Americans are less likely to see their greatest public benefits coming from transfers or services provided by the state than from the special deductions granted from its taxation—mortgage interest is only one of these major "tax expenditures."[7] A middle-class American taxpayer is thus hard put to develop the same practical affection for his government's civil functions as his French or German counterparts.

No doubt the American preference for private rather than

public arrangements is deeply implanted in the culture. But, given the practical consequences for household budgets, it is entirely reasonable for American taxpayers to resist paying European-level taxes. It is not the recalcitrant taxpayer who is irrational. Rather it is those analysts who rail against public "entitlements" but call for higher taxation. If Americans were to pay more taxes, they would have every right to expect more public benefits. As it is, from the perspective of the taxpayer as a consumer of public goods, the American state is not a particularly good deal.

STRUCTURAL IMPEDIMENTS TO HIGHER AMERICAN TAXES: INCIDENCE

Not only does the individual American taxpayer get less from the state than most of his Western European counterparts, but taxes fall upon him more directly, particularly if he is middle-class and prosperous.

The largest part of American revenue comes from taxes on incomes and profits; personal income tax yields the biggest share.[8] Such taxes obviously strike the taxpayer very directly. By contrast, social security taxes are the greatest single source of French and German revenues. Employers pay a share and the results, for the individual taxpayer, are generous state pensions, even for the well-to-do. Benefits, which are closely geared to previous income, go much higher than in the United

TABLE 5.1

Major Sources of Government Taxation, 1987 (Percent)

	INCOME/ PROFITS	SOCIAL SECURITY	GOODS/ SERVICES	USER FEES
U.S.	50.1	33.9	4.0	9.5
France	17.7	41.7	29.4	7.6
Germany	17.4	53.2	21.8	7.3
Industrial Country Average	40.1	33.6	14.6	9.0

Source: IMF, *Government Finance Statistics* (Washington, D.C.: International Monetary Fund, 1989), pp. 52–56.

States. Even for wealthy French or German taxpayers, a state pension is a perfectly reasonable way to secure an adequate future income.[9]

Social security taxes also form a major and growing share of United States revenues, although much less than in France or Germany. However, the benefit payments provided by social security in America are not sufficient to maintain the pre-retirement living standard of even the moderately well-to-do taxpayer.[10] For an adequate pension, the American middle-class taxpayer turns either to a private plan, or to government plans for civil servants or the military. But the social security system itself is merely a minimal pension scheme for the poor.[11] Even as such it is not very generous by European standards. Regarded as a pension scheme, in other words, social security is insufficient for the better half of the population. Regarded simply as another form of taxation, it seems regressive—a perception of growing significance as rates jumped by 22 percent over the 1980s.[12] In short, American social security taxes can easily be perceived as a bad deal for both the rich and the poor.

The European states also rely much more on consumption taxes than the United States. These indirect taxes are imposed across the board on nearly all goods and services and probably arouse less public opposition than direct income taxes. Economically, the arrangement favors those who save over those who consume. Families with ample incomes have greater potential for saving than the poor. But in Europe, these inequalities are heavily compensated by the overall structure of the tax system.[13] Large households, rich and poor, also receive generous family allowances, along with free medical care and free public education through the university level.

Public revenue in America also relies much more heavily on property tax—a critical source for most local governments and school jurisdictions.[14] Taxes on property, mostly real estate, fall particularly heavily on lower-income families and elderly citizens whose principal asset is a house.[15]

In short, compared with the European states, both the distribution of benefits and the incidence of taxation in America discourage higher taxation. Direct state benefits to households are lower and particularly ungenerous to the middle class. Taxes also fall more directly on that same middle class. Under the circumstances, widespread resistance in America to further general taxation is neither surprising nor illogical.

BRACKET CREEP AND THE TAX REVOLT

The tax revolt that dominated politics in the 1980s began in the late 1970s but its foundations stretched back to the 1960s. Although the Revenue Act of 1964 had reduced individual income tax rates, from the middle to the end of that decade effective overall tax rates rose for almost all income groups, increasing the ratio of their taxes to their incomes. State and local taxes rose from 9.4 percent of GNP in 1966 to 12.2 percent in 1977.[16] While changes in tax laws during the 1970s brought considerable relief at the lower end of incomes, the position of the middle class improved less or actually worsened. Meanwhile, the tax position of the top 10 percent improved markedly.[17]

In the later 1970s, certain broad trends began to foment a major public reaction. The main cause was the decade's record inflation. Nominally higher incomes pushed taxpayers into higher tax brackets. Income taxes began to rise rather sharply relative to family incomes.[18] By 1980, double-digit inflation was coexisting with a severe recession. Public alarm at higher and accelerating taxes was hardly surprising. At the same time, in many cities and regions, inflation, demography and urbanization greatly appreciated the market value of residences. Assessments and taxes jumped accordingly. Many middle-class households thus saw a further sharp increase in their tax burden. While the appreciated value of the house was fictional in practical terms—since it yielded no increased income—the increased taxes were very real. For families whose incomes were not keeping up with inflation, a group that included a large segment of the middle class, the exploding real estate taxes were outrageous and frightening. They played a key role in the outburst of antitax and anti-inflationary feeling that by the late 1970s was beginning to dominate politics in many parts of the country, notably California with its large retired population.[19]

In 1978, while income and property taxes were already rising more rapidly than usual, Congress passed a major in-

TABLE 5.2

Federal, State and Local Tax Receipts, 1971 to 1985 (As a Percentage of GDP)

	TOTAL	FEDERAL	STATE AND LOCAL
1971	29.7	18.4	11.3
1973	30.9	19.4	11.5
1975	30.0	18.4	11.6
1977	31.0	19.3	11.7
1979	31.1	20.1	11.0
1981	32.0	20.9	11.1
1983	31.2	19.4	11.8
1985	31.7	19.7	12.0

Source: Joseph A. Pechman, *Federal Tax Policy*, 5th ed. (Washington, D.C.: Brookings Institution, 1987), p. 368.

crease in social security taxes—to be phased in over a number of years. The increases were justified by a combination of demography and inflation. By 1982, high unemployment plus low productivity promised to undermine earlier estimates, and the system's future solvency was once more in question. Contribution levels were raised still further. All in all, social security taxes jumped by 22 percent over the 1980s. By the latter part of the decade, the levies began to weigh heavily.[20]

In short, by 1980, between bracket creep propelled by inflation and the heavy increases in social security taxes, a major jump in federal taxation was in progress. In some parts of the country, it was accompanied by higher state and local taxes—increases that grew stronger in the 1980s.[21] The Reagan Revolution has to be understood in this context.

Ronald Reagan's tax cuts halted the federal rise, but did not, in the end, actually reverse it. The tax reforms of 1981 did not greatly lower the overall federal tax burden, even if they seriously undermined federal finances. Indeed, by 1985, federal taxes were absorbing more of the gross national product than in almost any year of the 1970s, while the overall tax burden had almost returned to its record level of 1981.

TAXES AND INCOMES: THE DECLINING MIDDLE CLASS

Obviously, the effect of rising taxes, pushed up by inflation, depends on the degree that incomes themselves keep up. America's income patterns have shifted in directions that also help explain the tax revolt. There are several ways of looking at the figures. One is to chart how income is distributed among the population—the balance of rich, poor, and middle class. From the 1970s through the 1980s, the proportion of families with low incomes remained about the same. Families with in-

TABLE 5.3

Real Median Family Income (1989 Dollars)

Year	Median Family Income
1970	31,543
1971	31,490
1972	32,976
1973	33,656
1974	32,451
1975	31,620
1976	32,597
1977	32,758
1978	33,548
1979	33,454
1980	31,637
1981	30,540
1982	30,111
1983	30,719
1984	31,547
1985	31,962
1986	33,328
1987	33,805
1988	33,742
1989	34,213

Source: *Economic Report of the President, 1991* (Washington, D.C.: U.S. Government Printing Office, 1991), p. 320.

comes below $20,000 (in constant 1987 dollars) formed 31 percent of all families in 1973 and the same percentage in 1986. Those having incomes of $20,000 to $50,000 actually declined from 53 percent to 47 percent in the same period. But those earning over $50,000 rose from 16 percent to 22 percent of families. In other words, the proportion of poor families stayed about the same; the middle ranks grew smaller, but only because an increasing proportion rose into the higher brackets. The middle class appears to have been shrinking through upward mobility.[22] In the 1980s, the rich did very well indeed. Not only was there a notably higher proportion of the population in the higher income brackets, but the be-fore-tax income share of the richest 15 percent grew by 24 percent, of the top 5 percent by 40 percent, of the top 1 per-cent by 81 percent.[23]

Looking at the median income of the American family, however, suggests a less complacent view.

As the table shows, median family income, adjusted for inflation, stagnated after 1973, shrank rather sharply with the deep recession of the 1980s, and did not recover the 1973 level until 1987. Behind this pattern of stagnation, decline, and limited recovery lie some fundamental economic, social, and demographic changes with profound effects on the nature of family life in America.

Spreading poverty and the general stagnation of incomes is related to, among other things, the slow growth of labor productivity, the rapid rise in the number of single-parent, female-headed families, as well as to the proliferation of jobs in low-paying service industries.[24] On the other hand, the broadly based but tepid recovery in family income in the later 1980s is partly owed to a rise in the number of two wage-earner families.[25] Typically, both husband and wife worked in service jobs to regain the level of income formerly reached by the husband alone in a manufacturing or construction job. The rise of family incomes in the upper brackets in the mid to late 1980s also appears related to the same broad switch from one to two wage-earners per family.[26]

Except perhaps for the top 10 percent, these changing income and employment patterns do not so much indicate any widespread new affluence as a trading away of traditional family values in order to maintain money income. This pattern puts the feminist movement in a rather ironical perspective. Outside the upper brackets, women have not so much been liberated from the family as driven from it by economic necessity. The income gains made as a result of these social changes, moreover, cannot be repeated ad infinitum. Once a large proportion of families already has two wage-earners, the future growth of median income will depend more on the general rise of productivity. In the United States, with continuing low investment, and correspondingly low productivity gains, the prospects for big rises are not brilliant.[27] Even with higher joint incomes, the economic situation of many families has grown more precarious than formerly. Jobs in the service sector have little security and lesser benefits, particularly medical coverage. Urban middle-class families, moreover, increasingly feel compelled to educate their children in private schools. Tuition for schools and universities is a very heavy burden.[28]

This perspective helps explain the malaise that has hung over the American economy, despite what appears to be a sharp gain in the number of wealthier families. The social cost of the gains has been high. In general, what might be called the existential situation of many families has actually worsened. In short, it is not surprising that a large number of Americans feel economically insecure and resist paying higher taxes to governments that offer them a limited package of public benefits. European public sectors that provide free medical care and higher education, and generous pensions, family allowances and unemployment benefits certainly present a greater incentive to pay higher taxes.

The taxpayer's standard of living is affected not only by his earnings and taxes, but also by the costs of vital goods and services. Among those are health care and education. Since the American public sector provides substantially less of those social goods than in most countries of Western Europe, the difference falls on the private sector—and consequently absorbs a larger share of private budgets. In America, costs for those goods have increased far more rapidly than incomes or other costs. Medical care has been particularly dramatic. It was 5 percent of total personal consumption in 1960 and has risen to 13 percent by 1989.[29] Logically, when the cost of such functions increases more rapidly than real income and other costs, it tends to squeeze private budgets and limits still further the willingness—or the capacity—of private households to pay more in taxes. Rapidly rising costs for health care thus threaten to impoverish the private sector directly and the public sector indirectly.[30]

All these trends together form the background to the tax revolt of the late 1970s, and to the Reaganite ascendancy that followed: Inflation was pushing taxpayers into higher brackets; sharp rises were scheduled for social security taxes; general state and local taxes were at high levels historically, while inflation and urbanization were rapidly raising real estate taxes in many locations. Meanwhile, real median family income was stagnant or falling, and revived somewhat only with the widespread shift from one to two wage-earners per family. Public and especially private budgets were being squeezed by the rapidly rising costs of certain general services, in particular, medical care.

THE GREAT TAX DEBATE OF THE 1980s RECONSIDERED

The data just reviewed makes it tempting to conclude that the great debate over taxes in the 1980s was misconceived, misdirected, and had little real effect. While Reagan did stop the rapid rise in federal income taxes that seemed ready to occur, he did not significantly lower the level that had already been achieved.

Thanks to inflation and bracket creep, federal taxes did jump from 20.2 percent of net national product (NNP) in 1975 to a high of 23.3 percent in 1981. Rapid inflation eventually stopped, thanks to the tight monetary policies initiated at the end of the 1970s by the Federal Reserve, under its unusually resolute new chairman, Paul Volcker. The inflation rate was halved in 1982, and again in 1983—a fall in the consumer price index (CPI) from 10.3 percent to 3.2 percent. And Reagan's tax bill of 1981 did sharply lower top rates and, eventually, install an indexing scheme to block bracket creep.[31] By 1984, the ratio of federal taxation to NNP had fallen to 21.2 percent. But by 1987, after a series of piecemeal revenue increases, a further "rescue" of the social security system, and a

TABLE 5.4

**Taxation in the 1980s
(As Percent of NNP)**

YEAR	TOTAL	FEDERAL	STATE/LOCAL
1980	33.2	22.5	10.7
1981	34.0	23.3	10.7
1982	33.5	22.4	11.1
1983	32.8	21.5	11.3
1984	32.5	21.2	11.2
1985	33.0	21.6	11.4
1986	33.0	21.5	11.5
1987	33.8	22.3	11.6
1988	33.5	22.0	11.5
1989	33.8	22.4	11.4

Source: The Tax Foundation, *Facts and Figures on Government Finance: 1990 Edition* (Baltimore: Johns Hopkins University Press, 1990), p. 35.

major tax reform (1986), the level was back to 22.3 percent.[32] Meanwhile, the combined federal, state and local tax burden, which had dropped to a low of 32.5 percent of NNP in 1984, was over 33 percent again by 1985, higher than it had been in the late 1970s. By 1987, it stood at 33.8 percent—its highest point in history. In short, Reagan, with Volcker's help, did head off the major rise in store for American taxes. But he did not reverse for long the high levels that had already been reached.[33]

Much has been made of the great inequities that have supposedly resulted from various tax changes since the 1970s. The following table gives a breakdown of "effective" tax rates, rates that take into account transfer payments, employee fringe benefits, net imputed rent, and corporate earnings allocated to shareholders. It shows that from 1980 to 1988, the real tax burden fell both for the bottom 30 percent of the population and for the top 10 percent. The rest were taxed somewhat more. None of the changes in the 1980s is particularly dramatic, even after the comprehensive tax reform of 1986. For the bulk of the population, the changes between 1970 and 1975 were far more significant.

These general figures for the nation as a whole do pass

TABLE 5.5

**Effective Tax Rates for Total Government, 1970 to 1988
(Tax Rate as a Percent of Total Income)**

POPULATION	1970	1975	1980	1985	1988
1st decile	18.8	19.7	17.1	17.0	16.4
2nd decile	19.5	17.6	17.1	15.9	15.8
3rd decile	20.8	18.9	18.9	18.1	18.0
4th decile	23.2	21.7	20.8	21.2	21.5
5th decile	24.0	23.5	22.7	23.4	23.9
6th decile	24.1	23.9	23.4	23.8	24.3
7th decile	24.3	24.2	24.4	24.7	25.2
8th decile	24.6	24.7	25.5	25.4	25.6
9th decile	25.0	25.4	26.5	26.2	26.8
10th decile	30.7	27.8	28.5	26.4	27.7
Top 5 percent	33.0	28.4	28.9	26.0	27.4
Top 1 percent	39.0	29.0	28.4	25.3	26.8

Source: Joseph A. Pechman, "The Future of the Income Tax," *Brookings General Series Reprints #437* (Washington, D.C.: Brookings Institution, 1990), p. 4.

over, however, the very considerable regional variations that have often provided the flashpoints for public unrest over taxation. Extreme regional differences do exist, sometimes among cities, towns, and rural counties within the same state. Great disparities also exist in federal outlays to various regions of the country, and hence in "effective" federal taxation from one region to the next. Eastern urbanized states and the Midwest pay more to Washington than they receive, whereas for much of the South and the West it is the other way around.[34]

THE REAGAN DEFICIT

If the Reagan tax cuts did not significantly lower the level of federal taxation, why was there such a spectacular increase in the federal deficit? In the official table below, the third column states the actual deficit (as a percent of GNP) while the fourth column estimates what the deficit would have been with Carter tax rates and Reagan expenditures.

Clearly, Reagan's tax cuts do not, in themselves, explain the whole of the sustained increases in the fiscal deficit. In the Reagan years before 1986, the rise in federal spending was as

TABLE 5.6

Federal Expenditure Growth and the Deficit, 1970 to 1990 (Percent of GNP)

YEAR	EXPENDITURES	RECEIPTS	DEFICIT	DEFICIT AT 1981 RECEIPTS/GNP RATIO
1970	19.8	19.5	0.3	
1975	21.8	18.3	3.5	
1980	22.1	19.4	2.8	
1981	22.7	20.1	2.6	
1982	23.8	19.7	4.1	3.7
1983	24.3	18.1	6.3	3.2
1984	23.1	18.1	5.0	3.0
1985	23.9	18.6	5.4	2.8
1986	23.7	18.4	5.3	2.6
1987	22.7	19.3	3.4	2.6
1988	22.2	19.0	3.2	2.1
1989	22.3	19.3	3.0	2.2
1990	23.2	19.1	4.1	3.1

Source: *Budget of the United States Government, Fiscal Year 1992* (Washington, D.C.: U.S. Government Printing Office, 1991), Part Seven-15.[35]

significant as the decline in federal revenue. Defense outlays accounted for a significant portion of that rise. Real outlays for human resources also continued to go up, with very large increases in Medicare. Real outlays for net interest also went up sharply. Physical resources fell drastically, but not enough to compensate. In short, Reagan's deficits can most plausibly be blamed not on his tax cuts alone, but also on the increases in spending for defense, human resources, and net interest.[36] The rise in military spending was particularly significant because it reversed the sharp declines in real spending from 1970 to 1977. Instead of being, as before, a major source of annual budgetary savings, defense was transformed into the most significant increase. What if the Reagan tax cuts had not been passed? Had the pre-Reagan tax regime stayed in place, and bracket creep done its work, the deficits of the 1980s would very probably have been lower. Federal tax rates and the government share of national income, however, would have been pushed to levels unprecedented in our national history. By 1981, before the Reagan tax cut, federal receipts were already at 20.1 percent of GNP.[37] In the postwar era, this ratio had been achieved only in 1969, the peak year of taxation during the Vietnam War. By contrast, in 1944, the peak year of World War II spending, federal receipts were only 21.7 percent of GNP.[38]

In summary, the Reagan Revolution was not so much a tax cut as a rejecting of major tax increases. From this perspective, the fiscal crisis of the 1980s was less a tax problem than a spending problem. The 1970s had seen a pattern of rising civil outlays compensated both by falling military outlays and by unlegislated tax increases (bracket creep). The 1980s sharply reversed the decline in military spending but without imposing either a corresponding reversal in civil spending or adequate tax increases. To blame the fiscal crisis on excessive civil consumption, because the public elected an administration that blocked a tax increase, is a rather elliptical way of analyzing the problem. It might better be said that the public, its own budget squeezed, balked at paying a higher price for the federal government's package of goods and services, including the sharply augmented outlays for defense. With fiscal policy thus frozen in a political and economic deadlock, a fiscal deficit was the path of least resistance.

AMERICAN DEFICITS RECONSIDERED

The past three chapters have been examining the causes of America's fiscal deficit. In particular, they have weighed whether the blame should fall on too much spending or too little taxation. From a purely historical American perspective, the growth of civil spending since 1950 does not seem excessive, once demographic changes and the general rise of national income are taken into account. From a Western European perspective, American federal outlays seem either too low or too high. They are too low in that the federal government fails to provide the taxpayer with public goods at a European level. But the outlays are too high for what the federal government actually does provide in civil goods and services. The obvious reasons are America's higher military spending and different division of labor between the public and private sectors. But there is also the American government's notable inefficiency in providing certain critical public goods—clearly medical care and perhaps education as well. In other words, neither a historical nor a comparative perspective offers much support for the belief that American fiscal problems should be blamed on excessive civil spending.

The historical and comparative study of taxation suggests a similar conclusion. If American taxes are not high enough, it may well be because spending on civil public goods is too low. In any event, raising taxes, under present circumstances, would mean a real decline in America's standard of living. Since real income has scarcely risen in two decades, the resistance of a broad segment of the middle class to higher taxes is hardly mysterious or, indeed, illogical. In brief, it seems difficult to resolve the American fiscal problem by raising taxes or by cutting civil spending.

Short of reducing the country's standard of living, relief for the deficit has to come from one of three sources: a reduced geopolitical role that allows serious and sustainable cuts in military spending, a more efficient provision of public goods by government and private sectors together, or greater economic growth. The first two are probably not obtainable without fundamental political and institutional changes. Like any other political system, the United States would prefer to be rescued by growth. Politically, it has been easier to run deficits while waiting for growth. And thanks to the dollar's international appeal, financing large fiscal deficits has turned out to be relatively easy in the short term. For years, moreover, economists have been telling politicians that deficits are the key to growth. But although we have had all the deficits anyone might want, rapid sustained growth has not followed. Instead, chronic large deficits appear to have had a corrosive effect on America's real economic strength. That effect, in turn, reflects how the deficits have been financed, the topic of the next chapter.

Chapter 6 *Financing the Deficit: The International Dimension*

*T*he United States has run fiscal and external deficits of one sort or another since the 1960s. Since the mid-1970s, both deficits have been very substantial. Given America's low savings rate, financing these deficits has often depended heavily on borrowing or otherwise appropriating the savings of foreigners. That capacity, in turn, has depended upon America's special position in the world economy. Throughout the postwar era, although others have obviously played critical roles, the United States has been the global system's principal leader—the benevolent hegemon of a Pax Americana. American preeminence has been not just economic, but military, political, intellectual, and cultural. American wealth provided the means to initiate the building of the postwar world economy and American liberalism provided the global vision. Thereafter, American military power underwrote the system against more than four decades of Soviet challenge.

One of history's ironies is that a hegemonic power often benefits less from a liberal system than other powers who participate in it. Almost inevitably, the hegemon provides a disproportionate share of certain common goods, like security, for which it is not adequately recompensed. "Free-riders" profit accordingly and, in time, grow relatively stronger as the hegemon grows relatively weaker. Free-riding aside, a liberal system that opens markets and disperses technology through global investment tends naturally to reduce the initial advantages of the leading power. In the early postwar decades, American policy deliberately hastened the process. The United States encouraged the European Economic Community, sent aid to undeveloped countries, and reconciled itself to mercantilistic practices from its allies in order to build up their economies and deflate their local communist movements. The success of such policies almost inevitably diminished America's relative preeminence. But America's burdens and habits of hegemony have never been adjusted accordingly, and America's own political economy has shown signs of increasing strain. Chronic fiscal and external deficits are a sign of that strain.

From a long-term perspective, hegemony thus seems a deceptive benefit for those who exercise it. From a short-term perspective, however, it does offer particular advantages. The United States has been seizing financial advantage from its international position at least since the 1960s—often for the best of motives—in particular to sustain the expensive military forces that have kept the liberal global order secure. Nevertheless, the direct and indirect costs have grown increasingly heavy—both to the United States and to the rest of the world. The United States has come to look increasingly like a hegemon in decay—using its leading role within the international monetary system to sustain its flagging resources, with practices that ultimately undermine both the system and America's own power within it.[1]

America's monetary manipulations have gone through various stages, each representing a different conjunction between America's growing deficits and its special position within the world economy. Three distinct formulas stand out over the years. The first is the Bretton Woods formula that characterized the 1960s. The second is the Nixon formula that prevailed throughout most of the 1970s. And the third is the Reagan formula that flourished in the early to mid-1980s. Naturally, each formula was bound up with the international monetary arrangements that prevailed in its period. The first formula takes its name from the international monetary agreement signed at Bretton Woods in Vermont during World War II. It spelled out a postwar international regime with fixed exchange rates to be oriented around gold and the dollar. As a "gold-exchange standard," it was technically similar to the regime that had prevailed in the 1920s and collapsed in 1931.[2] The Nixon and Reagan formulas both operated within an international system of floating exchange rates, the regime that ensued as the Bretton Woods system finally collapsed in the early 1970s.

BRETTON WOODS: KENNEDY AND JOHNSON'S FORMULA

The Bretton Woods formula is perhaps the most interesting. The early and middle 1960s are often looked upon as a golden age for the American economy. Internally, fiscal deficits were modest, at least by later standards. A regular trade surplus, fattened by increasing earnings from overseas investments, royalties and fees, meant a comfortable current-account surplus, despite considerable outflows for military forces, aid, travel, and remittances.

The capital side of the balance of payments told a differ-

TABLE 6.1

U.S. Balance of Payments Statistics, 1960 to 1970 (In Millions of Dollars)

	1960	1962	1964	1966	1968	1970
Trade Balance	4892	4521	6801	3817	635	2603
Net Investment Income	3378	4298	5041	5047	5989	6233
Net Military Transactions	−2752	−2449	−2133	−2939	−3143	−3354
Net Travel and Transportation	−964	−1152	−1146	−1331	−1548	−2038
Other Services	639	912	1161	1497	1759	2330
Other Transfers	−2367	−2740	−2901	−3064	−3082	−3443
Current Balance	2824	3388	6822	3034	621	2360
Long-term Capital	−3962	−4874	−7187	−6079	−2750	−6251
Basic Balance	−1138	−1486	−366	−3045	−2129	−3891

Note: Numbers may not add because of rounding.
Sources: *Economic Report of the President, 1990* (Washington, D.C.: U.S. Government Printing Office, 1990), p. 410; OECD, *Balance of Payments of OECD Countries: 1960–1977* (Paris: OECD, 1979), pp. 10–11.

ent story. The recurring deficits in America's "basic" balance of payments, a measurement that includes long-term capital flows as well as the current account, disclosed that the real economy was spending and investing abroad more than it was earning, despite its current-account surplus.[3] A detailed look at the elements of that basic balance showed that the net surplus on merchandise trade, foreign investment income, and other services was regularly overwhelmed by the outflow for net military transactions, government aid, and net private investment.

This phenomenon—a basic balance of payments deficit together with a current-account surplus—suggests a certain redefinition of the concept of "absorption." Normally, the term includes only investment and consumption at home. But in an interdependent global economy, many countries—and particularly a global superpower like the United States—also consume and invest heavily abroad. When this "overseas absorption"—for such purposes as military bases or corporate investments—exceeds the current-account surplus, the country may be said to be overabsorbing. In other words, the United States in the 1960s was not producing enough—at home or abroad—to cover its combined domestic and foreign consumption, investment, and government spending. By the same calculation, it was not saving enough to finance both its domestic and foreign investment. In short, despite its current-account surplus it was overabsorbing and was thus in real disequilibrium with the rest of the world economy.

No other country could have continued in such a posture for long, particularly in a fixed-rate system like Bretton Woods. Normally, when a country overabsorbs, it shows a balance of payments deficit and either runs out of reserves or devalues its currency. But since the Bretton Woods system was not a gold standard but a "gold-exchange standard," it designated certain currencies, most notably the dollar, as "reserve currencies." That meant that other countries could choose to hold dollars as monetary reserves or use them in international transactions in place of gold. Under postwar conditions, with America playing such a predominant role militarily as well as economically, such an arrangement confirmed the United States as the world's monetary hegemon. Its currency was everyone else's real money. In effect, the United States owned a paper gold mine.

In theory, foreigners could exchange all their dollars for gold upon demand. But in practice, the system encouraged and ultimately constrained foreign central banks to hold their accumulated dollars as reserves, rather than convert them into gold. The system also encouraged the private firms and individuals abroad to hold dollars rather than to exchange them for their own national currencies.[4] A giant "offshore" capital market, the Eurodollar market, grew up to mobilize those expatriate dollars and began to attract funds from central banks as well as private holders. The regular outflow of American credit thus resulted in a huge "overhang" of American obligations to foreigners, a debt that soon far exceeded America's own reserves, and indeed the reserves of all other central banks combined.[5] Ultimately, the overhang forced the United States to default on its contractual obligation to maintain a fixed exchange rate.

While it lasted, however, the system permitted the United States to finance its basic balance of payments deficit simply by creating more credit at home and exporting it abroad. This gave the United States numerous advantages. It created the buying power that American investors wanted but without requiring commensurate domestic saving. Instead of producing price inflation at home, the exported credit helped push up prices abroad, particularly in Europe, the principal recipient of American overseas investment in the 1950s and 1960s.[6] Exporting inflation to Europe through a negative basic balance actually helped to keep the United States trade balance positive, just as the growing overseas earnings repatriated from America's foreign investments, financed through the negative basic balance, helped to keep the current-account balance positive. As the manager of the world's reserve currency, the United States had thus moved into the position of a bank, making profits by issuing credit in excess of its own reserves. In this case, however, the credit was being spent by the banker, his IOU then being used by everyone else as money. This gave the United States a formidable advantage for accumulating real assets abroad.

The system was indubitably "hegemonic." In the gold-exchange standard, all national currencies were not created equal. A United States deficit with another country could be paid in dollars—of which the United States had no shortage—as opposed to gold—of which it had a finite supply. The exploitative and unstable nature of the process was understood well enough by the governments of America's allies. The French were the most vocal critics. They had disliked the gold-exchange standard ever since its first appearance in 1923, and blamed the subsequent monetary collapse and Great Depression on that standard's asymmetrical anomalies and inflationary propensities.[7]

European resentments became a major political issue as early as 1965, when General de Gaulle made the exploitative, inflationary, and unstable character of the Bretton Woods system a subject for one of his magisterial press conferences.[8] The growing presence of United States corporations in Europe's national economies made the "American challenge" a hot political topic.[9]

The Bretton Woods formula, of course, had an Achilles' heel. The United States was pledged to redeem foreign dollar holdings with gold. American reserves were grossly inadequate if major central banks or private holders of the huge overhang began demanding conversion. In due course, that is what happened. The United States defaulted in stages, starting with the "two-tier" gold market in 1968.[10]

The historical problem is not explaining why the Bretton Woods system collapsed but rather why it lasted so long. It had, of course, ardent academic defenders. The growing world economy needed liquidity to grow, they argued, and America's balance of payments deficits were the only means available to provide that liquidity.[11] Throughout the 1960s, however, the United States did try a series of measures to reduce the dollar outflow, including capital controls on corporate investment abroad. But such measures were hardly compatible with America's historic role as patron of an integrating global economy. Nor were the Kennedy and Johnson administrations, bent on growth, willing to tolerate domestic interest rates sufficient to reverse the capital outflow. The United States was thus driven to taking a more direct political approach to defending the dollar. Pressures and blandishments focused on Canada, Germany, and Japan—America's three principal creditors—and helped sustain the dollar through the late 1960s. So long as the Europeans and Japanese depended on United States military protection, they were reluctant to diminish American prestige or alienate American opinion. And it was in no one's interest, as even de Gaulle made abundantly clear, to precipitate a general monetary collapse.

In the end, it took a series of major shocks before the Bretton Woods system finally did break down. The Vietnam War was the greatest of these shocks. A large part of Western public opinion began to see the United States as an imperialist oppressor, bringing a loss of good reputation that was all the more painful after the near euphoric prestige of the Kennedy era. American public opinion itself grew distracted, divided, and even violent. The country also began losing its economic balance. Inflationary pressures accelerated as added military spending piled on top of President Johnson's ambitious civil programs. Johnson, fearful that critics of his social programs and the war would somehow combine, delayed pressing for a tax increase and castigated the Federal Reserve when it tried to tighten monetary conditions in 1966.

Even by 1965, however, domestic price inflation was growing visible. Credit inflation was no longer merely for export, it had begun leaking out at home. Higher domestic prices helped undermine the trade balance, which generated a sharp reaction among Americans themselves. Influential economists, in and out of government, began complaining of the "overvalued" dollar and arguing for a new policy of "benign neglect" of the dollar's exchange rate. The stage was being set for an international monetary system with floating rates and, with it, a new formula for financing America's worsening fiscal and external deficits. Delivering the coup de grace, however, was put off until Richard Nixon's presidency. In 1968, the last year of the Johnson administration, the United States switched abruptly to tight monetary and fiscal policies. As Nixon came into office in 1969, the consequences were a slowing of price inflation and a respite from pressure on the dollar, together with a severe recession. The United States had caught the British disease of stagflation.[12] Nixon, with an eye on the congressional elections, abandoned austerity in 1970. His reflation led to a massive run on the dollar in 1971, whereupon he gave up trying to keep the old rules and instead let the dollar float. With floating exchange rates, Nixon hoped to escape from the straitjacket of stop-go, while addressing the country's basic economic and geopolitical problems.

NIXON'S PROBLEMS

The American situation in 1969 gave Richard Nixon good cause to regret his defeat in 1960. Instead of inheriting great opportunities from the frugal Eisenhower, Nixon inherited big problems from Eisenhower's successors. Extricating the United States from Vietnam was the biggest problem. If not managed properly, Nixon feared, withdrawal could lead to a general assault on American positions around the world, and greatly increase the danger of nuclear war. And within the United States, "neoisolationist" reactions on both left and right might severely limit America's world role in the future.

Neoisolationism also had an economic dimension. The faltering trade balance in the late 1960s suggested a decline of America's industrial competitiveness. With fixed exchange rates, America's inflation had made the dollar increasingly "overvalued," which disadvantaged domestic American producers and provoked a wave of protectionist feeling in important segments of industry and labor.[13] But while domestic producers were demanding protection, internationally oriented firms were demanding deregulation. As the dollar grew weaker in the 1960s, the Kennedy and Johnson administrations had imposed capital controls to lessen the outflow. Multinational enterprise in general was fed up with these, and big banks chafed at regulations that kept them out of the rapidly growing Eurodollar business.

As time went on, the Nixon administration also faced an increasingly severe fiscal squeeze. By the end of the Johnson administration, inflation, "bracket creep," and the temporary tax increase of 1968 had considerably strengthened the government's revenue base.[14] But by the early 1970s, the tax surcharge had lapsed and outlays for the civil initiatives of the Kennedy and Johnson era—including Medicare—were gaining momentum.[15] And demographic trends—more young and more old people—were pushing up retirement benefits and education costs. Demographic and social trends had also changed the work force in ways that led to structurally higher unemployment.[16] Meanwhile, Nixon's "neofederalist" policy pushed up federal contributions to state and local governments.[17] By 1971, federal deficits were rising sharply. By the mid-1970s, they would be at a new order of magnitude for peacetime.

In addition to its growing fiscal problem, the Nixon administration also faced deeply entrenched domestic price inflation. Although the Bretton Woods mechanism had transmitted a good part of America's excess credit creation of the 1960s to the rest of the world, the rate of domestic price inflation had nevertheless more than trebled from 1964 to 1966—from 1.0 percent to 3.5 percent. It had nearly doubled again by 1970—to 5.6 percent.[18]

By the 1970s, moreover, a significant amount of the ex-

TABLE 6.2

**Growth in the Federal Budget Deficit,
1960 to 1980
(In Billions of Dollars)**

YEAR	CURRENT DOLLARS	CONSTANT 1982 DOLLARS	PERCENT OF GNP
1967	− 8.6	− 26.8	−1.1
1968	−25.2	− 74.2	−3.0
1969	3.2	9.0	0.3
1970	− 2.8	− 7.4	−0.3
1971	−23.0	− 55.4	−2.2
1972	−23.4	− 53.5	−2.0
1973	−14.9	− 32.0	−1.2
1974	− 6.1	− 12.0	−0.4
1975	−53.2	− 93.9	−3.5
1976	−73.7	−120.9	−4.3
1977	−53.6	− 81.6	−2.8
1978	−59.2	− 84.1	−2.7
1979	−40.2	− 52.7	−1.6
1980	−73.8	− 87.3	−2.8

Figures include both on and off-budget receipts and outlays.
Source: *Historical Tables: Budget of the United States Government, Fiscal Year 1990* (Washington, D.C.: U.S. Government Printing Office, 1989), p. 17.

ported inflation that had accumulated abroad began to be reexported back to the United States through the exploding prices of primary commodities—especially food and oil. Oil prices, which had been trending downward since the 1950s, were boosted abruptly by the producers' cartel, OPEC (Organization of Petroleum Exporting Countries), galvanized into action by the Arab-Israeli War of 1973. Their success rested on long-accumulating changes in the oil market, together with the already sharp upsurge of inflation throughout the world, a trend which their action greatly accelerated. The fourfold increase in oil prices set at the end of 1973 had a major effect on economic conditions for the next decade. But United States domestic prices were already increasing at a rate of around 9 percent a year by the time the oil shock occurred.[19]

THE NIXON FORMULA

Nixon's "New Economic Policy" was his major initiative to cope with America's mounting economic difficulties. In a dramatic announcement on August 15, 1971, in the midst of a gigantic run on the dollar, Nixon suspended convertibility indefinitely, put a surcharge of 10 percent on half of America's imports, controlled wages and prices for ninety days, and proposed new tax and spending cuts, including a 10-percent cut in foreign aid.[20]

Nixon's measures reflected a broad new formula that was to prevail in American policy through most of the decade. His rhetoric tried to make a virtue out of necessity. By abandoning deflation in 1970, he himself had made the dollar's fall inevitable. He tried to salvage American prestige by treating devaluation as a major victory. The United States was reneging on its Bretton Woods obligations not out of weakness, the administration claimed, but crack down on its freeloading allies.[21] For a time, Nixon's formula worked well. The dollar declined significantly but gradually, and American exports picked up significantly.[22] Politically, the jingoist rhetoric appealed to neo-isolationist sentiment without making any real concessions to it. The actual policy pleased the various economic constituencies most immediately involved. Floating the dollar liberated America's banking and other internationally oriented businesses from the capital controls that impeded them in the rapidly growing global economy. Devaluing also helped domestic-based industrial producers by raising the cost of foreign goods.

From a classic economic perspective, however, Nixon's solution was only cosmetic. To give lasting benefits to trade, a devaluation has to be accompanied by domestic deflation. If demand is not deflated at home, consumption of imports will not be squeezed from the domestic market, nor will domestic production be liberated for exporting abroad. Instead, more expensive imports will help push up domestic prices and general price inflation will cancel the effects of devaluation.

Nixon, however, had devalued to escape deflation, not to embrace it. Reluctant to cut military spending more drastically, and unable to stop the rapidly rising civil spending, he relied on the Federal Reserve to monetize the growing fiscal deficits. The Fed acquiesced. Monetary restraint was applied only in times of acute price inflation, as in 1973. The rest of the time, monetary conditions were easy.[23] Internationally, therefore, Nixon's formula could not be a once-for-all adjustment of the dollar's parity. Instead, it was a policy of relying on repeated devaluations to accommodate domestic inflation. Bretton Woods could never be restored, as the Europeans hoped, because the dollar would never really stabilize. A regime of floating rates was inevitable. How much the dollar declined (or rose) would ultimately depend on how America's credit inflation interacted with that of its major partners. While America's huge capital exports continued to stoke inflation overseas, the dollar nevertheless declined 47 percent against the German deutschemark from 1971 to 1979.[24]

Like the Bretton Woods formula, the Nixon formula based itself on America's special international advantages. A European country that devalues its currency, but refuses to limit domestic demand, soon finds its domestic prices and wages skyrocketing, because such a large part of the goods sold in its domestic market are imported from abroad. Rising food prices, for example, quickly translate into inflationary wage demands while rising raw material prices easily turn into inflated prices for manufactured goods. In other words, price inflation soon cancels the foreign trade advantages of devaluation and further devaluation simply accelerates the inflationary spiral. The

United States is in a somewhat different position. As a large and relatively autarchic economy, America supplies a large part of its own food and raw materials, and many of the raw materials it does import heavily, oil for example, are priced in dollars. The United States thus has a comparative advantage in beggar-thy-neighbor devaluations.

At the time, America's competitors were not in a good position to retaliate. Europeans faced a Hobson's choice. If they bought in the currency markets to support the dollar, they would be importing inflation as they had under the Bretton Woods system. If they remained inactive as the dollar fell, their trade would suffer—particularly in key areas like aircraft, armaments, or other high-technology products where they were struggling to become competitive with more powerful American firms. Putting up tariffs on these depreciated American exports invited American retaliation and was, in any event, difficult to reconcile with continuing dependency on American military protection. Faced with such unpromising alternatives, America's affluent allies complained and temporized. Gradually, they grew more serious about constructing a monetary bloc of their own.[25]

If Nixon's formula was a success in the short term, its natural consequence, domestic price inflation, could not be held off forever—certainly not while record federal deficits were being financed by credit inflation. For a time, Nixon used wage and price controls to suppress the consequences. Political power, in effect, substituted for economics. When the 1972 presidential election was over, the controls came off. Prices exploded. The consumer price index jumped from 3.4 percent in 1972 to 8.7 percent in 1973—to 12.3 percent in 1974![26] By 1974, the Fed's frightened reaction, the food and oil price shocks, and the general effects of inflation on purchasing power all combined to push the economy into its deepest recession since World War II. Nixon, crippled by the Watergate scandal, was bundled out of office. His formula, however, was resurrected in 1975 and survived through most of the decade.

NIXON'S FORMULA AND THE OIL CRISIS

The huge oil price increase that fell upon the world economy in 1974 changed the basic patterns of American policy

very little. After an interlude of deflation, America's ultimate
reaction was merely a variation on Nixon's overall formula.
When the oil shock actually was felt in 1974, the Fed was already sharply tightening monetary conditions in reaction to
the exploding price inflation of 1973. Tight money and rising
prices—first for food and then for fuel—squeezed consumer
budgets and depressed consumption of other products. A
recession was the natural result. With domestic demand re-
strained, the trade balance moved back into surplus, despite
the oil shocks, and the current-account balance grew strongly
positive.[27] When the Fed began to reflate in 1975, the reviving
economy brought a rising demand for imports, oil included,
which eventually pushed the whole current account into record deficit, where it remained stuck until the next recession.[28]

From a classic liberal perspective, any sustained reflation
under the circumstances of the oil shock was perversely
wrongheaded. A nation faced with a long-term increase in the
price of a fundamental import like oil should let the price effects deflate general demand in order to free production for
more exports. Essentially, that was the policy followed by Europeans and Japanese. Europeans, following such a regime,
saw their rates of growth diminish very sharply. The United
States, by contrast, continued to stimulate growth, finance its

TABLE 6.3

**Annual Growth of Real GNP/GDP
(Percentage Change)**

	1960–73 (ANNUAL AVERAGE)	1974	1975	1976	1977	1978	1979	1974–79 AVG.
U.S.	3.8	−0.5	−1.3	4.9	4.7	5.3	2.5	3.0
Germany	4.3	0.2	−1.4	5.6	2.7	3.3	4.0	2.4
France	5.7	3.2	0.2	5.2	3.1	3.8	3.3	3.1
Total EEC	4.7	1.8	−0.9	4.9	2.4	3.1	3.2	2.4
Total OECD	4.9	0.8	−0.2	4.8	3.5	4.0	3.1	2.6

Note: Figures for France, EEC, and OECD are in terms of GDP.
Sources: *Economic Report of the President, 1990* (Washington, D.C.: U.S. Government
Printing Office, 1990), p. 419; OECD, *Economic Outlook, Historical Statistics, 1960–1985*
(Paris: OECD, 1987), p. 44; and *Economic Outlook, 48* (Paris: OECD, December, 1990),
p. 181.

fiscal disequilibrium in part through inflation, and treat its external disequilibrium with benign neglect. While a falling dollar did not cure the American external disequilibrium, except during a recession, it did keep American exporters relatively competitive. And United States growth rates, sharply lower than European growth rates in the 1960s, held up better in the 1970s.

When Europeans complained about the Nixon formula's chronic beggar-thy-neighbor depreciation of the dollar, the Carter administration countered with a "locomotive theory"— a Keynesian analysis of the interwar depression applied to the effects of the oil shock.[29] The huge oil price increase, it was argued, had taken a substantial chunk of the world's income away from high-consuming societies, like Europe and the United States, and given it to high-saving countries, like most members of OPEC. The oil shock had thus brutally deflated overall demand within the world economy. Oversaving and collapsing demand would lead to a new depression just as, in the Keynesian view, they had caused the Great Depression of the 1930s. Catastrophe could be avoided only if rich countries pumped up their domestic demand and ran balance of payments deficits to counteract the excessive saving of the OPEC countries. That was the way to keep the world economy out of a deflationary spiral.[30] The United States was itself clearly fulfilling its obligation to spend freely. The Europeans should join the locomotive, in other words coordinate their policies to inflate as rapidly as the Americans. Doing so would also take care of the falling dollar.[31] While the allies resisted in theory, several did adopt more expansive policies.[32]

The oil shock, combined as it was with America's expansive monetary policy and benign neglect of the dollar, proved a particular bonanza for American banks. With credit easy and OPEC savings high, American banks bid vigorously to "recycle" funds to borrowers, often in the third world, who were having trouble adjusting their economies to the new oil price. Spectacular United States bank profits were the result, but set the stage for the banking crisis of the 1980s.

THE FALL OF THE NIXON FORMULA

By 1979, domestic and foreign reactions finally forced the United States to abandon the Nixon formula. Domestic American inflation rates had reached a startling annual 13.3 percent. OPEC had engineered a second major rise in oil prices, to regain in one blow what had been lost to the dollar's depreciation since 1974. Bond prices had fallen sharply and the price of gold soared from $300 to $875 per ounce. The dollar was threatening to go into a free fall. In effect, oil, gold, foreign exchange, and domestic credit markets all coalesced in a general revolt against American inflation. President Carter responded in 1979 by appointing a new and strong-minded chairman of the Federal Reserve, Paul Volcker, who quickly imposed severe monetary restraint. Real interest rates jumped to unprecedented levels.[33] The 1970s thus closed like the 1960s—with a recession caused by the collapse of the prevailing policy formula.

Volcker initially hoped to move the economy decisively toward price stability and fiscal and external balance. Prolonged monetary restraint was to wring inflation out of the nation's economic culture. Lower real interest rates could then prompt investment and bring a noninflationary recovery. Success required fiscal restraint, so that federal borrowing could be reduced sharply. Interest rates could then be brought down without having to inflate credit. There seemed reasonable hope for a decisive fiscal improvement. Inflation and bracket creep had generated a substantially higher revenue base for income taxes, while Congress had mandated increases in social security taxes.[34]

THE REAGAN FORMULA

The incoming Reagan administration, however, had quite different ideas. It supported Volcker's campaign to root out price inflation, but not the fiscal restraint that his overall strategy required. Instead, the administration pushed through big "supply-side" income tax cuts in 1981, along with an indexing of tax brackets.[35] In theory, the tax cut was supposed to stimulate rapid growth of the economy, and a corresponding jump in federal revenue. In fact, the big revenue increases of the 1970s abruptly ceased. Meanwhile, defense spending in constant dollars gradually returned to the levels of the Vietnam and Korean wars. Civil programs continued to grow, albeit at a slower rate. The chronic deficits of the 1970s thus rose to a historic extreme. The 1982 deficit, in constant dollars, was already the largest in the postwar era.[36]

Volcker's determination to keep money tight had produced a severe credit squeeze by 1979. Real interest rates that had long been negative became abruptly positive.[37] Reagan's big fiscal deficit in 1981 intensified the pressure. The postwar era's most severe recession resulted. After the long inflationary debt binge of the 1970s, the consequences were highly destabilizing for both domestic and international economies. Mexico had fallen into a debt crisis so severe that it alone threatened the solvency of the United States banking system.[38] By 1982, the Fed felt constrained to start easing credit. Interest rates fell and the economy began to recover, but by the latter part of 1983, the Fed felt safe to resume its anti-inflationary vocation. The fiscal deficit, meanwhile, continued to grow. A new jump in domestic interest rates was only natural.[39] More surprising was the large inflow of foreign savings that rushed to the United States to take advantage of the higher yields and lower taxes.[40] The inflow eased credit conditions and the recovery resumed.[41] The United States had now found a new formula to replace the Nixon policy. Deficits were being financed not by credit inflation but by borrowing foreign savings. In effect, the United States was borrowing back the inflated dollars that had been exported throughout the 1960s and 1970s.

With the heavy inflow of foreign capital came a radical increase in the dollar's exchange rate. The high dollar, together with a domestic boom, naturally meant a large trade deficit.

The inflow of foreign goods, made cheap by the high dollar, helped keep down domestic American prices, at least for goods traded internationally. Thus, the Reagan boom could continue without the domestic price inflation that had sapped the Nixon and Carter booms. In other words, foreign savings financed America's fiscal deficit, while foreign goods kept down America's domestic prices.

Europe and Japan were able to assume this complementary role because they were following restrictive macroeconomic policies that naturally gave them a surplus of savings and production. Like the United States, Germany and later

TABLE 6.4

**Balance on Merchandise and Current Accounts
(In Billion of Dollars)**

| YEAR | MERCHANDISE ACCOUNTS | | | CURRENT ACCOUNT | |
	EXPORTS	IMPORTS	NET	CURRENT	CONSTANT*
1980	224.3	−249.7	−25.5	1.5	1.8
1981	237.1	−265.1	−28.0	8.2	8.7
1982	211.2	−247.6	−36.4	−7.0	−7.0
1983	201.8	−268.9	−67.1	−44.3	−42.6
1984	219.9	−332.4	−112.5	−104.2	−96.7
1985	215.9	−338.1	−122.1	−112.7	−101.6
1986	223.4	−368.4	−145.1	−133.2	−117.1
1987	250.3	−409.8	−159.5	−143.7	−122.4
1988	319.3	−446.5	−127.2	−126.5	−104.3

*1982 dollars. Totals may not add due to rounding.
Source: *Economic Report of the President, 1990,* p. 410; author's calculations of constant dollars.

France had embarked upon a supply-side policy. They, too, sought to raise business profits to spur investment and productivity, but their strategy was very different from the American. Their first priority was not lowering taxes but lowering the cost of borrowing by reducing their fiscal deficits. At the same time, their monetary policy was kept tight enough to dampen domestic demand, and thus to keep down prices and wages. Relatively lower borrowing costs, prices, and wages were, they thought, the way to reach and preserve higher profit margins. The cost of this strategy was unusually high unemployment.

American policy both helped and harmed European policy. America's strong demand for capital sucked away European savings and kept up European interest rates. The strong dollar also raised the relative price of oil and other raw materials, further squeezing European business margins and keeping up unemployment. But America's strong demand for foreign products also greatly helped the European strategy. European governments could suppress domestic demand, and thus lower wage and capital costs, in part because the strong

American demand took its place. In other words, German and Japanese savings helped to finance American debt, but American consumption—made possible through borrowing—also encouraged the Germans and Japanese to produce, save, and invest.[42]

Ironically, the Reagan supply-side formula thus provided more favorable supply-side conditions for production and investment abroad than in the United States itself. The overvalued dollar gravely handicapped a large part of American manufacturing and agriculture, despite a continuing American consumer boom. Since foreign goods were cheaper, American profit margins were severely cut and many farms and manufacturers went bankrupt. United States investment was thus directed away from industries that had to compete with foreign goods toward the service sector, tax shelters, or real estate and financial speculation generally. Failing firms and speculative overheating began to prepare a new financial crisis, signaled in May 1984 by the failure of Continental Illinois, a major regional bank. By 1985, these troubles forced the Fed to relent once more. A new credit expansion refreshed the consumer boom and fueled a great speculative boom in real estate and corporate takeovers. But thanks to the still unfavorable profit margins in manufacturing, there was little investment in new productive capacity. Foreign savings continued to flow in for the speculative bonanza, despite attempts among the major central banks to coordinate an "orderly decline" of the dollar.[43] With the dollar still high, cheapened imports continued to keep United States price inflation at bay—and American manufacturing profits down.

The situation carried the seeds of its own demise. Borrowing to finance consumption or investments that add little to production makes the stock of debt grow faster than the stock of productive investment. Interest costs began to grow more rapidly than income. By 1986, the economy's ratio of overall debt to GNP reached levels not seen since just before the crash of 1929. The pattern's unsustainability grew obvious and confidence in the dollar rapidly eroded. Private foreign capital flows ceased and the faltering dollar had to be shored up by massive support from foreign governments.[44] By the year's end, household borrowing also began to fall. A major stock market crash ensued in October 1987. The Fed reacted with a huge outpouring of liquidity that pushed the dollar to a historic low against the yen and the deutschemark by the end of the year. The Reagan formula, as such, had run its course. The boom sputtered on until 1990, helped by an export boom generated by the now low dollar, together with a shift to expansive policies in Europe. But by 1990, the United States was in a recession brought on, in good part, by speculative collapses and a debt crisis throughout the economy.

THE FORMULAS REVISITED

However much America's formulas have varied from one decade to the next, there have been two constants. One is the inability to match fiscal outlays with fiscal income. The other is the ability to command whatever extra resources are needed from the rest of the world. At no time were these two features more notorious than during the Reagan era. Fiscal and external deficits reached a new order of magnitude, yet foreign savings flowed in freely to finance the gap. The dollar's strength defied all the economic laws of gravity meant to explain currency flows and exchange rate movements. Exchange rates are supposed to adjust to "purchasing power parity." Most of the time in the 1980s, the dollar was clearly overvalued.[45] Similarly, an oversupply of a national money in world markets is supposed to trigger a fall in that currency's value. Perpetual and huge United States current-account deficits continued to flood currency markets throughout the decade. But an infinite supply of foreign investors nevertheless seemed confident in the dollar's value as a safe haven, or in the Fed's capacity to control inflation. By the middle of the 1980s, the United States was drawing the bulk of internationally available savings not only from its rich allies but from impoverished third world countries as well.[46] The grossly overvalued dollar finally came down only when it became flagrantly obvious that United States authorities were determined themselves to bring it down. In short, the huge sums sucked in to finance the Reagan era's deficits suggested that America's capacity to command foreign resources was greater than ever.

That the world's richest country should go on borrowing such a large part of the world's capital to support its government spending and general standard of living seems difficult to regard as a rational allocation of global resources. Yet, one way or another, the practice has endured for several decades. Two obvious questions arise: How does America's global appropriation affect its real economy—in particular productivity and therefore the ability to compete over the long term? And how much longer can America expect to go on with it? Chapter 7 takes up the first question and Chapter 8 adds the second.

Chapter 7 *Fiscal Deficits, Public Goods, and the Real Economy*

Showing precise links between government policy and what actually happens in the "real" economy of working and selling is inevitably uncertain and controversial. No mechanistic model can capture the copious variety of America's sprawling economy; and analyzing government policy alone can seldom explain that economy's performance. But government policy does matter. The national state does have vital economic functions to perform. And if its policies are ill-conceived—if it does not adequately provide certain public goods—the economy may adapt, but there will be a cost.

One of the most vital public goods is sound money. Thanks in large part to the various ways of financing America's chronic fiscal deficits described in the last chapter, sound money is a public good that has long been lacking to the American economy. With highly volatile interest, inflation, or exchange rates, the dollar has been unstable, domestically or internationally, since the 1960s. On the surface, America's market economy has adapted well enough. But the by-product is a chain of chronic pathological symptoms. When considered together with fundamental changes in the world economy, those symptoms do not bode well for America's long-term economic future.

This chapter explores some of the symptoms of the 1980s, and the inadequacies of macroeconomic policy that have contributed to them. In particular, the chapter discusses America's lagging productivity and incomes, its increased business debt, its propensity for speculation over long-term investment, and its crisis in the financial industry. All those symptoms are discouraging. Bad and inconstant public policy has fed them all.

THE GENERAL CHALLENGE

The United States is not, of course, the only country that needs to worry about long-term economic trends. Europe has been bedeviled with "Eurosclerosis" since the 1970s. The Soviet economy has for some time been on the verge of collapse. Even Japan has had a considerable crisis of confidence in recent years.[1] Every advanced economy has felt itself challenged by rapid historical changes and feared that its responses were inadequate. There are, moreover, very good reasons for these feelings.

After the spectacular growth of the earlier postwar decades, the 1970s and 1980s were comparatively difficult. The progress of democratic welfare capitalism, part of the unprecedented prosperity of the 1960s, saddled most Western economies with high labor and social costs, a decline in profit margins, and a deterioration of investment prospects. Meanwhile, the cold war continued to impose military burdens— heavy for the United States, very heavy for the Soviet Union, but also significant for several states in Western Europe. Among the major capitalist economies, only Japan largely avoided this twin burden of welfare and arms.[2]

To sustain these high costs and still remain competitive, Western economies must keep increasing their productivity— their ratio of output to input. That has meant straining to stay ahead in those high value-added technologies, products, and services that generate high returns. Productivity, however, is not the only concern. There is also full employment. Even in economic terms, it cannot be satisfactory to achieve high productivity in one part of an economy if, at the same time, a substantial part of a country's human and other capital is left unemployed. Such a result is even less acceptable culturally, socially, and politically. The modern Western man tends to find his identity, self-respect, and place in society through his job. Increasingly, this is true of the modern Western woman as well. Satisfactory employment for the adult population is thus an end in itself, quite apart from the income that results. High unemployment, even when assuaged by generous welfare benefits, seems a corrosive evil that undermines the society's vitality and cohesion. Thus, high productivity and high employment are the twin and sometimes conflicting goals of public policy.

The struggle to achieve those goals has grown increasingly arduous. The various shocks that ushered in the 1970s—the social unrest, the floating of the dollar, and the abruptly escalating oil prices—did more than reflect the assorted breakdowns and conspiracies of the day. They also marked the onset of a severe technological and industrial challenge to all advanced societies. Exceptionally rapid technological change promised revolutionary changes in productivity that could create, destroy, or transform whole industries overnight.[3] At the same time, formidable industrial competition in traditional products such as textiles, shoes, steel, and consumer electronics was building up from rapidly industrializing countries with cheap labor.[4] These twin challenges, at both the upper and lower ends of industry, provided a harsh new framework for national policy and international competition.

In the complex process of economic and social adaptation that has followed, every advanced nation has demonstrated its own mixture of strengths and liabilities. In the end, performance has depended heavily on such elusive elements as economic and social culture, managerial skills, entrepreneurship, or luck. But government policy has certainly hindered or helped. Every government has made mistakes, but some have proved more persistently dysfunctional than others. The American government has been a particularly heavy cross for its economy to bear.

AMERICA'S CHRONIC IMBALANCES

As might be expected, the American economy's performance since the 1970s has shown many strengths. American firms began ahead in most of the rapidly growing technological, consumer, and service industries. America's commercial technology has been able to profit from the abundance of uni-

versities and research centers and a lavish, if inefficient, sub-
sidy from the military budget. And the United States continues
to form a huge, rich, and naturally protected market, with ample capital and labor, easily supplemented from the rest of
the world.

By the end of the 1980s, the United States could still take
pride in a respectable growth rate, measured by the GDP, and
a comparatively low unemployment rate, made possible by an
impressive record in creating jobs.[5] But productivity growth
was lagging compared with Japan and most Western European countries. And there were a series of chronic and deeply
structured imbalances: the fiscal, trade and current-account
deficits, the need to borrow abroad, and a persistent tendency
toward inflation. All were related and at their core lay the fiscal deficit itself, along with the three major formulas for financing it that were discussed in Chapter 6.

Over the years, each of these formulas has had its own
particular syndrome of imbalances and bad effects. In each
case, a frequently unstable dollar has been the natural consequence. The cost has been high over the long term—for the
world, but particularly for the United States itself. An erratic
dollar has helped blight American productivity and incomes,
encouraged excessive speculation and debt, and then worked
to make the debt unmanageable. And it has done severe in-
jury to the financial industry itself. Tracing those consequences for the real economy through three formulas and over
three decades would obviously be a large and speculative work
in itself. But even a summary look at the workings of the Reagan formula in the 1980s gives ample illustration of the general damage.

UNSTABLE MONEY AND THE REAL ECONOMY:
THE 1980s

The government's macroeconomic policy in the 1980s was
set by the need to finance huge fiscal deficits without the price
inflation of the Nixon formula. In the resulting Reagan formula, Reagan contributed fiscal deficits, Volcker tight money
and high interest rates, and foreigners their savings. Together, they pushed up the dollar, which greatly expanded the
current-account deficit but kept down price inflation.

The consequences varied across the spectrum of American business. They were particularly severe for businesses based in the United States competing with producers based abroad. A large part of America's agricultural and manufacturing enterprises fall into this category. The Reagan formula's combination of big fiscal deficits and tight money meant high real interest rates that squeezed profit margins. It also made for a high dollar that kept import prices down, so that American producers could not raise their prices to recoup. Price inflation thus remained low in the parts of the economy subject to international competition, but so did profits.[6] Occasional periods of relative monetary ease and a falling dollar never lasted long enough to change the long-term prospects for these American producers, but instead sparked consumer booms that sucked in imports and speculative booms that pushed up stock and real estate prices.

Among manufacturing firms, strategies to meet the situation varied widely. Insofar as firms were benefiting from heavy military spending, they were exempt from the profit squeeze and could invest to meet the heavy new demand. Others, facing shrinking profits, invested heavily to improve their productivity. As a result, some firms began to reap outstanding productivity gains. Near the end of the decade, as the dollar declined sharply and European and Japanese economies began to reflate, these firms were in a strong position to raise their market share. Taken together, the record of such firms makes American productivity increases per worker in manufacturing look very respectable in the 1980s.[7]

At the same time, however, overall employment in the domestic manufacturing sector shrank relatively sharply in the United States. While investment in new labor-saving equipment was no doubt partly responsible, employment in manufacturing also fell because many American firms shifted their operations abroad, restructured, or went out of business altogether.[8] Domestic business investment that was not financial speculation tended to gravitate toward tax shelters or sectors insulated from international competition, notably commercial real estate, services, or manufacturing tied to the military budget.[9] Jobs in manufacturing fell 7.7 percent from 1979 to 1989, but jobs in the service sector increased 31.1 percent. The ratio of service sector to manufacturing jobs was two to one in 1960, three to one in 1979, and over four to one in 1989.[10] Creating new jobs was the American economy's most notable accomplishment in the 1980s. It looks particularly impressive by comparison with French and German economies in the same period. The United States had relatively lower unemployment, despite its comparatively high number of new workers.

LOW PRODUCTIVITY AND INCOME

America's record in creating jobs is blighted, however, by its relatively poor performance in raising productivity per person employed or hour worked. Between 1982 and 1989, the average annual increase in productivity per working hour was 2.7 percent in the Federal Republic of Germany, 3.1 percent in Japan, and 1 percent in the United States. This pattern, unfortunately, is of long duration.

Since the United States began the postwar era with a great lead in absolute productivity, American analysts have been able to console themselves that the country remains well ahead—

TABLE 7.1

Relative Productivity, 1960 to 1988
(Average Annual Percent Change)

	1960–68	1968–73	1973–79	1979–88
REAL GDP PER CAPITA				
U.S.	3.1	2.0	1.4	1.8
France	4.2	4.6	2.3	1.4
Germany	3.1	4.0	2.5	1.7
Japan	9.1	7.1	2.5	3.4
OECD less U.S.	4.4	4.6	2.1	2.1
REAL GDP PER EMPLOYED PERSON				
U.S.	2.6	1.0	0.0	1.1
France	4.9	4.3	2.5	2.0
Germany*	4.2	4.1	2.9	1.5
Japan	8.5	7.6	2.9	3.0
OECD less U.S.	4.9	4.7	2.4	1.9

*Germany: 1979–87.
Source: OECD, *Historical Statistics: 1960–1988* (Paris: OECD, 1990), pp. 48, 51.

even if the margin has been steadily shrinking. Some recent studies suggest that the moment of overtaking is near, or already past.[11] Comparing the absolute productivity of one nation with another is admittedly tricky. There is little doubt, however, about figures that have consistently shown overall United States productivity increasing more slowly than French, German, or Japanese over several decades. Such trends cannot go on indefinitely among advanced economies without affecting rankings.

The causes for America's lagging productivity in the 1980s do not seem mysterious. With competitive conditions unfavorable, thanks to the high dollar, and long-term costs and returns uncertain, thanks to fluctuating macroeconomic policies, capital was more attracted to speculation than to real investment. Aside from the defense industry, what investment there was in the real economy shifted away from manufacturing toward services. Since investment in manufacturing normally produces the greatest gains in productivity, the shift away from manufacturing meant comparatively low productivity growth for the economy as a whole. Growing services, however, created many new jobs. Thus, there was a trade-off between productivity and jobs.

America's relative shift of employment to services also went hand in hand with a sharply declining level of working-class income. Over the past three decades, wages in services have fallen sharply in relation to wages in manufacturing. In 1960, hourly rates in services were 64 percent of those in manufacturing. By 1988, they were 44 percent. For the work force as a whole, real hourly compensation had not risen appreciably since the second half of the 1970s. Figures for hourly earnings actually give too optimistic a picture, since many service jobs are part-time. Average real earnings per week of an American worker had actually fallen, by 1989, to below the level of 1961. By 1990, they were not even at the level of 1959! The fall in working-class incomes also contributed to a decline in private savings and rise in private debt.[12]

RECESSION, DEBT, AND SPECULATION

As was noted in Chapter 6, the Reagan era's selective hard times forced the Fed sporadically to relax its tight money—as during the 1982 Mexican debt crisis, or in 1984 with the failure of Continental Illinois. In 1985, depressed conditions prompted a serious effort to push down the dollar, and the stock market crash in October 1987 led to an intense shower of liquidity.[13] The combination of poor basic conditions for real investment with intermittently easy credit gradually fostered both a severe domestic debt crisis and a monstrous speculative bubble. In the end, the financial industry itself was deeply injured.

The causes for the general growth of debt in the 1980s go beyond the special needs of beleaguered farmers and manufacturers. Despite the straitened circumstances of so many producers, and the stagnant real earnings of the work force as a whole, consumption in America remained robust throughout the decade. It is because its consumption remained so strong that America's growth of GNP continued to look vigorous by comparison with that of most other Western economies.[14]

If real earnings were stagnant, what was fueling the strong consumption? The short answer is debt. With consumption growing and earnings stagnant or falling, savings obviously fell and private and public indebtedness increased to record levels.[15] The biggest relative growth of consumption in the economy was in the government sector.[16] It was made possible by a record peacetime growth in the public debt—an increasing portion of which was sold to foreigners.[17] The rise in government consumption was essentially for defense. Indeed, increased military spending accounted for about one third of the rise of consumption in the economy as a whole.[18] But private consumption also rose, despite stagnant real incomes. Here the government's general inadequacy in providing certain public goods played a critical role. The rise in private consumption could be laid to the rapid growth of medical care. The absolute rise in private consumption spending on health care was equal to the overall rise in private consumption outlays.[19]

Because of the high dollar, Reagan's consumption boom was, as we have seen, a bust for a large part of America's producers. Thus, alongside public and private debt for consumption was a growing business debt of a rather more desperate kind.[20] As stricken firms and regions fell further and further into debt, many regional banks assumed greater risks as they tried to save foundering clients.[21] This great increase in business debt began to be matched by a decline in its quality. Some bank loans began to degenerate from "hedge financing," where cash flow repays principal and interest, to "speculative financing," where cash flow covers interest but not principal. Many loans represented what may be called "Ponzi finance" (after the famous Boston swindler), where cash flow is so low that fresh borrowing is needed to cover even the interest payments.[22] Thus, the restraining effects on overall borrowing from tight money and high interest rates were undermined by lower standards for creditworthiness. Washington's fashion for banking "deregulation" helped the whole process along. Tight money was further mitigated, of course, by the Fed's own periodic bursts of credit inflation to stanch fears of a banking crisis, or to push down the dollar to help beleaguered farmers and manufacturers.

A business environment with unpromising prospects but at least intermittently abundant credit naturally encourages speculation. Moreover, the high real interest rates that handicapped many businesses also greatly facilitated speculation with their assets. High rates, particularly when resulting from tight monetary policy rather than high investment demand, naturally devalue shares as well as bonds. Stock prices are depressed further when corporate profits are low—another natural result of high real interest rates. In the 1980s, many firms saw their share prices fall even below the replacement value of their real net assets. Such a situation encouraged takeover bids and asset stripping, since speculators saw large profits from buying the devalued shares and selling off the real assets. Hard times were pushing firms to restructure in any event.

Banks, pressed into "creative financing" by the worsening position of so many of their clients, turned to financing takeovers. "Junk bonds" came into fashion—high-yield and high-risk instruments, their value based on the putative worth of assets to be taken over. Financial institutions and pension funds, worried by the prospect of large losses from deteriorating traditional investments, stocked up on these high-yield bonds to boost their current incomes. Meanwhile, the prevailing speculative climate encouraged business firms generally to borrow rather than to save, as often for defensive as for speculative reasons. Firms leery of a takeover threat were inclined to divest themselves of all liquid assets, since those were added incentive to corporate raiders. Many firms used their liquidity to buy back their own shares. To raise investment or working capital, they borrowed, since saving profits only made them more attractive targets, while selling their depressed equity shares left them more vulnerable to corporate raiders.[23] In addition, United States tax laws traditionally favor borrowing over accumulating profits or selling equity. Interest on loans is deductible from corporate profits whereas dividends, paid out of profits, are taxed. Indeed, they are taxed twice—first as part of net company earnings and then as part of the shareholder's income. Thanks to the tax laws, firms, especially in the noncorporate sector, found it easier to go into debt than to attract investment based on profit. This left them, however, with debt rather than equity—with creditors rather than shareholders.[24]

Speculators bidding for control of companies often pushed share prices well beyond the firm's real value. But once the takeover was achieved, the consequences were visited upon the captured company itself, now stripped of its liquid resources and loaded with the obligation to pay off the high-yield junk bonds used to finance its own pillage.[25] Original shareholders bought out at unnatural prices did very well, but original bondholders saw their assets decline radically in quality.[26] Many once well-established companies, thus stripped and laden, found themselves unable to continue without extensive new borrowing—often to meet operating costs and debt service. Such firms easily fell into a sort of rake's progress of unsound finance. Their degenerative spiral became a danger to their bankers. Once caught, banks had a powerful motive to try to keep such firms afloat in the hope that conditions would eventually improve. Where whole industries or regions were involved, banks themselves were at risk. The temptation to innovate new forms of credit and to market them aggressively grew difficult to resist. Banks became "Merchants of Debt."[27]

In due course, the financial industry itself has worked itself into a major crisis that threatens to affect the rest of the economy for a long time to come. Here again, the government bears heavy responsibility—not only because of its failure to regulate the industry properly, but because of its failure to create a stable monetary environment that would permit rational capital markets and efficient financial institutions.

THE FINANCIAL INDUSTRY'S STRUCTURAL PROBLEMS

Aside from greed, bad business judgment, and bad government policy, changing technology has anyway been making the whole financial industry progressively riskier. Thanks to computerization and radical improvements in international communications, large sums of money move instantaneously around the world and markets are ever more immediately integrated and responsive to each other. In domestic retail banking, credit cards, electronic transfers, automated cash machines, and money market funds have gradually made the traditional checking account seem an expensive and inefficient anachronism. "Disintermediation" has also extended to the investment end of banking, where innovations like private placements or a huge market for commercial paper and medium-term notes have permitted large corporations to bypass traditional bank lending for a good part of their financing needs. Such broad and revolutionary changes have naturally shaken the whole financial industry. Many American bankers have felt unfairly hindered by traditional regulatory arrangements to preserve small-scale retail banking and protect small depositors. Such arrangements have severely impeded that consolidation of financial institutions and national branch banking commonplace in Europe and Japan. Big foreign banks, moreover, have been pressing hard to enlarge their place in the American market.[28]

Under those circumstances, it is not surprising that the banking industry has grown more and more troubled and competitive. Since the 1960s, banks have seen a narrowing of the basic spreads between what they earn from putting out money and what they pay to get it. To squeeze more lending power out of their capital, deposits, and interbank borrowing, banks "innovate"—with riskier loans that charge higher rates or with "off-balance sheet" instruments that avoid reserve requirements. For many banks, innovation has paid off handsomely. Overall, real profits of banks have risen to new peaks in every decade in the postwar period.[29] But the creditworthiness of their loan portfolios has declined and their capital position has grown weaker. By the 1980s, the whole American banking structure had begun to appear fragile, and the risks to it from a severe recession more and more formidable.[30] Knowledgeable analysts regularly warned of the dangers hanging like a sword of Damocles over the entire financial system.[31]

Already in the 1970s, general financial instability was becoming a serious problem. Early in the decade, several large real estate investment trusts and a couple of big railroads went into bankruptcy. A few large banks joined the parade. The city of New York was heading toward bankruptcy. By the end of the decade, most big American banks had grown notoriously vulnerable to the Latin American debt crisis.[32] But each particular crisis along the way appeared to confirm the extraordinary resilience and inventiveness of the system as a whole. The government seemed always willing and able to float the financial industry off the rocks with fresh credit. By sustaining problem banks, the government was also ratifying the practices causing the problems. Big banks were emboldened by confidence that the government could never let them fail. Meanwhile, the government increased its guarantees to depositors and decreased its surveillance over institutions. Prolonged exposure to hypothetical risks that seldom were allowed to become actual bred further complacency. Over and over, it seemed, power and inventiveness could defy the traditional laws of economic balance.[33] Meanwhile, a great deal of money was being made.

Government policy was clearly responsible for a good part of the financial industry's later difficulties. Part of the problem lay with manifestly obsolescent regulations. No administration even attempted a systematic overhaul of banking legislation until the early 1990s, when a significant part of the industry was in bankruptcy or close to it.[34] Haphazard earlier changes, riding on a wave of ideological enthusiasm for "deregulation," merely opened the way to more speculation, while extending the government's own liabilities.[35] The American government's inadequacy, however, has had a more general and fundamental aspect. Banks are particularly vulnerable to radically fluctuating monetary policy that destabilizes the supply of credit and the demand for it. The fluctuating interest rates, exchange rates, and inflation rates that are the result greatly increase the risks and costs of banking.

THIRD WORLD DEBT

Bankers' problems with third world debt since the 1970s are a good illustration of how fluctuating monetary policy heightens risk. The oil shock of 1973 gave third world countries a choice between borrowing internationally or adjusting to higher energy prices by cutting domestic investment and consumption. The monetary conditions that prevailed in the United States through most of the 1970s made borrowing seem much preferable. The Nixon formula with its easy money, plus the high and rechanneled savings of OPEC countries, ensured ample international liquidity. Banks, awash with money, eagerly poured it out to supposedly safe "sovereign borrowers."[36] Rising price inflation actually offered domestic borrowers a negative real interest rate through significant periods of the decade. Foreign countries with large dollar earnings had similar advantages.[37]

When the United States switched to Volcker's tight money and then to the Reagan formula, it radically transformed the position of third world debtors. Formerly negative interest rates turned positive with a vengeance. Even for those with important dollar incomes, the dramatic appreciation of the United States currency sharply revalued the principal of their debts, as well as their real interest charges. It also had depressing consequences for export sales and thus for the dollar and other foreign currency earnings of many third world producers.[38] With credit markets tightened worldwide, new loans became difficult to arrange and old loans difficult to roll over. Banks, laden with portfolios of abruptly discounted loans, refused to lend long-term. Not surprisingly, third world and Eastern European borrowers began to default. The huge losses and potential losses have continued to blight bank earnings for more than a decade.[39]

THE SAVINGS AND LOAN DEBACLE

The same erratic swings in American macroeconomic policy have had similar effects on domestic debtors and their banks. Nowhere has the market cost of public inadequacy been more vividly illustrated than in the spectacular collapse of America's savings and loan industry. The disaster, brewing for two decades, seems difficult to exaggerate. By May of 1990, Secretary of the Treasury Nicholas Brady estimated that more than one thousand firms—around 40 percent of the industry—might have to be seized by the federal government for insolvency. According to the General Accounting Office, the minimum cost for bailing out the industry would be $325 billion over the next forty years.[40] With a serious recession, or higher interest rates than projected, the bill could easily accumulate to $500 billion by 2030. The price for this "economic Vietnam" will very probably exceed, in real terms, all the aid given to Europe under the Marshall Plan, plus the subsequent bailouts of Lockheed, Chrysler, Penn Central, and New York City combined.[41]

As usual, economic analysts rushed to show that the disaster was not nearly so bad as it seemed. The government, it was said, would merely borrow from capital markets to repay private savers. Those savers would presumably reinject their capital back into the credit markets. The macroeconomic effect would be limited largely to the government's interest and administrative costs. This relatively cheerful view was somewhat misleading. Much of the original capital had been squandered on foolish investments. The new capital to reimburse it was being taken from fresh savings that would otherwise have gone to other investments. Unless it is assumed that all investments in the American economy are invariably foolish, the lost opportunities were presumably real. In any event, the combined interest and administrative charges, estimated in mid-1990 at $170 billion, were hardly negligible and would increase the government's already heavy operating deficits for years to come.[42]

All sorts of indirect consequences are also part of the real cost. The continuing dangers of bankruptcy in the mortgage loan business may be expected to add a general risk premium to interest rates for the indefinite future. Considerable damage may be expected to the whole structure of housing credit and home ownership—a mainstay of the building industry and once thought a particular accomplishment of the American political economy. Home ownership has been declining for some time and actual homelessness is a major and growing social problem.[43] Meanwhile, a plethora of speculative commercial construction will depress and distort the real estate market in many parts of the country long into the future.[44] Much of this malinvestment can be traced to various forms of public inadequacy. A corrupt and foolish tax code has encouraged commercial overbuilding.[45] Depressed prices and the fluctuating dollar have brought a swarm of foreign as well as domestic speculators.

How the S and L failure came to pass illustrates very well the interaction between erratic federal macroeconomic policy and the troubles of the financial sector, as well as the consequences for the real economy. The federal government has guaranteed S and L deposits since the 1930s, both to encourage an adequate flow of savings into home building and to subsidize lower interest rates for home mortgages. Solvency for S and Ls depends upon interest rates. Rates paid to depositors have to remain low enough to balance the rates offered in long-term fixed mortgages. According to the traditional formula, mortgage rates were fixed long-term at 6 percent and depositors paid 3 percent.[46] In 1965, average mortgage rates for new houses stood at 5.81 percent, the average interest return on outstanding mortgages was 5.93, and the average cost of funds was 4.25 percent. Under those conditions, an S and L run with elementary prudence was eminently secure. But as inflation and the government's borrowing needs began to weigh more heavily on credit markets, interest rates and yields began to climb. By 1970, after the monetary crunch that began in 1968, the average cost of funds rose to 5.30 percent. With average interest returns on outstanding mortgages at 6.56 percent, S and Ls were growing precarious. By 1980, average interest returns on outstanding mortgages were at 9.31 percent, while the average cost of funds was at 8.94 percent. Thrifts were competing with new money market funds paying depositors a spread over six-month U.S. Treasury bills, which were themselves yielding 11.37 percent. In 1981 and 1982, the average cost of funds rose above the average return on mortgages.[47] S and Ls, as originally conceived, were structurally bankrupt.[48]

The drama played itself out through the further monetary vicissitudes of the 1980s. Congress and the Reagan administration sought a solution through deregulation. New legislation permitted S and Ls to loan for purposes other than home mortgages.[49] Minimum capital requirements were reduced and the range of assets eligible for meeting those requirements was greatly expanded. S and Ls were also free to pay market interest rates to depositors. Thus liberated, they were supposed to float themselves out of the bankruptcy inherent in their original mandate by joining the parade of fancy finance and dubious commercial investment that was the decade's specialty. Not surprisingly, owners and managers of S and Ls were not particularly adept at speculation. Their newly liberated capital helped build a huge bubble in commercial real estate. But they did not escape from bankruptcy; instead, their ruin took on a much grander scale. Bad luck played its usual part. Sectoral depressions in agricultural, oil, and industrial regions took a deadly toll in regional real estate markets.

Fraud was also commonplace. In effect, deregulation gave managements of the S and Ls a license to gamble, if not to steal. As Congress deregulated the S and Ls, it also raised federal guarantees to depositors—from $40,000 to $100,000 per individual account and with no effective limit on the number of accounts. At the same time, federal oversight was notoriously inadequate and the Reagan administration opposed increasing regulatory staffs. Regulators frequently took several years to close an insolvent institution. Meanwhile, its management could go on trying to recoup by speculating with federally guaranteed capital.[50] Members of Congress frequently interceded with the regulators—not always with disinterested motives. Scandals involved several senators and their staffs. Prolonged hearings amply exposed the corruption inherent in American political campaigns and the congressional process in general.[51] In short, the S and L crisis combined the chronic faults of American economic policy with the endemic debility of the political system. The result was a monstrous financial mess whose effects will blight the real economy long into the future.

PUBLIC GOODS AND NATIONAL PERFORMANCE

This chapter began by noting the difficult times through which all advanced economies have been passing. Rapid technological change and heightened competition have challenged every nation to adapt quickly and successfully, or watch its standard of living decline. Under such circumstances, problems in the real economy have been serious enough. Certainly general economic conditions since the 1970s would anyway have made bank lending unusually risky and forced great changes on banking practices. But in the United States, dysfunctional government policies have added greatly to the difficulties, both for the economy as a whole and for banking in particular. Not only has the American government failed to set and sustain a proper regulatory framework, it has also failed to set a proper macroeconomic framework. Its fiscal deficits have raised capital costs, while its tax policies have channeled investment in unproductive directions. Above all, its monetary policy has greatly increased the risks of long-term productive investment, while adding to the allure of speculation. That monetary policy has been dictated to a great extent by the exigencies of avoiding price inflation while financing a radically unbalanced fiscal policy.

MARKET COMPENSATION

A reasonably stable macroeconomic policy, favorable to rational long-term business investment, is in the nature of a public good. When the state does not provide such a policy, a market system does, of course, react to repair the public sector's inadequacy. Monetary instability since the 1970s has, for example, induced an enormous increase in hedging, swapping, and arbitrage. Those practices have absorbed the talents and furnished the livelihood of many bankers, dealers, and traders. They have greatly increased the size and profits of the financial industry as a whole. In effect, the industry has provided the techniques for traders, investors, and corporate treasurers to protect themselves against swings in exchange or interest rates. The high risks of holding foreign currencies or trading without hedging have been vividly demonstrated over and over again by the huge losses regularly suffered by presumably experienced firms.[52] But protection comes at a cost.

Since hedging is not magic, technically every gain must bring someone else a corresponding loss. A hedging contract, however, can allow two parties to an international transaction to lock in their original prices, regardless of subsequent changes in exchange rates. Each party renounces any gains, so that neither will suffer any loss. Both prefer stable prices to uncertain prospects for windfall profit. Hedging contracts cannot, however, be extended more than a year or two, without increasing costs astronomically. They cannot, therefore, protect a long-term investor indefinitely against radical changes in the terms of trade. Since the switch to floating exchange rates in the early 1970s, such changes have been regular occurrences among the United States, Europe, or Japan. Even for short-term protection, firms pay a cost to set up the hedge. For economies as a whole, there is the diversion of talent and capital into financial services—a lesser evil than leaving transactions uncovered, no doubt, but a cost all the same.

Monetary instability has also helped push the whole financial industry toward concentration. Today's high and unpredictable losses mean that very large financial conglomerates are needed to ride out the risks. Hence the unprecedented worldwide merging of banks, investment banks, brokerage houses, underwriters, and insurance firms. By 1991, the Bush administration was proposing legislation to encourage mergers between banks and large industrial firms. The long-term economic costs and political dangers of the trend toward concentration can only be imagined.[53] It may represent the market's best way of adjusting to instability, but it is highly unlikely to enhance the libertarian values of the market's most sincere defenders.

Much of the market's actual adjustment in recent years has merely confirmed the ability of the strong to visit the costs of instability upon the weak. Since hedging and concentration do not eliminate the extra risk and cost of monetary instability, but merely externalize it, the chief losers are those "widows and orphans" unable to command the institutions and techniques to protect their capital. Meanwhile, a large part of those working in the financial industry spend their time chasing interest rates through world markets in a sort of global video game. The game burdens the real economy with extra costs. Not the least of those costs is diverting too much business talent into the lucrative but relatively unproductive byways of fancy finance. In short, the market cannot substitute for the public good of stable money. The market does not work properly without an orderly framework of public regulation and sound public finance.

MARKET LICENSE AND MARKET FREEDOM

Paradoxically, inadequate public policy frequently leads to growing public intervention in the market economy. Where the market is not framed and regulated so that it can function properly, something eventually must substitute for it. The United States has thus been witnessing a growing demand for protectionism and industrial policy from the state, or for enough corporate concentration to permit effective planning from within the private sector. When the market grows too erratic to perform its functions properly, more statism or more corporatism is the almost inevitable remedy.

Every national political economy has, of course, its own particular blend of state, market, and corporatist elements. Some blends work better than others. Germany, for example, with its powerful and independent central banks has long enjoyed relatively stable domestic monetary conditions that encourage savings and investment. Much of German industry is caught up in a highly effective private corporatist structure organized through the big banks. France has always had a comparatively active interventionist state. In recent years, state policy has been trying to achieve the monetary stability it has traditionally been unable to provide by submitting the French economy to the discipline of a German-dominated European Monetary System. In other words, it has borrowed the Bundesbank. Both France and Germany, of course, have long used the European Community to structure and stabilize a wider competition, among other things, to guard against the excesses to which both statism and corporatism are susceptible, particularly when confined to a protected national area.

Throughout the 1980s, both France and Germany worked

with some success to develop and correct their own distinctive national systems—toward providing a more efficient and coherent allocation of resources and thus strengthening their economies for an increasingly competitive world. Doubtless, many shortcomings remain. And a reunited Germany has acquired many new structural difficulties. By comparison, however, the capacity for institutional progress in the American economy seems deficient. The fiscal incubus means that erratic macroeconomic policy continues to deprive the United States of stable monetary conditions for an effective capital market. Nevertheless, the United States has been very slow to develop those practices that may help to compensate. Unlike France, the United States has little coherent state industrial planning—even within the huge subsidized military sector. At the same time, the American economy's size, diversity, and strong antitrust traditions have impeded the effective private corporatism typical of the Germans and Japanese. Perhaps the incursion of huge foreign firms will provide the American economy with an imported substitute for its stunted native corporatism. That cannot be a formula that will bring universal satisfaction.

In many respects, the practical problems of the American economy stem from a certain deep-seated intellectual confusion. While the United States is full of fierce partisans of market economics, a clear understanding of what is required to run a proper market economy seems lacking. The state and the market are not natural enemies. A market cannot function properly without a state that sets a proper framework of regulation and policy. In sustaining a healthy free-market economy, the old-fashioned liberal rhetoric of laissez-faire is no substitute for a coherent and balanced state policy. Ironically, nothing illustrates this home truth better than the problems of the American economy during the 1980s—the decade of Reaganite ascendancy.

Chapter 8 *The Future According to Present Trends*

*N*o matter how discouraging long-term economic trends may seem, someone authoritative is always handy to explain why things are really getting better. No sooner had the giant twin deficits appeared in the early 1980s, than they were said to be curing themselves. In the last years of the decade, those complacent expectations were brutally disappointed, but similarly optimistic predictions were already blooming for the 1990s.

In fact, better expectations have often seemed plausible. Improving trends have been there to be found. But they have been superficial eddies rather than an underlying current. At the same time, the economy's capacity to bounce back regularly, even while slowly declining, indicates an enduring vigor that feeds hope for a healthier future. But for any lasting improvement in the structural imbalances that manifest our decline, something more is required than better luck with business as usual. If government policy has brought us to our present pass, government policy will have to rescue us. Only fundamental changes in policy, and probably significant alterations in political habits and structures, can dissolve the malign syndrome slowly dragging down the American economy. This seems clear—both from the record of the 1980s, and from any reasonable survey of what lies ahead for the rest of this century.

DISAPPOINTED HOPES IN THE 1980s

The federal deficit that mushroomed so explosively in 1982 and 1983 was sharply lower by 1987, even if still astronomical by historical standards. For two more years, it did not grow in real terms and therefore fell as a percentage of GNP—from 5.3 percent in 1985, to 3.0 percent in 1989.[1] By 1988, the current-account deficit had also begun to fall significantly, as the campaign to bring down the dollar, initiated in 1985, was showing some effect on trade, and as European economies entered a new phase of expansion.[2]

The end of the decade saw all hopes for fiscal self-correction dashed. In fiscal 1990, the official federal deficit had climbed to over $220 billion. Estimates for fiscal 1991 were running to over $300 billion and beyond.[3] Changes in the government's net borrowing requirements revealed an even more sober picture. In fiscal 1990, the gross federal debt grew by $330 billion. Estimates for 1991 were for over $400 billion. Meanwhile, the current-account deficit for 1990 remained stuck at a very high level despite the weaker dollar, together with falling United States and rising Western European demand.[4]

As in the 1970s, it was tempting to blame external shocks. Obviously, the savings and loan and Persian Gulf crises did have major economic consequences. The S and L debacle sub-

TABLE 8.1

**Outstanding Federal Debt at Year End,
1981 to 1991
(In Trillions of Dollars)**

	1981	1982	1983	1984	1985	1986	1987	1988	1989	1990	1991*
Gross	0.99	1.14	1.37	1.56	1.82	2.12	2.35	2.60	2.87	3.20	3.62
Held by Gov't	0.21	0.22	0.24	0.26	0.32	0.38	0.46	0.55	0.68	0.79	0.90
Held by Public	0.78	0.92	1.13	1.30	1.50	1.74	1.89	2.05	2.19	2.41	2.72

*Estimated
Source: *Economic Report of the President, 1991* (Washington, D.C.: U.S. Government Printing Office, 1991), pp. 376–77.

stantially increased federal expenditures and greatly increased federal borrowing requirements. The Gulf war led to fresh military spending and to an explosion of oil prices. Neither the domestic nor the foreign shock, however, was a fortuitous piece of bad luck unrelated to the government's own policies. The S and L crisis was intimately connected with long-standing macroeconomic and regulatory policies. And the oil shock arising from the Iraqi invasion of Kuwait could not be understood apart from America's growing dependence on foreign oil, itself a consequence of America's response to the first and second oil shocks.[5] Even the war with Iraq, with its immediate and ultimate effects on military spending, could scarcely be separated from America's well-established and often proclaimed geopolitical role in the Persian Gulf, militantly embraced by the Bush administration. Hegemonic regional policies, let alone a "New World Order," are unlikely to avoid occasional fighting and heavy expense. In short, the fiscal shocks at the end of the decade may not have been expected by the administration, but they were entirely logical consequences of long-standing policies.

In any event, it was not the S and L crisis or the Gulf war and its oil prices that prevented the fiscal deficit from resolving itself in the late 1980s. The improvement for 1985 to 1989 mainly reflected a business cycle moving out of recession toward full employment and was certain to reverse itself well short of any genuine balance. Federal deficits, interrupted only once in more than three decades, were "structural" rather than merely cyclical. Even at "full employment," they would remain substantial in size, as the 1984 *Economic Report of the President* had candidly admitted.[6] Thus, the 1989 fiscal deficit, before the impact of either the S and L crisis or the Gulf war, was still around $160 billion. This was after six years without a recession and with unemployment at only slightly more than 5 percent.

The causes for so large a structural fiscal imbalance in the 1980s were hardly arcane. To begin with, there was a substantial fiscal deficit already in 1980. It was a recession year—with unemployment at 7 percent of the work force. Fiscal 1989, however, was at the end of a boom, with unemployment at 5.2 percent. Yet the deficit, in real terms, was 40 percent higher.

TABLE 8.2

Economic Indicators for the United States, 1980 to 1990

YEAR	DEFICIT IN 1982 BILLIONS	GNP GROWTH	UNEMPLOYMENT	INFLATION*
1980	−$ 87.3	−0.2%	7.0%	12.5%
1981	−$ 84.6	1.9%	7.5%	8.9%
1982	−$127.9	−2.5%	9.5%	3.8%
1983	−$199.2	3.6%	9.5%	3.8%
1984	−$171.5	6.8%	7.4%	3.9%
1985	−$190.6	3.4%	7.1%	3.8%
1986	−$193.9	2.7%	6.9%	1.1%
1987	−$128.0	3.4%	6.1%	4.4%
1988	−$128.4	4.5%	5.4%	4.4%
1989	−$121.9	2.5%	5.2%	4.6%
1990	−$168.2	0.9%	5.4%	6.1%

*Consumer Price Index, December to December.
Sources: *Economic Report of the President, 1991* (Washington, D.C.: U.S. Government Printing Office, 1991), p. 356; *Budget of the U.S. Government, Fiscal Year 1992* (Washington, D.C.: U.S. Government Printing Office, 1991), Part Seven: 17.

In the interim, the level of real federal receipts was up 28.75 percent, the level of outlays up 30.11 percent, and real GNP was up by 30.38 percent. In other words, federal expenditures stayed in line with the economy's growth but federal income did not. Chapter 5 discusses how, from 1981 through 1986, President Reagan's increases in spending were at least as important as the relative decline in taxes in explaining the record deficits of those years. It is also interesting to look at the composition of the increased federal spending. By the end of the decade, all three major superfunctions of the budget had significantly larger real outlays, but in different proportions.

Roughly speaking, real defense outlays had grown twice as fast as government revenue; human resources a third less quickly, and net interest nearly four times faster. The huge increase in net interest reveals what might be called the budget's "Ponzi factor." With compounding interest charges growing at a very much faster rate than new outlays for defense or human resources, and nearly equal to them in dollar terms, the underlying fiscal situation was actually deteriorating. Not

TABLE 8.3

Differences in Outlays for Superfunctions, 1980 and 1989 (All figures Based on 1982 Dollars)

	PERCENTAGE CHANGE	REAL DOLLAR INCREASE ($1982)	CHANGE IN PERCENTAGE OF FEDERAL OUTLAYS
Defense	+52.25%	+82.82	+4.0%
Human Resources	+21.95%	+81.38	−3.3%
Health	+40.36%	+11.06	+0.3%
Medicare	+77.94%	+29.59	+2.0%
Net Interest	+116.50%	+72.37	+5.9%
Physical Resources	−16.42%	−12.82	−3.9%
Other	−13.64%	−7.26	−2.6%
Total Revenue	+28.75%	+175.90	—
Total Outlays	+30.11%	+210.51	—
GNP Growth	+30.38%	+930.60	—

Sources: *Economic Report of the President, 1991* (Washington, D.C.: U.S. Government Printing Office, 1991), p. 288; *Budget of the U.S. Government, Fiscal Year 1992*, Part Seven: 35–36; author's calculations.

only were new expenditures outrunning new revenues, but compounding interest was taking a larger and larger proportion of total expenditures. The principal losers—human resources and physical resources (except for health and medicare)—could be expected to react with greater and greater intensity, which would increase pressure for larger deficits, and hence for more interest. Whenever the long boom ended and reversed, the federal deficit should have been expected to return to the peaks of the earlier 1980s and to surpass them, as in fact it did. The steady decline of the deficit measured in constant dollars after 1986 was sharply reversed in 1990, when it rose by 38 percent. A further rise of at least 37 percent was predicted for fiscal 1991, bringing the deficit, measured in current dollars, to its highest level ever.[7] Such a trend was eminently predictable before the S and L debacle or the Middle East crisis, since nothing had happened to improve the basic fiscal imbalance.

PROSPECTS FOR STRUCTURAL IMPROVEMENTS IN THE 1990s: MILITARY SPENDING

Without conscious changes, prospects for improving the underlying structural deficit seem no brighter in the 1990s. President Bush, to be sure, began the decade by recanting his pledge against new taxes. But tax increases sufficient to have any significant effect on the fiscal imbalance remain unlikely, for the reasons analyzed in Chapters 4 and 5. Opening the 1990s with a recession could not enhance the already dubious prospects and the bitter struggle to pass a largely cosmetic package of revenue increases in the fall of 1990 gave little new cause for optimism.[8]

For much of 1990, great hopes for fiscal improvement lay with a "peace dividend," the reduced defense outlays expected after the Soviet retreat from Europe. By the autumn, the administration had agreed to genuine cuts in the military budget.[9] This window of fiscal opportunity was already being shut, however, by President Bush's August decision to intervene massively in the Middle East. By April of 1991, the Persian Gulf War was already estimated to be adding about $50 billion to military outlays. But the United States also eventually extracted pledges from its allies of more than $53 billion. No one could tell what the ultimate costs of war and reconstruction might be.[10]

As the Gulf crisis indicated, even the demise of Soviet power would not, in itself, relieve the United States of its outsized military burden. Any durable cuts in military spending would depend on a more modest definition of America's geopolitical role in the world. If the Soviet military retreat from Europe should ultimately induce the United States to define itself as the world's only superpower and principal policeman, no lasting cuts in the defense budget are likely. On the contrary, America's geopolitical role could grow more rather than less costly. Grouping states into two superpower spheres of influence used to give the world a certain stability, strongly reinforced by the fear of a nuclear confrontation between the strategic giants. That threat also limited the need for conventional forces. A more plural world, experiencing rapid social, economic, and cultural changes, and loaded with many arbitrary boundaries and artificial regimes, has, if anything, a greater potential for conflict. In short, even the end of the cold war will not, by itself, bring any automatic or lasting fiscal improvement.

TRENDS IN THE CIVIL BUDGET

If a peace dividend is problematic in the 1990s, overall cuts in the civil budget seem close to impossible. The fiscal shocks of the late 1980s have, by no means, yet run their course. A formidable portfolio of potential shocks remains. By the end of 1990, the Federal Deposit Insurance Corporation, the federal guarantor of bank accounts, was running short of funds because the recession was swelling an already record number of bank failures.[11] Banks were suffering heavily from both foreign and domestic loan defaults. A deep debt crisis had continued in the third world and in Eastern Europe; volatile oil prices and a global recession had deteriorated conditions further. At home, the speculative bubbles of the mid-1980s were bursting—notably in the real estate and junk bond markets. Bankruptcy was also widespread among firms crippled by takeover debts. With assets devalued and clients sinking, banks themselves were tottering in many parts of the country.

Beyond the overhang of pending financial shocks is a large catalog of long-deferred public needs. The federal government is, for example, responsible for a number of substantial and seemingly unavoidable environmental costs. Cleaning up the sites of the Atomic Energy Commission's plants for manufacturing nuclear weapons is alone estimated to cost eventually some $200 billion.[12] Broad pressure is also building for more federal spending on highways, bridges, airports, rapid transit, urban redevelopment, and a whole range of other improvements. An increasingly dilapidated infrastructure is widely condemned for injuring the country's general economic productivity and growth, which is not surprising since the federal government cut its real spending on physical resources by nearly a quarter during the 1980s.[13] While state and local governments tried to compensate, the recession of the early 1990s put those governments themselves under intense fiscal pressure. Unlike the federal government, they cannot finance sustained large deficits. A further shift of civil burdens away from

Washington is therefore less and less likely. But a further starving of funds seems more and more self-defeating.[14]

The same economic rationale feeds demands to upgrade America's spending on primary and secondary education. The federal government cut its education spending by roughly a quarter in the 1980s.[15] State and local governments, which carry most of the cost of education in any case, were hard put to keep making up for the federal decline. Again, the political case for more spending has a powerful economic logic. Not investing enough to educate the future work force makes the whole country poorer, as well as less governable. An uneducated, crime- and drug-ridden underclass is not only a shameful moral hazard but a severe economic drag.

Chapter 3 notes how much demography drives spending on human resources. Today's demographic trends bring double bad news for tomorrow's fiscal trends. The birth rate is declining and life expectancy is lengthening. In other words, while the school-age population is falling, the percentage of the population over sixty-five is growing. In 1950, only 8.1 percent of the population was over sixty-five years old. By 1990, the proportion was 12.6 percent. By 2020, it is projected to be 17.7 percent and by 2030, 21.8 percent. For every three people of working age (eighteen to sixty-four) in the year 2030, two people will be either under eighteen or of retirement age. The future burden on the federal budget can only be imagined.[16] Having more older people creates more demand for health services, the costs of which continue to rise rapidly, despite their already comparatively high level.

In summary, the 1990s offer little prospect for any automatic or lasting fiscal improvement. The deficit seems fated to remain structural and not merely cyclical. Little progress toward structural readjustment was made during the boom years of the 1980s. Even the most promising prospect, a peace dividend, is made doubtful by the Gulf war. Meanwhile, the S and L debacle, the banking crisis, the recession, a large inventory of other off-budget obligations, pressing environmental costs and infrastructure needs, growing public dissatisfaction with educational and health standards, concern over the economic and social costs of a growing underclass, and demography itself all stand in the way of major lasting declines in civil spending. On the contrary, real spending can be expected to rise sharply—more sharply than during the 1980s. Meanwhile, nothing gives hope for any structural improvement in revenues. Complacent faith in automatic adjustment, in other words, has a very slim foundation. Business as usual is heading into bankruptcy.

PONZI'S DANCE

Taken altogether the trends at the beginning of the 1990s point toward a progressive increase in federal borrowing. In 1980, the accumulated net federal debt was equal to 22 percent of the GNP. By 1990, it was equal to 44 percent of the GNP. In the same period, net interest grew by 91 percent in real terms, while its share of annual federal spending jumped from 8.89 percent to 14.77 percent. Indebtedness of that kind grows by its own momentum. Debt can be expected to snowball, and interest payments to take an increasing share of federal revenue. The federal government is caught in its own version of Ponzi finance. Under such circumstances, not only does government borrowing crowd out private investment, but debt service crowds out other government spending.[17]

Heavy government borrowing could, of course, be defended if prevailing inflation and money illusion provided a negative real interest rate. Arguably, that was the case in some years between 1970 and 1981. In addition, so long as inflation kept pushing up the nominal GNP, bracket creep often produced disproportionate increases in federal income taxes.[18] These sorts of arguments form a general apology for a systematically induced mild inflation, a policy fashionable in the neo-Keynesian era and discussed in Chapter 2. A little inflation was thought necessary to sustain full employment—and hence to boost investment, productivity, general economic growth, and disproportionately higher federal revenues.

As was observed in Chapter 2, these arguments for inflationary finance were questionable, even when real interest rates actually were negative. Inflation has all sorts of harmful side effects on investment, saving, prices, wage demands, and general financial and social stability. The dynamics of money illusion, moreover, make it impossible to stabilize inflation at a steady rate. Stop-go policies are inevitable and stagflation follows with all its dire consequences for the real economy.

In any event, real interest rates were clearly no longer negative by the 1980s. Positive rates were back with a vengeance, thanks in good part to a general revulsion against the effects of price inflation. Meanwhile, the decade's various tax bills largely eliminated bracket creep.[19] Ponzi finance no longer made sense for the government, even in narrow accounting terms. So long as real interest rates remained positive, higher federal debt meant higher real interest payments. And without bracket creep, higher interest charges would take a growing portion of federal revenue.[20]

In theory, more rapid growth of the real economy could raise federal revenues enough to break the Ponzi pattern of compounding debt. But as was indicated in Chapter 7, the budget deficit has itself become a principal obstacle to sustained economic growth. Meanwhile, as interest payments continue to grow faster than revenues, rising debt saps the government's real resources. If net interest's share of the federal budget increases as rapidly in the 1990s and afterward as it did in the 1980s, it will take nearly 25 percent of federal spending by the year 2000, and 43 percent by 2010! America's debt is now self-propelled. For Washington, the miracle of compound interest has become the nightmare of compounding debt. As a result, the federal government will have to borrow more and more—or have less and less to spend.

FINANCING THE DEBT: CAPITAL'S NEW FRONTIER IN EUROPE

Financing a self-propelled debt obviously requires more and more capital. America's borrowing needs have long since outgrown its own savings.[21] In the past, the United States has always been able, one way or another, to summon savings from the rest of the world. Throughout the 1980s, the Reagan formula—laced with an occasional dash of credit inflation—attracted record inflows of foreign capital. In good part, that was because government policies in Western Europe and Japan restricted consumption and government borrowing, and thus created a large pool of savings for America. The situation for the 1990s promises to be more difficult. The European Community's rapid progress toward a single market, Ger-

many's reunification, Eastern Europe's liberation, and the Soviet Union's own opening have created tremendous long-term
investment needs for a new "Pan-Europe." If Europe's capital
goes to its own central and eastern portions on anything like
the scale required, America's new debt will no longer be
matched by Europe's new saving.[22]

Political need may redirect Europe's investment as much
as economic opportunity. The formidable social, political, and
financial problems of the new Pan-Europe must somehow be
managed, if Western Europe's own safety and prosperity are
not to be put at risk. Europeans may well conclude that capital
investment to build up Eastern economies is a better investment than more spending on armaments. The Japanese will
note the same political risks and economic opportunities and
perhaps feel a similar need to help the Soviets. If all goes well,
moreover, the long-term prospects for real economic growth
in Pan-Europe are quite fabulous. The European Community
is already the world's richest market; its potential for growth
is now greatly enhanced. If the Soviet Union's economy and
politics can ever be liberalized and stabilized, it too is an enormous market, with vast natural resources to be developed.

Insofar as Pan-Europe does succeed, the United States will
no longer be in the same geopolitical position to command
capital from its old allies. A domesticated Russia would significantly devalue America's role as Europe's protector. Even if
the world remains a dangerous place, as it most assuredly will,
America's allies are likely to adopt a less dependent course. By
comparison with Pan-Europe's own needs and possibilities,
continuing to finance America's fiscal mess may come to seem
uninspiring and unpromising. By the 1990s, America's financial problems are beginning to be well understood abroad. That
a large part of European savings should go regularly to finance America's improvident government, while Europe itself
has urgent need, is bound to seem more and more unnatural.
In other words, the Western triumph in Europe, if sustained,
could bring the United States to the edge of a fundamental
crisis in its postwar political and economic policy.

The Gulf war in early 1991 had some of the same Pyrrhic
characteristics. It was a triumph for American arms but also a
threat to America's future solvency.[23] Not only did the war

require higher United States military spending in the present, and encourage it in the future, but the devastation removed Kuwait from the dwindling roster of the world's major savers. With Iraq freshly ruined and Iran still suffering the devastation of its long war, the Middle East will urgently need capital for a long time to come and the rich regional powers remaining will be hard-pressed to provide it. In short, considering pressing European and Middle Eastern demand, global prospects for cheap and abundant capital are much diminished. The United States will be competing with needs elsewhere that the world's major savers will find difficult to ignore.[24]

SCENARIOS FOR TRANSITION

Like the 1960s and the 1970s, the 1980s ended with a dollar crisis and a recession. The dollar fell 17.1 percent against the German mark in 1990 and the real GNP declined 1.6 percent in the fourth quarter. Another American formula for financing imbalances had apparently run its course. In the later years of the 1980s, many experts hoped that this Reagan formula could end with a "soft landing." To achieve it, the United States was supposed to reduce its fiscal deficit and the rest of the world to expand its domestic demand. A new global trade agreement, the Uruguay Round, would reduce trade barriers and boost American exports of services and farm products, while central banks would intervene to steady the dollar's decline and prevent its overshooting.[25] For a time, conditions looked promising. Japanese and Europeans did reflate their economies. Central banks were cooperating to manage a limited fall of the dollar, and conditions seemed much better for a turnaround in the trade balance. The Uruguay Round was proceeding toward a new agreement that was expected to meet several major American concerns. Fiscal prospects looked brighter; the federal deficit was falling as a percentage of GNP and a peace dividend seemed imminent. In effect, this soft landing was to be a relatively automatic and painless drifting into a real adjustment of America's internal and external imbalances.

As we know, conditions for a soft landing never really materialized. Improvement in the fiscal balance was ephemeral. The structural situation was deteriorating. By the end of 1990,

the S and L debacle, the Gulf war, and a recession were pushing the federal deficit to a new record. More shocks and pent-
up demands for big new federal expenditures were waiting in
the wings. Meanwhile, the trade deficit had stopped falling and
trade negotiations were temporarily suspended.[26]

By March 1991, a stunningly easy victory in the Gulf war
brought a sharp recovery to the dollar and the stock market.
Still, the basic economic news remained discouraging.[27] The
recession did, however, have one useful consequence. Business and consumer borrowing were so depressed that financing the record fiscal deficit was relatively easy; short-term
interest rates thus remained relatively low. But all this depended on a continuing recession. In effect, the United States
had maneuvered itself into what might be called the standard
"IMF formula" for financing a prolonged fiscal deficit. In the
absence of a formula for exporting it, the United States was
being forced to carry much more of its own debt burden. The
Fed was being put in a more and more difficult position, where
it was harder and harder to muddle through in a fashion
pleasing to both its domestic and foreign constituencies. Its
still cautious policies offered little but the dreary prospect of
prolonged stagnation, with living standards declining still
further.

Under such circumstances, pressure was likely to grow
stronger for America to use its international monetary power
once more to transfer the cost of its excessive debts. Many
third world and Eastern European countries grew heavily in-
debted in the 1970s. Creditors eventually stopped lending fresh
capital and forced these countries to cut living standards in
order to service their loans. The IMF was even able to force
Britain into prolonged austerity in the 1970s.[28] The American
political economy would be unlikely to tolerate a similar regime. While no one can say for certain what form America's
shrugging off of debt might take, past experience offers three
models. One, the Reagan, is no longer functioning. Another—
Bretton Woods with its fixed exchange rates and hegemonic
dollar—seems unlikely to return in the foreseeable future. This
leaves the Nixon formula—inflation checked by periodic bouts
of monetary penance. As an alternative to protracted stagflation, a return to Nixonian finance might well grow highly ap-

pealing, particularly to politicians worried about reelection. With the recession, the Gulf war, and the pending budgetary shocks chasing away hope for fiscal improvement, and foreign needs likely to make basic borrowing conditions more difficult, the stage could be set for more vigorous monetary stimulation from the Fed. Instead of a soft or hard landing, there could be a new inflation.

Some crisis might provide the occasion. A collapse of the dollar would, in theory, do wonders for American trade—and might be rationalized in that way. Americans would probably not feel guilty about the capital or trade losses of their allies, who could, not altogether unfairly, be depicted as longtime freeloaders on American military spending. Outraged American reactions to German and Japanese diffidence about "burden-sharing" in the Gulf war have perhaps already suggested the tone. Americans might also expect their foreign creditors to return soon enough. A prosperous country that has just sloughed off a good part of its unmanageable debts is logically a better investment than one still struggling. Inflation and dollar depreciation cut a good deal of American debt in the 1970s, yet foreign capital rushed to America in the 1980s.

On the face of it, inflating away the debt might seem more difficult in the 1990s than in Nixon's time. By the mid-1970s, for example, the average maturity of federal debt had shifted sharply from long- to short-term. Whenever so much of the national debt held is short-term, an alert market, smelling inflation, can be expected to transfer the debt burden quickly from eroding principal to rising interest.[29] By the end of the 1980s, however, the average maturity of the publicly held federal debt was actually longer than in Nixon's time—nearly as long as in the early 1950s.[30] Foreign credit, of course, had grown much more important for domestic financing than in the 1970s.[31] Openly inflationary policies might well provoke a big capital flight, with domestic consequences in the United States more significant than before. But assets have to be held somewhere, and massive dumping causing the dollar to collapse would prove self-defeating for the large foreign holders themselves.

There would, however, be other costs. Foreign creditors would have a strong incentive to switch from financial to real

assets within the United States. More xenophobic reactions could
be expected from the public, along with more inflation in stock
and real estate prices. High inflation's domestic social and political fallout would probably be severe. Saving and investment
patterns would be further distorted. Eventually, accelerating
inflation would compel a new phase of brutal monetary tightening. Still, purging debt in this fashion could presage a real
cure for the basic fiscal and external imbalances. Repudiation
could buy a new chance, at a high price, to make the adjustments that ought to have been made long before. But if the
adjustments were not made, the debt would probably soon reconstitute itself.

REGENERATION FROM CRISIS?

The last decade of this "American Century" thus holds
forth a troubled prospect for the United States itself. The accumulating debts of chronic public and private overabsorption
severely hamper macroeconomic policy and point toward a
significant drop in living standards. The most recent formula
for summoning foreign savings seems to have reached its natural end. Changes in the world that represent the triumph of
American policy have also undercut America's geopolitical position, and perhaps undermined more fundamentally its capacity to commandeer foreign resources.

Like many other well-anticipated crises, this one may never
occur—or at least may be postponed for another generation.
Other events may intervene. Europeans, for example, face their
own formidable internal dislocations. Sandwiched between
Russians and Arabs, they are also much more vulnerable to
violent external disruptions than Americans. The great European hopes of 1989 may thus fritter away and European capital may rediscover the virtues of an American refuge. Even
the European Community may falter under the double stress
of a united Germany and a chaotic East.

In early 1991, the Gulf war reinforced American complacency. Many began to suspect, or hope, that America's leadership and easy military triumph over Iraq indicated a new
phase of the Pax Americana—with the United States, the only
remaining global power, installed as the world's policeman, and
able at last to demand adequate "burden sharing" from its

protectorates. From this perspective, the United States, even without its old economic predominance, could finally attain that global sway imagined by early enthusiasts of the American Century, before the cold war blighted their hopes.[32]

Events seldom evolve quite as anyone expects. The United States will certainly remain the world's leading military power and single richest economy, with all its traditional advantages of huge space and relative isolation. Nevertheless, it seems unwise to count on a reflowering of American global hegemony. Since the recovery of Europe and Japan, and with decolonization and development in the third world, some very robust long-term trends and logical connections have been pointing the world toward a more plural order. Such trends are not likely to be reversed by America's tour de force in the Persian Gulf. European integration, for example, has been one of the principal forces shaping the postwar order. Its powerful geopolitical logic is now embodied in several decades of successful institutional evolution. Enlarging free Europe may slow this process, but is unlikely to stop it. In any event, resting America's future prosperity on hopes for the collapse of Europe's dreams would be a sad end for the Atlantic Alliance—and an ironical conclusion to the cold war. It is a strategy whose success, moreover, would prove highly dangerous for America itself. American hegemony is no substitute for the European Community. The United States cannot manage Europe. And a fragmented Europe, cut loose from its moorings, is not a reassuring prospect for America's own safety. In Europe, as in the world at large, America's best course is to accommodate and guide a more plural order, rather than to oppose it.

These geopolitical considerations are inextricably related to American macroeconomic policy. In the long run, probably the only way for the United States both to lead and to accommodate a more plural world is to accept for itself the discipline needed to sustain an orderly and liberal plural system. That means renouncing the abuse of America's special monetary position in the global economy. It means no longer regularly financing America's deficits by monetary manipulations that shift the burdens of adjustment abroad. It means beginning seriously to make the long-deferred adjustments at home. In particular, it means undertaking a long-term commitment to get rid of the structural fiscal deficit, and to restore monetary conditions favorable to long-term investment in the real economy. Refusing to make these internal adjustments more or less compels the United States to go on asserting its hegemonic outward power. Failure and decline at home will have to be masked by more and more vigorous assertions of economic and military power abroad.

The conditions of a more plural world are not, in themselves, discouraging for the kind of domestic American transformation required to accommodate it. The great world changes that began at the end of the 1980s could make America's rebalancing easier, as well as more essential. In particular, the new situation in Europe could present the United States with an extraordinary chance to regain its fiscal balance and cure its chronic overabsorption. Historically, the Pax Americana reached its triumphal fulfillment with the voluntary Soviet retreat from central Europe. Circumstances in a plural world order should be propitious for the United States to make that basic geopolitical adjustment required for its own fiscal rebalancing. The United States should be able to shed a significant part of the heavy arms spending of the cold war, not only because of the Soviet retreat, but also because it should be possible to build a new and broader coalition to sustain order in the world.

With serious progress toward fiscal balances, a more plural world also offers the United States much more promising conditions for external rebalancing. Europe's new investment needs and prospects, while implying an end to foreign subsidies to the American economy, also offer the United States an unprecedented chance to restore its own trade balance and thus free itself from dependency on foreign savings. Before the Soviet retreat and transformation, the prospects for turning around the American trade balance never were very promising. Two or three decades of overabsorption and speculative malinvestment have turned the American economy into a sort of carcass to feed the energetic exporters of Europe and Japan. The American market is so large, and the American capacity for borrowing has been so infinite, that a good part of the rest of the world's industrial structure has been built around America's overabsorption. Short of a real collapse of the dollar, a depression, or some other pretext for a violent turn toward protectionism, it has been difficult to imagine how the United States could reverse so large an imbalance. Resorting to the draconian remedies needed would inevitably carry very high costs. Serious American protectionism could easily break down the world economy, as could a prolonged bout of inflation that radically depreciated the dollar. The cure could then easily begin to seem worse than the disease.

Opening Eastern Europe and the Soviet Union could provide a historic opportunity to escape from this dilemma. With luck, Russia could be the new carcass, a role for which it is particularly well-suited and from which everyone could profit. To complement its great need for Western goods, Russia possesses vast untapped resources that Europe, Japan, and the United States itself need. Should Russia stabilize its politics, and achieve a more open economy, the prospect of developing its resources not only could attract much of the world's free investment capital but the subsequent products could finance a large appetite for imports. A very substantial rise in overall world demand could be expected. This could be the window providing America the opportunity to correct its overabsorption, without requiring a beggar-thy-neighbor confrontation with its European and Asian partners.[33]

In short, not only does the trend toward a more plural world put increasing pressure on the United States to change, it also offers an unprecedented opportunity to do so with success. Thus, the trend to a more plural world does not impose decline on America. Rather, it challenges us to reverse decline at home and to set a new, more solid foundation for continuing leadership abroad. But as the history of the 1980s indicates, there are no automatic solutions. The United States cannot expect to drift into salvation. As in the 1940s, history beckons but America will have to rise to the occasion.

Chapter 9 *Decline Revisited*

*B*y our analysis, the causes of America's fiscal crisis go very deep. They have to do with the nation's postwar political structures and geopolitical role, together with some of its most cherished ideas about politics and economics. Those things are not easily altered. Small wonder that every administration since the 1960s, trying to ride out the swirling events of its time, has shrunk from cures that seemed worse than the disease and convinced itself that time and a little adjustment would eventually repair the country's problems. Pusillanimous politicians, moreover, have never lacked firm intellectual backing. It is tempting to say that if half the creative energy had gone into confronting America's problems that has gone into explaining them away, our Republic would be in much better shape than it now is. But in a country as rich and powerful as the United States, decline is hard to take seriously. More complacent interpretations seem more reasonable.

Two currently fashionable views seem particularly worthy of attention. The first interprets America's economic troubles as that purging of obsolescent structures required before a new stage of rapid progress. The second sees our domestic industrial decline as only one part of what is, on the whole, America's successful adaptation to the global economy.

CREATIVE DESTRUCTION?

In market theory, bankruptcy has a vital role. If the incompetent and unlucky are not allowed to fail, the system cannot keep its promise to maximize efficiency. Some theorists carry their appreciation for bankruptcy to heroic limits. The noted economist, Joseph Schumpeter, celebrated the Great Depression of the 1930s as that "creative destruction" of obsolescent firms and managers needed to open the way for new industries nurtured by advancing technology.[1] Not surprisingly, Schumpeter's ideas have enjoyed a certain revival in recent years.[2] Deftly applied, they can make today's widespread indebtedness and bankruptcy seem a sign of healthy rejuvenation. Financial buccaneers and asset strippers are transformed into emissaries from a technological world spirit. Schumpeter's views are, in fact, highly relevant to present circumstances. In a time of rapidly changing technology, radical industrial restructuring is clearly needed and can never be entirely painless or orderly. Our question, however, is not whether adjustments are necessary, but whether America's public policy has for the most part mainly hindered them, and added to their pain.

Each country has tended to handle restructuring in its own characteristic way. In France, for example, the socialist government of the early 1980s nationalized several major industrial companies along with the remnants of the private banking system. The principal economic aim was to create viable firms for the big new European market. The state injected fresh capital and new technocratic management and restructured whole sectors of industry.[3] When the conservatives formed a government in 1986, they "privatized" many public firms—a step that some socialists asserted they would eventually have taken as well. Many of the plans for their nationalizations had, they claimed, been drawn up by the previous conservative government. When the socialists returned to full power in early 1989, no move was made either to reverse privatization or to extend it. In any event, the firms, public or private, that emerged from this process seemed in much better shape to cope with an increasingly competitive world.[4] Germany, too, saw extensive industrial restructuring, but the state's part was a good deal less direct than in France. Instead, the major banks played their traditional role of arranging the alliances needed to keep Germany's producers in the forefront of world competition.[5]

To say that every country does the same thing in its own way is not to say that all countries succeed equally well. Statist France and corporatist Germany came to have one thing in common in the 1980s. Whether led by socialists or conservatives, their governments were making a determined effort to improve the basic financial conditions for industrial investment. That, they believed, was the best way to strengthen national productivity and competitiveness. During the 1970s, both countries had, for the first time since the early postwar era, experienced major unemployment. They had also seen, like the United States, sharp declines in the growth of output and productivity.[6] Thanks to inflation, oil shocks, stop-go policies, and recessions, business profit had fallen and investment with it.

Not only had investment fallen, but it had been misdirected by the perverse combination of high labor costs and unnaturally low real interest rates. High labor costs continued despite record unemployment, thanks to unions and employ-

TABLE 9.1

Real Gross Fixed Capital Formation

	U.S.	FRANCE	GERMANY	JAPAN
AVERAGE ANNUAL PERCENTAGE CHANGES			
1960–68	5.0	8.0	3.1	15.2
1968–73	3.7	7.1	5.5	12.5
1973–79	1.9	0.2	0.5	1.5
1979–88	2.8	1.2	0.8	4.7
AVERAGE PERCENTAGE OF GDP			
1960–67	18.0	23.2	25.2	31.0
1968–73	18.4	24.6	24.4	34.6
1974–79	18.7	23.6	20.8	31.8
1980–88	17.8	20.4	20.5	29.2

Source: OECD, *Historical Statistics, 1960–1988* (Paris: OECD, 1990), pp. 57, 69.

ment taxes. Low real interest rates prevailed, thanks to credit inflation and the recycled savings of the oil producers.[7] The malinvestment encouraged by these conditions left a legacy of relatively unproductive debt. In some industries, cheap capital built overcapacity and preserved obsolescent firms. In others, debt fed unemployment because labor-saving investment was unnaturally cheap in relation to labor costs. Meanwhile, paying heavy unemployment relief kept governments themselves adding to national indebtedness.

Trying to cope with these knotted problems, German and then French economic policy-making gradually evolved a new continental version of "supply-side" economics. Its basic axiom was simple: If projected profits do not equal the long-term rate of interest, plus a premium for risk, rational investors will stick with purely financial instruments or invest abroad.[8] With profitability the touchstone, both countries adopted roughly the same strategies: Restrain labor costs, squelch inflation, and reduce fiscal deficits so that their financing is possible without credit inflation, high interest rates, or heavy new taxes. While neither country tried to renounce its elaborate postwar welfare system or its long-standing military plans and obligations, each did make a determined effort to control costs. In tandem with strictly disciplined fiscal policies, monetary policies were designed to keep capital costs down without stoking price inflation. For France, traditionally inclined to trade inflation for growth, the conversion to monetary stability was a radical shift. To reinforce it, the French joined the Germans to build the European Monetary System (EMS), designed to impose stable money and noninflationary finance throughout the European Community.

All in all, Western Europe's two biggest economies made considerable progress by the end of the decade.[9] Both significantly strengthened their international competitive positions. France, whose outlook had seemed so unpromising earlier in the decade, brought its external accounts back into rough balance, cut inflation, labor costs, and fiscal deficits. Germany's changes were less dramatic but no less impressive. France, to be sure, still has many of its old structural problems, and unification has endowed Germany with unprecedented new ones.

But both countries came out of the decade strengthened for whatever trials lay ahead. Sensible and stable government policies were a major factor in their improvement.

The United States, by comparison, entered the 1990s with its overabsorption still huge and its combined public and private debt burdens still rising rapidly. In contrast to the sustained European efforts to maintain stable policies favorable to business investment, American policy was driven by the imperious and erratic demands of an undisciplined budget and unprecedented financial disorder. Thus, despite a great deal of destruction, American policy has not set a propitious environment for the creative investment needed to build adequate long-term productivity and prosperous domestic employment.[10]

Despite all the talk of supply-side growth, American policy appears not to have grasped the axiom that ought to be self-evident to any avowed supply-sider: When monetary conditions are too volatile for confident long-term predictions, liberal markets cannot be expected to allocate capital adequately for long-term real investment. Chronic stop-go makes long-term investment too risky. Money flows instead to highly liquid financial instruments or service industries that require little fixed capital. In brief, the American government is failing to set the environment needed for American business to surmount the technological and industrial challenges of the late twentieth century. The American economy is thus distracted and hampered from performing according to Schumpeter's scenerio. But not all governments, it seems, are always equally dysfunctional.

AN IMPERIAL ECONOMY?

One of the major causes for America's declining industry and productivity has been the heavy tendency among American firms to relocate their manufacturing abroad. Given the right theoretical perspective, however, declines in domestic manufacturing can be transformed from a sign of weakness to the natural bent of a superpower. American firms, it can be said, remain preeminent in those economic activities that will generate wealth in the future and draw particular strength from their global approach to production. They consolidate their global predominance by employing cheap foreign labor—either by using manufacturing facilities abroad, or perhaps by importing cheap labor into the United States. If manufacturing declines inside the United States, it is because American firms can conduct it more efficiently elsewhere. Americans at home no longer wear the blue collars of those who labor, but the white collars of those who direct the labor of others. America is thus not declining, but has merely entered a new phase of global hegemony.[11] The principal bad effects of America's disequilibria rain down on others, rather than upon the United States itself.

The argument is essentially a geopolitical variation of the "product-cycle theory," itself a modern updating of the theory of comparative advantage that lies at the heart of liberal economics. According to the theory, once the technology for making a particular product has become routine and widely available, its profit margins shrink and its manufacturing ought to migrate to peripheral countries. Advanced economies, their comparative advantage lying in highly educated work forces and well-developed infrastructures, should specialize in those new products and services that will presumably generate bigger profit margins. When firms from advanced countries regularly employ and control manufacturing in peripheral countries, the theory takes on a geopolitical as well as an economic aspect.[12]

The theory can no longer offer so comfortable an apology for the performance of America's real economy as it formerly did. American companies still remain well represented among the world's giants and fast-growing new firms, but a safe American lead in most of the high value-added areas of manufacturing and services cannot now be taken for granted. America's aerospace industry has more competition than ever before. Even the computer giants—like IBM or Cray—are more challenged and troubled than at any time since the war.[13] The old giants—automobiles and steel—are beleaguered. In some fields, like consumer electronics, American firms have nearly disappeared.[14]

Part of the trouble with American manufacturing could be blamed on a widespread misapplication of the product-cycle theory. In many sectors, American firms may suffer from often preferring cheap labor abroad over better use of more expensive workers at home.[15] The true comparative advantage of rich and developed countries, after all, ought to lie in the high productivity of their own well-educated labor. With such labor, they should be able to take quick and flexible advantage of new technological possibilities. Japanese industry seems particularly impressive in this respect. Japanese carmakers, for example, design and produce new models in three years; American carmakers still take five. Developing an American work force capable of such prodigies is not, however, easily compatible with the relentless search for cheaper labor—at home or abroad. Firms in Japan or Europe, where it is difficult to fire workers, have often responded by investing heavily in their own employees and equipment. Such firms seem more likely to benefit from the marriage of superior labor and technology that is supposedly the real comparative advantage of an advanced society.

Transferring manufacturing abroad may also not be easily compatible with continuing to generate creative products at home. Separating manufacturing in the factory from design and engineering in the laboratory perhaps reflects an unfortunate trend in American economic and social culture. America was once a nation of tinkerers, some of whom were inspired to innovate. Putting an ocean between white-collar and blue-collar employees portends, among other things, a drying up of the human springs that feed technological innovation.

America's comparative strength in high technology should presumably rest heavily on its superb system of higher education. But if American universities and research institutes still remain preeminent, the training of America's own technicians and engineers seem to have fallen off drastically, particularly by comparison with our principal economic rivals. A high percentage of graduates in America's top engineering and scientific schools are foreigners. Of American graduates, a high percentage are recent immigrants.[16] The presence of so many foreigners should be a source of pride, but the diminishing number of Americans should not. The United States seems to be evolving a two-tier educational system. Top American universities and elite secondary schools are, arguably, the best in the world. But the general level of public education in primary and secondary schools seems to have slipped badly. The pattern seems unpromising for continued technological predominance.[17] America's heavy preoccupation with military weapons is a further vulnerability. Military technology does not translate easily into competitive civilian products and huge outlays for military research do not yield proportionate results for civilian competitiveness. Instead, so much military spending, while it swells the nation's scientific, engineering, and industrial establishment, also impedes its contribution to the economy's competitiveness.[18]

Aside from the question of how well American industry has actually been making use of the nation's comparative advantage, there remains an "identity problem" involving America's business firms and the nation as a whole. To what extent is the United States as a nation or economy coterminal with the reach or success of its global corporations? Even if following the supposed dictates of the product-cycle theory produces a successful strategy for individual firms, it does not automatically produce happy effects for the nation's employment, social cohesion, or general welfare.

This identity question is closely tied to the shift of employment away from manufacturing toward services, a trend characteristic of all advanced societies but more pronounced in the United States than in most European countries or Japan. Over the 1980s, the rapid growth of employment in services, and its decline in manufacturing, is often taken as proof of America's successful adaptation to the product-cycle theory. On the face of it, creating so many new jobs in services does seem a notable achievement, particularly in comparison with the high unemployment that has accompanied industrial restructuring in France and Germany. But this swelling employment in the service sector hardly seems to reflect any comparative advantage for the United States as an advanced economy, or triumphantly vindicate the benefits of a global strategy for manufacturing. Most of the new service jobs can hardly be described as high-technology or high value-added. The great majority are in fast-food chains, discount retail stores, hospitals, building maintenance, and similar low-wage sectors.

Looked at more carefully, America's job creation seems less a successful adaptation of the skilled labor force at home than its impoverishment, catalyzed by heavy importing of cheap labor from abroad. Many newly created service jobs are, in fact, filled by regular large influxes of immigrant labor—a substantial part of it illegal.[19] The result is a two-tier work force, with the bottom filled by a swelling underclass of immigrants, older racial minorities never fully absorbed into the work force, or discarded blue-collar workers from declining industries and depressed regions.[20] Many from this last group appear to drift from high-paying jobs into long-term unemployment.[21]

Even financial services, which was a service industry in the 1980s that grew rapidly and provided many high-paying jobs, has not sustained its promise.[22] Growth was linked to recycling OPEC capital to third world debtors, funding takeovers with junk bonds, or arranging swaps and hedges. Many of those once highly profitable practices have now produced a legacy of bad debts, mortgaged equities, and tottering banks. Profits have fled and the whole industry has fallen on hard times. America's big banks, once the world's largest, are today well down the chart of the world's giants.[23] Employment on Wall Street has dropped precipitously and many of its proudest firms have been forced into mergers and liquidations. Several now depend on Japanese or European backers.

Trying to understand what has been happening to American jobs and incomes is obscured by the traditional classification of employment into manufacturing and services. As a category, services lumps together bankers, scholars, and building cleaners. The distinctions seem more significant than any similarities. Even in the old manufacturing sector itself, the changing nature of production and business organization has gradually blurred the line between manufacturing and service jobs. Robert Reich's influential study, *The Work of Nations*, attempts a new classification more relevant to the major trends in technology and business structure. Business organization has been changing radically, he believes. Whereas the corporation of the past was typically a hierarchically organized "high-volume" producer of standardized goods, the new corporation is a "high-value" enterprise whose key assets are the skills and reputations it can summon for "linking solutions to particular needs."[24] Increasingly, moreover, resolving problems successfully means assembling an ad hoc coalition of producers around the world, a global "enterprise web." According to Reich:

> America's core corporation no longer plans and implements the production of a large volume of goods and services; it no longer owns or invests in a vast array of factories, machinery, laboratories, warehouses, and other tangible assets; it no longer employs armies of production workers and middle-level managers; it no longer serves as gateway to the American middle class. In fact, the core corporation is no longer even American. It is, increasingly, a facade, behind which teems an array of decentralized groups and subgroups continuously contracting with similarly diffuse working units all over the world.[25]

With this view of business organization in mind, Reich reclassifies employment into "routine production services," "in-person services," and "symbolic-analytic services."[26] Routine production encompasses what remains of the old industrial working class. With manufacturing now bringing together components produced around the globe, a good part of this function is most efficiently carried out by cheap labor in the third world. Hence the decline within the United States of traditional manufacturing jobs. Personal service, by contrast, encompasses those routine jobs—like restaurant and hospital workers, building cleaners, security guards, and clerks of all kinds—that generally require workers to be physically near their customers. Those jobs cannot be exported abroad, but the cheap labor needed for them can be imported.

Reich's third category—symbolic-analytic services—embodies the new elite that the product-cycle theory is supposed to spawn. It performs those "problem-solving, -identifying, and brokering" services critical to the now dispersed and specialized global economy. Its skills add high value, and competitive advantage, and are therefore rewarded with a growing share of national income.[27]

Whether Reich's symbolic managers really contribute enough added value to justify their lion's share of the rewards may not seem self-evident to all observers. Marx would very probably see concepts like global enterprise webs as a refurbished ideology to justify the latest incarnation of the hustling bourgeoisie. Reich himself occasionally doubts whether the lawyers, financial manipulators, and public relations experts in his elite category add quite as much value as they extract, even in narrow economic terms—let alone from any broader social perspective.[28] Clearly, however, they are in a much better competitive position than America's routine production workers, now forced to bid their labor against millions of other production workers abroad, who are growing productive but remain cheap: "Twelve thousand people are added to the world's population every hour, most of whom, eventually, will happily work for a small fraction of the wages of routine producers in America."[29]

The result of these trends, Reich notes, is to fragment the national economic interest. America's three categories of workers are less and less in the same national boat. National wealth may depend more and more on the symbolic analysts. But this top fifth, able to summon labor from anywhere around the globe, depends less and less on the other four fifths. In short, there is no common national boat. Each category of the work force has a boat of its own. As the top boat rises, the other two sink. Since symbolic analysts can often perform their services from widely dispersed locations, they can even escape paying their share of national taxes. Increasingly, they retreat into privileged residential and educational enclaves. The top simply secedes from the rest.

Thus, as Reich himself is the first to admit, the globalization of the American economy is hardly an excuse for complacent self-satisfaction. On the contrary, the long-term social and political implications are deeply disturbing. They point toward a future of social alienation and conflict—a definition of national decline far broader and more deadly than anything purely economic.

In America's past, despite the heterogeneity of our society, abundant economic opportunity obviated the hard class lines and antagonisms that dominated European society and politics.[30] Land was cheap, jobs paid enough to raise a family, and an admirable system of public education gave the bold and lucky a chance to rise up the economic and social ladder. America's strength was refreshed in every generation by immigrants drawn from the enterprising poor and dispossessed around the world. Today, immigration continues apace, albeit from regions probably more difficult to assimilate into a Western culture. For first generations fleeing poverty and oppression, America remains a good deal. Jobs for cheap labor exist in abundance. In this realm of employment, new immigrants more than hold their own with downwardly mobile blue-collar workers, or with the increasingly demoralized old racial minorities. But if jobs for ordinary workers in the high value-added and high-productivity parts of the economy continue to shrink, how satisfactory will the successor generation of the present immigrants find America? No doubt, there will continue to be opportunities for bright, hardworking, and lucky children to rise into the symbol-managing elites. But even those opportunities will narrow if productivity growth continues to lag behind Europe and Japan. And productivity will not grow— in old- or new-style industry and services—without a climate that favors real investment. Both opportunity and productivity will narrow still more if the old public school system, sadly degenerated in much of the country, is not reinvigorated. There will simply be less opportunity in America for ordinary children—those of old immigrants or new.

The present trend toward impoverishment of the nation's working class may easily grow much worse. When the United States finally can no longer borrow easily abroad, the real weight of servicing the accumulated debt will fall still more heavily on the country's living standards. If America is fated to become a more stagnant two-tier society, with the bottom increasingly stuck, a different sort of politics is likely to follow.

In this sort of national decline, corporations and elites are themselves unlikely to escape the general consequences. Insofar as America's own continental base deteriorates, they are likely to deteriorate with it. America's principal rivals—Japan, Germany, and most of Europe—are all countries whose international reach is firmly rooted in their national societies. In a world of such rivals, the richer parts of the American economy are unlikely to flourish, like orchids, as gorgeous and exotic parasites living off the roots of others. Instead, therefore, of rushing to exploit cheap labor abroad, a true reckoning of comparative advantage suggests that American corporations should, like the Japanese and Germans, take care to build and preserve a superior work force at home. But if this is to be done, something must be done to train that work force and to improve conditions for long-term investment in America's real economy. Not much progress seems likely so long as the fiscal incubus continues to ravish America's capital markets. Nor is success likely if the American state cannot ensure the levels of general education and health common to other advanced societies.

For so developed an economy, America's present evolution seems a perverse application of any product-cycle theory. The advanced part of the economy seems a more and more prosperous and cosmopolitan enclave, barricaded within a deteriorating nation. Rather than providing a model for the third world, the United States appears to be imitating it. As in most third world countries, the state seems unable to provide the public goods that are the necessary foundation for advanced private enterprise. America's budgetary crisis embodies the persistent failure to provide those public goods, including a stable macroeconomic policy conducive to real long-term growth. It is this compounding failure of the American state itself that handicaps the nation as it faces the challenges of globalization and new technology, and slowly fritters away a magnificent social, economic, and political inheritance.

Chapter 10 *Rebalancing America*

*E*ven if we put aside all obfuscations and distractions and admit that fiscal deficits do harm the country a great deal, what can we do about them? By now, they are deeply rooted in our whole political economy and world role. No quick and easy remedy exists. Time itself will not cure them. We are not going to grow out of them merely by waiting. A serious burst of inflation could relieve the debt burden for a time, albeit at a heavy price in disruption and injustice. But if the basic imbalances continued, the relief would be temporary and the debt would soon reconstitute itself. Spending can hardly fall. Deep civilian cuts are as unlikely as they would be undesirable. Even a "peace dividend" will continue to elude us without significant changes in foreign policy. The stagnant incomes of much of the population, and the low level of public services, make tax increases improbable on the scale that would be needed. All these points have been explained at length in earlier chapters. Now that we are at the end, there are no rabbits to be pulled out of a hat.

In theory, of course, what needs to be done is clear enough. If the nation's economy is to have its proper chance to compete and flourish in a more demanding world, the federal government has to end its own "dissaving," misallocation, and inefficiency, along with its chronic ruinous forms of financing.

To reach fiscal balance will certainly require higher taxes, but to get them the federal government will need to make itself a better deal for its own citizens. It will have to spend more on the civil sector in ways that improve the country's productivity. To do that, it will have to find a geopolitical strategy that permits spending substantially less on the military. In general, it will have to spend more efficiently and cut back its notorious waste in producing public goods. It will have to gain rational control over defense costs, and provide health and education with standards and costs equivalent to those of European countries like France and Germany. This means a more efficacious relationship between public needs and private enterprise. It also means a rigorous and sustained commitment to professional and efficient public administration.

Changes of this kind will not occur spontaneously. They require a well-thought-out and coordinated set of policies, along with an exceptionally determined and principled political leadership. Behind the policies and the leadership must be a deep, widespread, and self-conscious consensus for national regeneration. To mobilize public will for a policy of discipline and sacrifice, something more is needed than a clever patchwork of special interests. The will to reform has to be informed by adequate ideas about how to reform—ideas understood intellectually by elites as well as intuitively by the public. Developing, refining, and spreading such ideas is a great task in itself. The deep structural problems revealed in the budget crisis are not only the result of political, administrative, or even moral failings. At heart, the failings are also intellectual and philosophical. As the budget crisis ought to make clear, Americans today are particularly deficient in their ideas about public power and responsibility. On the one hand, we are too enamored of using national power abroad. On the other, we are too diffident and confused about using it at home. If the American federal state is a superpower abroad, it is a pitiful, helpless giant at home.

Many Americans may think they prefer things that way. Power abroad and liberty at home seems not such a bad formula, particularly for those who enjoy both in good measure. Our study suggests, however, that the costs of the present dispensation are too high and growing unsustainable. The United

States is a national community, not simply an aircraft carrier launching its power around the world. In any event, the aircraft carrier is slowly sinking.

These twin needs—the self-limitation of our national power abroad and its regeneration at home—are challenges enough for many new studies—certainly by others and perhaps one or two more of my own. Finding a better intellectual and institutional formula for state power is a great collective task. Happily, many people are turning their attention to it. Perhaps this book will encourage still others to realize its urgency. We have a rich national tradition of public philosophy. We need to renew it—and also learn something from the ideas and experiences of other Western democracies.

In closing, it may help to pull together some further thoughts on the two broad topics that this study of the budget suggests are ripe for reconsideration: the role of our nation in the world and the role of our government at home. Since we have stressed the deficiency of ideas, it may not be amiss also to say something about the public responsibility of economic and political theory. Finally, in these rather stirring times in the rest of the world, it may be appropriate to consider the changes needed in America in the light of the changes taking place all around us.

GEOPOLITICAL ADJUSTMENT

I have already spoken at some length about America's geopolitical role and its costs, and written about these questions extensively elsewhere. The link between heavy military spending, civilian inadequacy, and fiscal imbalance has been abundantly noted. It is true that military spending is a much lower portion of federal spending, or national GNP, than in the 1950s or 1960s. Nevertheless, in constant dollars it remains near its postwar peak. It still represents a substantially higher part of GNP than in any of our major competitors. At a time when unmet civilian needs are crying out for aid, defense still consumes a quarter of the federal budget. That we have paid a substantial economic price for our military prowess over the years is undeniable.

To say that the price has been high, however, is not to say that the money has been wasted. For nearly half a century, we and our democratic allies have been faced with an extremely well armed, ruthless, and ambitious enemy, driven by one of the most dangerous and repulsive regimes in modern history. Under the circumstances, heavy American military spending was inevitable. The real issue was not whether the United States needed to be strong militarily, but whether we were following the most appropriate political and military strategy. The real problem was how to keep the need for military strength from severely handicapping and distorting our political system and economy. Very little in American national experience had prepared us for such a sustained effort. Normally, we had gone all out in war and then disarmed rapidly in peace. The cold war presented us with the traditional problem of a continental European great power—the need to maintain heavy standing military forces all the time. And we had the additional expense of keeping and supplying a substantial part of those forces on the other sides of the Atlantic and Pacific oceans.

Initially, we were fortunate to have had an overwhelming lead in nuclear weaponry that permitted us to economize substantially on conventional forces. Our principal economic competitors, moreover, were ruined by the war and our lead over them seemed overwhelming. Gradually, both advantages began to disappear. The Soviets closed the gap in nuclear striking power, which meant that more and more conventional strength seemed necessary to hold our Eurasian commitments credibly. Hence, the swelling defense budgets of the 1980s, including President Reagan's celebrated Strategic Defense Initiative. Meanwhile, America's allies were becoming more and more formidable economic competitors. The strain over the years on our resources grew obvious. Hence, the increasingly sharp debate over "burden sharing," and a good part of our fiscal problem itself. Political and military strains within the alliance system grew more and more significant. Happily for the world, and no doubt for the Russians themselves, the problems of their system were much worse.

Even Soviet disintegration, however, will not automatically resolve the problem of America's geopolitical role, with its comparatively heavy strain of military spending on the economy. That is because the retreat of Soviet power signifies not merely the exhaustion of our enemy, but also the transformation of a bipolar world system into a more plural one. This new plural world represents, in many respects, the triumph of postwar American foreign policy. It was not our aim to build a new Roman Empire, but to revive the broken great powers of Europe and Asia and to coax them into a liberal and co-operative world order. It was also our aim to help the new nations of the third world toward self-determination, democracy, and modern prosperity. And under American protection and patronage, a liberal world political economy really has emerged—a Pax Americana that for all its shortcomings is a not unreasonable approximation of the high ideals of our wartime dreams.

The success of American policy has, however, inevitably brought the relative decline of American power. The rejuvenation of Europe and Japan, and the development of the third world, have all meant a relative diminishing of the enormous American superiority of the immediate postwar era. This has been most manifest in the economic sphere—where our allies have long since grown into formidable competitors, and where industrialization in the third world now presses on all advanced countries.

So long as the Soviet menace persisted in Central Europe, the United States felt compelled to retain much of its old superiority in the military sphere, although it pressed its allies to rearm conventionally. Britain and France became nuclear powers, but on the whole, our allies were happy enough to cede us our military preeminence. Having the Americans assume a protector's role both guarded them from the Soviets, and worked in the economic sphere to advance their own competitive position against us. Behind its American shield, Europe created its democratic welfare societies, many aspects of which Americans should envy. Europe also built its Community, giving itself, thereby, increasing economic and political weight in the world. The Americans have not only accepted this Community, but in its early and critical stages, they vigorously sought to promote it.

Today's plural world is, therefore, not a defeat for American policy, but its natural fulfillment. The grandeur of American policy after World War II has not been to outlast the Soviets, but to foster a brave new world emerging out of the wreckage of the old. In this new world, the United States will have formidable competitors, but it need not have dedicated enemies or much to fear from others. Our "decline" is only a matter of relative adjustment. It need not continue indefinitely. The United States is still the world's preeminent power. Given a reasonable policy, it is likely to remain so for the foreseeable future. America's greatest potential enemy is itself. The principal threat to the United States is the possibility that it will obstinately fail to recognize and adapt to the more plural world it has done so much to create. This would be entirely understandable, but tragically unfortunate.

As the United States has seen its economic prowess more and more challenged by its own allies, many Americans have looked for consolation to our still uncontested military strength. Like the Soviets, but with much less reason, some Americans have clung to a bipolar view of the world. Now that the Soviets have retreated from the game, these Americans see the world as unipolar. Only one true superpower remains, the United States. The position, in their view, carries very heavy responsibilities for world order. The United States is, in effect, more than ever the world's policeman—forever in need of arms against a sea of troubles. There will be no peace dividend. The Russians may escape from the burdens of the cold war, but not the Americans.

If the United States does turn resolutely in this direction, it will be risking a great historic tragedy. It will be setting itself against a pluralist trend that is probably irresistible and that it ought to regard as its own proudest accomplishment. Instead of using the end of the cold war to rejuvenate its own flagging economic prowess, the United States really will become one of Paul Kennedy's dinosaur great powers of the past, dooming itself to decline. More and more it will feel compelled to use its remaining political credit and military power to compensate for its economic weakness. And it will end up clinging to military power because it is economically weak. All this makes for a course that leads toward conflict, isolation, and exhaustion.

Many people immediately dismiss thoughts like these as "neoisolationism." American geopolitical analysts and geopolitically minded politicians seem caught in a curious time warp, where the problems of the late twentieth century can only be

addressed in terms of the shibboleths derived from World War
II. Isolationism—if it means a lack of concern with world politics—is hardly contemporary America's most pressing weakness. There is, in fact, little danger that the United States will
adopt a strategy of trying to take itself out of the world. Nor
does any reasonable person believe that it should.

The United States can easily remain the leading power in
a more plural world but its leadership, to remain effective,
needs a new formula. Taking on excessive responsibility for
collective welfare is not a wise policy in such a world. Leadership requires a different style. It has to be based on a vivid
sense of the limits of purely national power, and therefore the
need for more plural management and a greater division of
labor. At any given moment, plural management is doubtless
less efficient than the old hegemony, but not over the long
run. The reality of the new world lies in its wider dispersion
of resources. Hegemonic policies merely encourage free-riding and ensure the decline and exhaustion of the leader. The
task is to find a multilateral strategy that effectively engages
the plural world's dispersed resources behind its common
interests.

The United States will have to learn to devolve responsibility and initiative to others whenever possible, and to consult
fully with others when it is not. The others will have to accept
the responsibilities of their own power. These changes within
our alliances should doubtless be gradual, but not impercep-
tible. In many instances, such changes may well seem more a
further extension of old practices than a radical departure.
The pluralist trend has been at work for a long time. World
economic relations, for example, have long been multilateral
in character, as the summits of the "Group of Seven" have
made more and more obvious. Even NATO's policies and
strategies have always been based on a patiently negotiated
consensus. In the military arrangements themselves, however,
the United States has always jumped in to take the lead—and
the primary responsibility. In the 1960s, the United States in-
sisted on such a course even when it led to the withdrawal of
one of its principal European allies. However much that style
may have been justified in the past, it will clearly be counterproductive in the future.

America's different figure abroad should be matched by a more mature and less jingoist style at home. American politicians should talk less about America's being "number one," and more about being a good team player. Above all, American Presidents should resist the temptation to substitute the occasional parade of power abroad for serious leadership at home. And the American public should beware of that mentality, among politicians and scholars alike, that finds the welfare of Kuwait a more compelling concern than the welfare of New York, Detroit, or Los Angeles.

Such a distorted priority is a menace not only at home but abroad as well. In the long run, the principal threat to America—and the world—is a breakdown in the highly integrated and increasingly troubled global economy. America's own chronic imbalances weigh more and more heavily on that global system. The first duty every nation owes to the world is to put its own affairs in order.

A BETTER VIEW OF THE STATE AT HOME

The federal government's overbalancing of foreign over domestic concerns has been accompanied in recent years by a strange atrophy in our ideas about the domestic role of the government. Throughout this book, there have been frequent illustrations of how the absence of an efficient public authority or an adequate provision for public goods handicaps the economy. Paradoxically, that failure of the public sector to perform its proper function in a market system encourages, almost inexorably, a drift away from markets toward a much more direct state role. Many who profess to love free-market institutions the most are among those most responsible for this trend. Those who deny the state its proper functions—those, for example, whose response to every evidence of market failure is more "deregulation"—thereby nourish the statist and corporatist trends that are the natural reaction.

Behind these characteristic mistakes of our time lie some fundamental and widespread misconceptions about the nature of public authority. Since the time of the Greeks, Western political thought has been informed by the idea that a good public community or state, and a good life for the individual citizen, are not only compatible but necessary to each other. But this identity exists as an ideal—a potential. The state is not only an ideal summoning citizens to Burke's "partnership in all virtue." It is also a functioning institution run by politicians and bureaucrats, who often behave like any other interest group. If the state is indispensable for the freedom, safety and prosperity of its citizens, it can also eat out their substance and crowd out their liberty. The very ideal of a shared identity and will can be perverted to rob citizens of their rights, indeed of their souls. In the modern Western tradition, democratic self-government is supposed to help resolve the tension. But majorities, as Tocqueville pointed out early in the last century, can be even more tyrannical than kings—hence, the strong "libertarian" tradition that emphasizes the dangers of unchecked power, however democratic, and the need to protect individual "rights," private property included. Western countries thus have elaborate systems of constitutional checks and balances and, to varying degrees, see the market economy as the necessary complement to political liberty.

Human rights and political balances may keep the public authority from going wrong, but they cannot make it go right. Since, in our immensely complicated modern societies, public power needs to be positive, it also needs to be good. It cannot be made good merely by being kept weak, divided, and distracted. It needs a collective superego to govern its action—a vision that engages citizens in a broad social pact to live together in pursuit of happiness, and in as much decency, comfort, mutual respect, and fellowship as the human condition permits.

Giving this public ideal a concrete definition that is efficacious and acceptable is, of course, the great challenge before any political system. Modern constitutional democracies have no popes to do this for them. Modern democratic politics is a game where political entrepreneurs put together programs and symbols and bid for support from interests and voters. Consensus is supposed to arise in the free clash of conflicting proposals and visions. Ideally, this consensus is more than the averaging of enough private interests to create a majority. Ideally, it embodies a high degree of collective reasonableness. How well an actual state lives up to its ideal is obviously problematic. Some systems are so bad that the conscientious citizen needs to revolt against what his state is on behalf of what he believes it should be. Happily, most Western states have been spared such agonies in recent times, but the tribulations of nations in eastern Europe, not to mention the difficulties of political life in the third world, should be a warning against taking too much for granted.

That the actual in politics forever mocks the ideal is obvious. The practical task is to improve the performance of the state in action. Our question here is what view of the state is more useful in securing its benefits and controlling its abuses. A view that expects only the worst is self-defeating. A constitutional system based on nothing but low expectations is unlikely to exceed them. A public philosophy that treats the state merely as an interest group is counterproductive.

That, in my opinion, is the great fault of many contemporary libertarians. They regard the state as a sort of public disease. Government is a mindless parasitic fungus, spreading everywhere and sapping the vitality of the society in which it has taken root. This view is, no doubt, all too plausible. But if the state is not challenged and disciplined by a higher idea of itself, the libertarian view becomes a self-fulfilling prophecy. Obviously a bureaucracy can be nothing more than a vigorously intrusive but nonproductive interest group, eager for power but incompetent in administering to the needs of the society. But the way to control it is not by mindless opposition to all public power, but by acknowledging the critical role of public authority, and by insisting upon the highest standards of public idealism and professional competence among those who exercise it. Crippling public authority and denigrating any idea of public good will not get rid of the public sector. Still less will it prevent its self-generating intrusion into private life. It will merely guarantee that the bureaucracy will remain at its lowest level. The best way to control the state is through public reason, not blanket private contempt and opposition. To make this argument is not to advocate throwing away our rights and balances. But it is to say that we can no longer afford a system as wasteful and incoherent as ours has become. Every constitutional system has to find an efficacious balance between the power to govern and the power to obstruct. Ours has gone haywire.

The point may seem simple, but the failure to grasp and respect it has been costing the country dear. Every President, it is said, now runs against the government. In office, he does his best to disavow responsibility for what occurs during his tenure. Unfortunately, given our system, the disavowals have become all too credible. The American federal system has never been a model of efficiency. The country is too big and diverse to be efficient in European terms. Fortunately, through most of its history the United States has had a reserve of public resources well beyond its immediate needs. That is no longer true. As our public need has grown, our public efficiency has fallen very low—even by our own standards—hence the budget crisis.

The budget process is itself a definitive illustration of the present debility of our public sector. The President sends a draft budget to Congress. He knows it has little relation to what will emerge, and frames it accordingly. In the ensuing melee, any coherent policy is soon lost in the myriad of disconnected skirmishes and deals that determine where public resources actually go. No one can really be held responsible for what emerges. The President laments that he is often not even a player in the game. Congress itself cannot generate a coherent policy. Even its old baronies that used to control departmental budgets are largely gone. The legislature is simply a marketplace where several hundred political entrepreneurs compete to service the organized interests that are their customers. Where, in all this, is the public interest?

Ironically, this process of governmental disintegration has been watched with rapt admiration by a good part of America's professional students of politics. Like old aficionados of the French Fourth Republic, they have grown so fascinated with the mechanism that they have grown indifferent to the result. It is hard to believe that a machine so intricate and beautifully poised as Congress could be advancing toward its own self-destruction.

Similar thoughts come to mind about America's increasingly incoherent legal system. Here the dangers of administrative fungus are already well-advanced. The explosion of litigation and increasing intrusiveness of the courts, and the astonishing proliferation of lawyers, are a very heavy burden for the American political economy to bear. The problem is not that the courts are too strong. Rather it is that they seem incapable of declaring law in any definitive and stable fashion. Legal professionals—jurists and scholars alike—seem to have lost any shared vision of a collective public interest and will. Politics through litigation is the result, and an enormous burden on the society.

In summary, no one can deny that the machinery of the state ought to reconcile the need to govern effectively with the need to obstruct. But the American system is now seriously out of balance. In the face of the institutional bedlam that the budget crisis so faithfully reflects, something is called for other than fatuous admiration. The cure cannot come from still more obstruction and deregulation, as so many libertarians seem still to believe. If it is not to come from dictatorship, then it must arise from a more serious search for public reason and public interest.

ECONOMICS AND PUBLIC POWER

The science of economics, like the science of politics, has a critical moral responsibility in generating the public philosophy needed to ennoble and discipline state power. Unfortunately, economics as a fashionable discipline, particularly in Anglo-Saxon countries, suffers from the same problem that disables the contemporary study of politics—an inadequate conception of the state. Economics, even more than politics, is infused with the nineteenth-century vision of Benthamite utilitarianism—a tradition whose notions of the political community and human nature in general would be easy enough to dismiss as patently ludicrous, were they not so deeply embedded in our whole way of thinking about public policy. In this tradition, the individual, taken one by one, is the only reality; the community is simply an aggregate of producers and consumers, pursuing pleasure and avoiding pain. As a healthy corrective to overblown collectivism, the Benthamite tradition is admirable. As a dominating perspective for thinking about public policy, it is one of the great blind alleys of Western philosophy. All the same, it is very much with us—and nowhere more than in contemporary economics.

It is thanks in good part to this tradition's deficiency in

respect to the state that economists so easily fall into the view
that markets can and should exist in autonomous isolation from
politics. The critical role of the state in setting the legal and
macroeconomic framework is somehow overlooked. This same
sort of political obtuseness afflicts those who advocate "letting
the market decide" fundamental issues of public policy. The
market is promoted from a mechanism into a solution—a substitute for politics. As a mechanism, the market has incompa-
rable virtues for carrying out the basic choices of the political
system in as efficient a way as possible, and with a maximum
of individual liberty. But letting the economic market settle
political issues obviously favors heavily certain interests over
others. To argue that the market should be the principal locus
for political decisions is to be either obtuse or disingenuous.
Marx, of course, made this point long ago. Behind those im-
personal factors that supposedly determine the market's decisions are in fact, he noted, the individuals who control and
manipulate them. It is not necessary to embrace Marx's solution to appreciate the obvious force of his analysis. Market
economics can be simply an ideology for the interest of the
dominant economic actors. Their interests, as they emerge from
the market, are not necessarily the best determinants of the
welfare of the whole community. It is up to the state to set its
own public priorities.

The product-cycle theory is a case in point. It is often used
as a cover for particular interests not necessarily general to the
whole community. To imply, for example, that production
workers in America ought ideally to have the same living standards as production workers in Thailand is to promote a rather
biased view of economic efficiency, not to mention of the national interest. Conceivably, there are broader views that should
be heard.

That is not to say, however, that politics can simply ignore
the market—that political preferences, backed by state power,
can rewrite the laws of economics. The function of economics,
as a science, is presumably to inform power, and the community at large, of the real costs of its political options. In that
respect, contemporary economics not only suffers from the same
blindness about the community as libertarian individualism, it
has its own particular problem of hubris. Economists are to-

day's wizards at court. Instead of checking power, they offer the politicians the magical means to do whatever they please. They have the essential quality for selling their wares: They believe in their own product.

Economic policy-making in much of the postwar era has been dominated by various neo-Keynesian sects. In many respects, that postwar Keynesianism has been a particular American creation. It has lifted Keynes's analysis of the causes of the interwar depression—insufficient demand caused by excessive saving and too little investment—and blended it with a sort of frontier theory of limitless expansion. It is a remarkable medicine to apply in an age of inflation and overconsumption. Keynes would, no doubt, be astonished. But as a view of the economy it has naturally been popular with ambitious politicians of all persuasions—essentially because it encourages them to believe they can do whatever they please. It was used in *NSC-68* to justify a huge rearmamant, and used again by Kennedy and Johnson to justify rearmament plus an ambitious welfare program. Its latest incarnation has been the supply-side economics of the Reagan era. It has become, in short, an ideology to justify enthusiasm over prudence—the opposite, presumably, of what the political function of economic theory ought to be.

In the end, this sort of neo-Keynesianism is also self-defeating, politically as well as economically. Its combination of fiscal deficits and monetary accommodation grows inexorably inflationary. As inflation gathers speed, it threatens middle-class incomes and savings and provokes revulsion against government taxation and spending of all kinds—particularly that which seems to favor the "loafer class" against the saving middle class. This is essentially what happened in the 1970s, with results that probably set back America's social progress by a decade or more. Neo-Keynesian license can easily prove just as self-defeating for America's world role. The fundamental requirement for a successful imperial power is to find a workable balance for international ambitions, domestic needs, and economic resources. Overextension provokes an almost inevitable reaction. It was Vietnam—with the inflation it accelerated—that provoked the "neoisolationism" of the 1970s. Unless the fiscal disorder of the 1980s can be brought under control, we shall, no doubt, have neoisolationism again.

Neo-Keynesians have been out of official fashion over the past decade, although Reaganomics owes more to their ideas than is usually acknowledged. But in many respects, the fashionable monetarism that succeeded is even more undisciplined and manipulative. In the 1980s, rigorous control of the money supply became a way to avoid price inflation and summon foreign savings. In effect, it was a clever way to finance an extraordinarily profligate fiscal policy. With their tight monetary policy, monetarist gurus offered politicians the opportunity to avoid inflation while continuing to spend as they pleased. High interest rates under such conditions became a way to squeeze labor costs, but also starved investment and fed speculation—hardly an admirable program for the nation's long-term economic welfare.

Monetarist economists may not be responsible for the skewed priorities and fiscal indiscipline of their political masters, but they may certainly be faulted for neglecting the institutional structure needed to preserve monetary stability. Particularly egregious was the enthusiastic support so many monetarists gave to floating exchange rates at the end of the Bretton Woods era. Floating rates, blessed by the monetary magi, were hailed as an instrument of stability. In truth, of course, they were a sign of a major breakdown in the restraining constitutional structure of the postwar international order—a structure designed to limit government power in the interest of long-term stability and growth. Monetarists certainly did not cause the conditions that led to the breakdown of that order, but they legitimized, serviced, and blessed the immoral system that succeeded it. In doing so, they betrayed their own cardinal principle of stable money. Beginning as protestors against inflation, they ended up as the technicians of wayward power.

The problem has not been so much the lack of good people; many people of high intelligence and goodwill have struggled to manage and enlighten public power through these confusing times. But as the budget crisis makes all too clear, our ideas are deficient. As a result, we cannot bring order and efficiency to our institutions or balance to our accounts. If we want to do better in practice, we will have to do better in theory.

CRISIS OF THE NATION STATE: AN INTERNATIONAL PHENOMENON

Throughout this book, one aspect or another of America's fiscal situation has been compared with that of other countries, France and Germany in particular. As was discussed in Chapter 7, since the 1970s, rapid technological change and the globalization of economic activity have challenged all advanced industrial societies to sustain their high living standards. The challenge extended to the Soviet system, under strong pressure to narrow the notorious gap between its living standards and those of the Western countries. Eventually, any such sustained economic challenge tests a nation's political institutions also. It is not surprising that the decade of the 1980s saw remarkable political ferment in both Eastern and Western Europe.

Eastern Europe found the Soviet system more and more inadequate. Its shortcomings fed demands for market mechanisms in place of central control. Popular definitions of acceptable economic conditions began to include not only higher consumption but free markets and political liberty. Out of the widespread discontent in the Soviet Union itself came Glasnost and Perestroika, together with sweeping arms control concessions and the renunciation of imperial control over neighboring European states.

The collapse of the national communist autocracies that followed the Soviet retreat brought reunification to Germany, and revolutionary efforts to liberalize political and economic systems throughout the region. By the summer of 1991, communist power was broken in Moscow and the Soviet Union itself was undergoing profound restructuring, and perhaps disintegration. Eastern Europe's other federal state, Yugoslavia, was meanwhile breaking to pieces in civil war.

Western Europe's political and economic evolution, less spectacular and traumatic, may well prove no less significant. The problem for West European states has been to consolidate and defend their high levels of public and private welfare in the increasingly competitive international environment. The

European Community has been an integral part of their national strategies. With the EC, they have hoped to reconcile their medium-sized national states with the continental scale needed to remain competitive. West European states have thus engaged to complete a single market by the end of 1992, and appear to be moving toward tighter monetary union and more effective confederal arrangements for foreign and defense policies. Thus, it can be said, in Eastern Europe a centralized federal union is disintegrating into a group of new—or long-suppressed—nation states, while in Western Europe a group of old nation states is forming a confederal union.

No doubt the contrast is too simple-minded. Many observers note a certain nationalist revival in Western Europe and the forces of centralization may well reassert themselves in the East. But whatever the fate of the liberal and nationalist experiments that have shot up throughout the East, it seems improbable that the old centralized federal command economy will ever be reinstated in the Soviet Union. Even less likely is a serious reversal of Western European integration, a movement that has been gathering force over three decades. Unquestionably, however, the nature, role, and structuring of public power will continue to be the subject of intense debate and experimentation—in both the East and the West of Europe and, of course, between them.

The problems of the American political system should be considered in this broader international context. Traditional political structures are everywhere in need of serious revision. It flatters us to interpret events in the Soviet Union in cold-war terms—as a victory of "our" system over theirs. But other perspectives are probably more useful—for Americans particularly. Postwar Soviet history may be seen, for example, as an instructive illustration of the consequences of protracted geopolitical overcommitment for even a very big power. It might also be seen to illustrate what happens when a political class fails to pay attention to the growing alienation of a large part of the population, or when the balance remains uncorrected between overloaded central institutions and atrophied regional structures, or when the structures of government administration remain unrenovated, even after their inefficiency has grown notorious. Americans might also note how such prolonged maladjustments were possible only because so huge a country as the Soviet Union has an exceptional capacity to ignore its own shortcomings and continue with self-destructive policies.

Americans may derive more positive inspiration from a closer look at Western Europe. Progress toward European unity offers a major historic opportunity to devolve some of our own excessive geopolitical burden and Western Europe's leading nation states have, in many respects, been more successful in providing their citizens with public goods, in part at least because their governments are more efficient than the American. With its Community, moreover, Europe seems to be evolving a formula for governing a continental political economy that strikes a particularly efficacious balance between central institutions and regional vitality. Two centuries after the United States, Europeans are conducting their own grand federal experiment. Just as the Japanese have copied and improved on our industrial prowess, perhaps the Europeans may do the same with our continental political system. Europe, of course, has not yet mastered how to concentrate its power to play its proper role in the world. But that mastery can be a dangerous accomplishment, perhaps too well achieved in the American federation and perfected to self-destruction in the Soviet.

We should wish the Europeans well, and the Russians too. But nothing compels us to remain inert before the shortcomings of our own federal system. Economic relationships and political institutions are in ferment throughout the world. We cannot expect to escape the challenges that such ferment poses to our own prosperity and political system. Certainly anyone who wants the United States to play a great role in the coming century should be worrying about what is happening to the springs of our national strength. Complacency before so striking a sign of political debility as our huge and worsening budget deficits is not the right course for a true patriot. Our political system, like everyone else's, needs to adapt to a different world.

Great periods of renewal are not unheard of in modern democracies. The Germans succeeded in Adenauer's time and the French in de Gaulle's. Over the past decade, both Germany and France have been able to recall their economies to balance and strengthen their competitiveness. In two or three generations, postwar Europe has made its Community a towering monument to the possibilities of visionary ideals. The United States has had more than its own share of great periods of reform and leadership. It is clearly time for another. Have we grown so self-satisfied, or so mired in secret despair, that we have somehow lost the knack?

Tables and Graphs

TABLES

Short titles are used throughout this section as follows: *Budget of the U.S. Government, 1992* for *Budget of the U.S. Government,* Fiscal Year 1992 (Washington, D.C.: Government Printing Office, 1992); and *ERP 1991* for *Economic Report of the President, 1991* (Washington, D.C.: Government Printing Office, 1991).

Constant 1982 dollars. As used in several tables and graphs that follow, these are derived from the "Composite Deflator" that can be found in *Budget of the U.S. Government, 1992,* Table 1.3, Part Seven: 17.

TABLE 1

Human Resources, Outlays by Function (In Current Billions)

	1950	1960	1970	1980	1990
Education, etc.	1.2	3.6	22.5	37.7	29.4
Health	1.4	2.9	15.4	27.4	44.1
Medicare	0.0	0.0	16.2	38.0	74.9
Income Security	21.2	27.2	40.7	102.4	112.4
Social Security	4.0	42.8	78.8	140.2	189.8
Veterans Benefits	45.8	20.1	22.6	25.1	22.2

Source: *Budget of the U.S. Government, 1992,* Table 3.1, Part Seven: 31–36.

TABLE 2

Human Resources, Shares of Functions
(As Percent of Total)

	1950	1960	1970	1980	1990
Education, etc.	1.7	3.7	11.5	10.2	6.2
Health	1.9	3.0	7.8	7.4	9.3
Medicare	0.0	0.0	8.2	10.2	15.8
Income Security	28.8	28.2	20.8	27.6	23.8
Social Security	5.5	44.3	40.2	37.8	40.1
Veterans Benefits	62.1	20.8	11.5	6.8	4.7

Source: *Budget of the U.S. Government, 1992*, Table 3.1, Part Seven: 31–36; author's calculations.

TABLE 3

Key Statistics for France, Germany, and United States

	FRANCE	GERMANY	U.S.
Population in 1989 (Thousands)	56,160	61,990	248,777
1990 GDP (Billions) at 1990 Market Rates	$1,191	$1,490	$5,330
GDP Per Capita in 1988			
at current rates	$17,002	$19,581	$19,558
at PPP*	$13,577	$14,134	$19,558
Net Average Annual population increase over 10 years (1987)	0.4%	0.0%	1.0%
Ratio of Population Aged 65+ to 15–64			
1980	21.9%	23.4%	17.1%
2000 (estimate)	23.3%	25.4%	18.2%
Population Under Poverty Level (Early 1970s)	16.0%	9.3%	13.0%
Defense			
as % of GNP (1988)	3.9%	2.9%	6.3%
as % of Central Gov't. Outlays (1988)	8.8%	9.6%	27.5%
General Gov't. Share in Employment (1988)	23.0%	16.0%	14.4%

*Purchasing Power Parity.
Sources: IMF, *Government Finance Statistics Yearbook, 1989* (Washington, D.C.: IMF, 1990), p. 58; OECD, *The Role of the Public Sector* (Paris: OECD, 1985), p. 63; OECD, *Reforming Public Pensions* (1988), pp. 142–43; OECD, *Economic Report on Germany, 1989–90* (1990), p. 126; OECD, *Public Expenditure on Income Maintenance* (1976), p. 67; OECD, *Historical Statistics, 1960–1988* (Paris: OECD, 1990), p. 42; OECD, *Main Economic Indicators*, April 1991, pp. 172–73, 178; U.S. Arms Control and Disarmament Agency, *World Military Expenditures and Arms Transfers* (Washington, D.C.: U.S. Government Printing Office, 1990).

TABLE 4

Current Receipts of Government (All Levels) (As Percentage of GDP)

	1980	1982	1984	1986	1988
United States	30.8	31.1	30.7	31.4	31.5
Japan	27.6	29.5	30.4	31.5	34.3
Germany	44.7	45.4	45.3	44.9	43.7
France	44.5	45.9	47.5	47.1	47.1

Source: OECD, *Economic Outlook, 48* (Paris: OECD, December 1990), p. 190.

TABLE 5

U.S. General Government Current Receipts and Total Outlays (As Percentage of GDP)

	1980	1982	1984	1986	1988
Current Receipts	30.8	31.1	30.7	31.4	31.5
Total Outlays	33.7	36.5	35.8	37.0	36.3

Source: OECD, *Economic Outlook, 48* (Paris: OECD, December 1990), pp. 189–90.

TABLE 6

Federal Receipts and Outlays, 1940 to 1990 (As Percentage of GNP)

	RECEIPTS	OUTLAYS	SURPLUS OR DEFICIT (−)
1940	6.8	9.9	−3.0
1941	7.7	12.1	−4.4
1942	10.3	24.7	−14.4
1943	13.7	44.7	−31.0
1944	21.7	45.2	−23.5
1945	21.3	43.6	−22.4
1946	18.5	25.9	−7.5
1947	17.2	15.4	1.8
1948	16.8	12.0	4.8
1949	14.9	14.7	0.2
1950	14.8	16.0	−1.2
1951	16.4	14.4	1.9
1952	19.3	19.8	−0.4
1953	19.0	20.8	−1.8

TABLE 6 (*continued*)

	RECEIPTS	OUTLAYS	SURPLUS OR DEFICIT (−)
1954	18.9	19.2	−0.3
1955	16.9	17.7	−0.8
1956	17.8	16.9	0.9
1957	18.2	17.4	0.8
1958	17.7	18.3	−0.6
1959	16.5	19.1	−2.7
1960	18.3	18.2	0.1
1961	18.2	18.9	−0.6
1962	17.9	19.2	−1.3
1963	18.1	18.9	−0.8
1964	17.9	18.8	−0.9
1965	17.4	17.6	−0.2
1966	17.7	18.2	−0.5
1967	18.7	19.8	−1.1
1968	18.0	21.0	−3.0
1969	20.1	19.8	0.3
1970	19.5	19.8	−0.3
1971	17.7	19.9	−2.2
1972	18.0	20.0	−2.0
1973	18.0	19.2	−1.2
1974	18.6	19.0	−0.4
1975	18.3	21.8	−3.5
1976	17.6	21.9	−4.3
1977	18.4	21.2	−2.8
1978	18.4	21.1	−2.7
1979	18.9	20.6	−1.6
1980	19.4	22.1	−2.8
1981	20.1	22.7	−2.6
1982	19.7	23.8	−4.1
1983	18.1	24.3	−6.3
1984	18.1	23.1	−5.0
1985	18.6	23.9	−5.4
1986	18.4	23.7	−5.3
1987	19.3	22.7	−3.4
1988	19.0	22.3	−3.2
1989	19.3	22.3	−3.0
1990	19.1	23.2	−4.1

Source: *Budget of the United States Government, 1992*, Table 1.3, Part Seven: 17.

TABLE 7

Manufacturing: Productivity, Labor Costs, Profit Shares, GDP Shares, and Employment, 1950 to 1988 (Average Annual Percentage Changes)

	U.S.	FRANCE	GERMANY	JAPAN
Output per Hour in Manufacturing[1]				
1950–73	2.7	5.8	6.6	9.9
1973–79	1.6	4.6	4.3	5.5
1979–88	3.4	3.1	2.6	5.8
1984–88	3.9	3.1	2.4	5.7
Unit Labor Costs[1]				
1950–73	2.5	4.1	3.0	2.4
1973–79	8.0	11.2	4.9	6.9
1979–88	2.3	6.7	2.7	−1.0
1984–88	0.2	2.2	2.1	−1.3
Gross Operating Surplus as Percentage of Gross Value Added[2]				
1960–67	27.3	N/A	36.1	55.7
1968–73	25.4	34.7	33.9	53.8
1974–79	25.4	30.8	29.4	43.5
1980–88[3]	24.9	25.2	28.3	42.2
Value Added as a Percentage of GDP[2]				
1960–67	28.0	29.0	39.9	34.5
1968–73	25.5	28.4	37.3	35.2
1974–79	23.3	26.7	34.6	30.5
1980–88[4]	20.6	22.3	31.7	29.2
Civilian Employment[2]				
1960–68	2.3	0.5	0.3	4.1
1968–73	0.2	2.1	0.9	2.0
1973–79	1.1	−0.9	−1.4	−1.3
1979–88[5]	−0.6	−2.1	−0.9	1.0

[1] Average annual rate of change based on compound rate method (BLS).
[2] Simple average (OECD).
[3] U.S. and Germany: 1980–87; France: 1980–85.
[4] U.S.: 1980–87.
[5] Germany: 1979–86 and 1988.
Sources: Edwin R. Dean, *Productivity and the Labor Force* (Washington D.C.: U.S. Department of Labor, Bureau of Labor Statistics, 1989) and OECD, *Historical Statistics, 1960–1988* (Paris: OECD, 1990), pp. 32, 63, 78, and *Historical Statistics, 1960–1986* (Paris: OECD, 1988), p. 74.

TABLE 8

Total Employment, 1980 to 1989 (In Thousands)

	U.S.	FRANCE	GERMANY	JAPAN
1980	101,405	21,709	25,795	55,360
1989	117,326	21,972	27,793	61,271

Sources: OECD, *Economic Outlook, 48,* December 1990, p. 118, and *Historical Statistics, 1960–1980* (Paris: OECD, 1982), p. 18.

TABLE 9

Standardized Unemployment Rates, 1964 to 1988 (Average Percentages)

	1964–67	1968–73	1974–79	1980–88
U.S.	4.2	4.6	6.7	7.4
France	1.7	2.6	4.5	9.0
Germany	0.6	1.0	3.2	6.0
Japan	1.2	1.2	1.9	2.5

Source: OECD, *Historical Statistics: 1960–1988* (Paris: OECD, 1990), p. 45.

TABLE 10

Real GDP, 1960 to 1988 (Average Annual Percentage Growth)

	U.S.	FRANCE	GERMANY	JAPAN
1960–68	4.5	5.4	4.1	10.2
1968–73	3.2	5.5	4.9	8.7
1973–79	2.4	2.8	2.3	3.6
1979–88	2.8	1.9	1.7	4.1

Source: OECD, *Historical Statistics: 1960–1988* (Paris: OECD, 1990), p. 48.

TABLE 11

U.S. Long-Term Real Interest Rates, 1966 to 1988 (Percent)

Year	Rate
1966	1.4
1967	1.7
1968	1.0
1969	1.0
1970	1.2
1971	0.7
1972	1.4
1973	0.5
1974	−1.5
1975	−2.6
1976	0.5
1977	0.3
1978	0.6
1979	−0.2
1980	1.5
1981	3.1
1982	5.4
1983	7.2
1984	8.1
1985	7.8
1986	5.5
1987	5.5
1988	5.6

Source: OECD, *Historical Statistics* (Paris: OECD, 1982 and 1990), pp. 94, 106, respectively.

TABLE 12

**Military Expenditures as a Percentage of GNP,
1963 to 1988**

	U.S.	FRANCE	GERMANY	JAPAN
1963	8.9	5.6	5.2	1.0
1964	8.1	5.3	4.7	1.0
1965	7.6	5.2	4.3	1.0
1966	8.5	5.0	4.1	0.9
1967	9.5	5.0	4.3	0.9
1968	9.3	4.8	3.6	0.8
1969	8.8	4.3	3.6	0.8
1970	7.9	4.2	3.3	0.8
1971	7.0	4.0	3.4	0.9
1972	6.6	3.9	3.5	0.9
1973	6.0	3.8	3.5	0.8
1974	6.1	3.7	3.6	0.9
1975	5.9	3.8	3.6	0.9
1976	5.3	3.8	3.5	0.9
1977	5.3	3.9	3.4	0.9
1978	4.9	3.9	3.3	0.9
1979	4.9	3.9	3.3	0.9
1980	5.3	4.0	3.3	0.9
1981	5.6	4.1	3.4	0.9
1982	6.2	4.1	3.4	1.0
1983	6.4	4.1	3.4	1.0
1984	6.3	4.1	3.2	1.0
1985	6.6	4.0	3.2	1.0
1986	6.6	3.9	3.1	1.0
1987	6.5	4.0	3.0	1.0
1988	6.3	3.9	2.9	1.0

Sources: U.S. Arms Control and Disarmament Agency, *World Military Expenditures and Arms Transfers* (Washington, D.C.: U.S. Government Printing Office, 1975, 1982 and 1990).

TABLE 13

M2, 1960 to 1990 (Annual Percentage Change)

YEAR	M2
1960	4.9
1961	7.4
1962	8.1
1963	8.4
1964	8.0
1965	8.1
1966	4.5
1967	9.2
1968	8.0
1969	4.1
1970	6.5
1971	13.5
1972	13.0
1973	6.9
1974	5.5
1975	12.6
1976	13.7
1977	10.6
1978	8.0
1979	7.8
1980	8.9
1981	10.0
1982	8.9
1983	12.0
1984	8.5
1985	8.4
1986	9.5
1987	3.5
1988	5.5
1989	4.9
1990	3.2

Source: *Economic Report of the President, 1991* (Washington, D.C.: U.S. Government Printing Office, 1991), p. 363.

TABLE 14

National Saving and Borrowing, 1980 to 1989
(As Percentage of Total)

	1980	1985	1986	1987	1988	1989
Gross Private Saving	17.5	16.6	15.8	14.7	15.4	15.0
General Government Balance	−1.3	−3.3	−3.4	−2.4	−2.0	−1.7
Federal Budget Balance	−2.2	−4.9	−4.9	−3.5	−2.9	−2.6
Gross Domestic Savings	16.3	13.3	12.4	12.3	13.5	13.3
Gross Private Domestic Investment	16.0	16.0	15.6	15.5	15.3	14.8
Domestic Surplus [1]	0.3	−2.7	−3.2	−3.2	−1.9	−1.5
Net Foreign Saving [2]	−0.5	2.8	3.2	3.4	2.4	1.9

[1] Equivalent to net foreign saving plus errors and omissions.
[2] Current Account with opposite sign.
Source: OECD, *Economic Survey, United States, 1989–1990* (Paris: OECD, 1990), Table 26, p. 80.

TABLE 15

United States Trade and Current Accounts, 1980 to 1990
(In Billions of Dollars, Surplus or [−] Deficit)

	1980	1981	1982	1983	1984	1985	1986	1987	1988	1989	1990
Trade	−25	−28	−36	−67	−112	−122	−145	−159	−126	−115	−108
Current	1	7	−6	−40	−99	−113	−133	−144	−128	−110	−99

Sources: *ERP* 1991. For 1990 figures, U.S. Department of Commerce, *Survey of Current Business*, Table 4.1, Vol. 71, No. 4, April 1991, p. 14.

TABLE 16

Distribution of Civilian Employment by Sector
(As Percentage of Total)

	1960	1980	1985	1988	CHANGE 1980–88
MANUFACTURING					
United States	26.4	22.1	19.5	18.5	−16.3
France	27.3	25.8	23.2	21.6	−16.3
Germany	34.3	34.3	32.0	31.8	−7.3
Japan	21.3	24.7	25.0	24.2	−2.0
INDUSTRY					
United States	35.3	30.5	28.0	26.9	−11.8
France	37.6	35.9	32.0	30.3	−15.6
Germany	47.0	44.1	41.0	39.8	−9.8
Japan	28.5	35.3	34.9	34.1	−3.4
SERVICES					
United States	56.2	65.9	68.8	70.2	+6.5
France	39.9	55.4	60.4	62.9	+13.5
Germany	39.1	50.3	53.5	56.1	+11.5
Japan	41.3	54.2	56.4	58.0	+7.0
AGRICULTURE					
United States	8.5	3.6	3.1	2.9	−19.4
France	22.5	8.7	7.6	6.8	−21.8
Germany	14.0	5.6	5.4	4.0	−28.6
Japan	30.2	10.4	8.8	7.9	−24.0

Sources: OECD, *Historical Statistics, 1960–1988* (Paris: OECD, 1990), pp. 40–41.

TABLE 17

Long-Duration* Unemployment, 1973 to 1988
(As Percentage of Total Unemployed)

	1973	1979	1983	1986	1988
U.S.	3.3	4.2	13.3	8.7	7.4
Japan	N/A	16.5	15.5	17.2	20.2
Germany	8.5	19.9	28.5	32.0	32.6
France	21.6	30.3	42.2	47.8	44.8

* 12 months or over
Sources: OECD, *Economies in Transition: Structural Adjustment in OECD Countries* (Paris: OECD, 1989), p. 32, and OECD, *Labour Force Statistics, 1968–1988* (Paris: OECD, 1990).

TABLE 18

World's Largest Twenty-Five Banks Ranked by Shareholders' Equity and Assets, 1989

SHAREHOLDERS' EQUITY	ASSETS
1. Fuji Bank Group	Dai-Ichi Kangyo Bank
2. Dai-Ichi Kangyo Bank	Sumitomo Bank
3. Caisse Nationale de Crédit Agricole	Fuji Bank Corp.
4. Sumitomo Bank	Mitsubishi Bank
5. Barclays	Sanwa Bank
6. Mitsubishi Bank	Industrial Bank of Japan
7. Citicorp	Norinchukin Bank
8. National Westminster Bank	Caisse Nationale de Crédit Agricole
9. Sanwa Bank	Banque Nationale de Paris
10. Industrial Bank of Japan	Citicorp
11. Industrial and Commercial Bank of China	Tokai Bank
12. Deutsche Bank	Mitsubishi Trust and Banking
13. Union Bank of Switzerland	Crédit Lyonnais
14. Bank of China	Mitsui Bank
15. Hong Kong and Shanghai Banking Corp.	Barclays
16. Compagnie Financière de Paribas	Deutsche Bank
17. Crédit Lyonnais	Bank of Tokyo
18. Japan Development Bank	Sumitomo Trust and Banking
19. Tokai Bank	National Westminster Bank
20. Swiss Bank Corp.	Long-term Credit Bank of Japan
21. Mitsui Bank	Mitsui Trust and Banking
22. Bank America Corp.	Taiyo Kobe Bank
23. Banco do Brasil	Yasuda Trust and Banking
24. Long-term Credit Bank of Japan	Société Générale
25. Dresdner Bank	Daiwa Bank

Source: "The Euromoney 500," *Euromoney*, June 1990, pp. 73–120.

TABLE 19

Export Market Shares by Country and Commodity, 1980 to 1988 (Percentage)

COMMODITY (SITC CODE)	U.S.	FRANCE	GERMANY	JAPAN
Rubber, Synthetic, Reclaimed (233)				
1980	23.2	19.5	11.3	10.8
1985	18.9	15.9	11.7	10.9
1988	19.9	16.8	13.0	8.6
Hydrocarbons (511)				
1980	19.0	19.6	12.7	4.3
1985	17.0	20.2	10.7	3.4
1988	18.8	7.4	9.5	4.5
Nitrogen-Fnctn. Compounds (514)				
1980	13.1	5.5	23.1	9.3
1985	13.3	4.9	22.2	8.9
1988	13.6	9.7	18.4	8.2
Medicinal, Pharmaceutical Products (541)				
1980	15.0	11.0	16.7	2.1
1985	17.8	9.6	14.9	2.5
1988	14.5	9.4	17.5	3.2
Iron, Steel—Univ., Plate, Sheet (674)				
1980	4.7	10.4	17.2	26.5
1985	1.5	8.6	13.9	27.9
1988	3.1	9.7	14.1	20.3
Automatic Data Processing Equipment (752)				
1980	37.1	7.4	12.1	4.4
1985	28.4	4.1	9.9	17.8
1988	23.3	4.7	8.7	21.5
Telecom Equipment, Parts, Accessories (764)				
1980	15.1	6.3	12.2	20.7
1985	16.1	5.8	8.2	30.3
1988	14.6	3.2	8.0	34.8
Electro-Medical and X-ray Equipment (774)				
1980	30.8	5.6	22.9	7.4
1985	30.6	3.5	18.8	16.9
1988	28.2	5.4	23.2	14.3
Household-Type Equipment (775)				
1980	9.7	8.6	21.2	12.7
1985	6.2	6.0	16.3	21.0
1988	6.7	5.9	19.8	10.9
Electric Machinery (778)				
1980	16.3	8.5	18.8	15.8
1985	16.6	7.2	15.8	21.5
1988	13.8	6.2	18.3	22.0

TABLE 19 (*continued*)

COMMODITY (SITC CODE)	U.S.	FRANCE	GERMANY	JAPAN
Passenger Motor Vehicles—Excluding Buses (781)				
1980	7.2	11.5	24.8	27.4
1985	7.4	6.1	23.1	30.7
1988	6.6	7.1	24.0	27.9
Aircraft (792)				
1980	51.9	6.5	10.5	0.3
1985	50.3	8.4	11.6	0.4
1988	55.7	18.0	3.0	1.3
Medical Instruments (872)				
1980	21.3	5.9	19.4	10.5
1985	19.9	4.8	20.7	11.8
1988	20.3	6.1	20.1	12.9

Source: United Nations, Department of International Economic and Social Affairs, Statistical Office, *International Trade Statistics Yearbook,* Vol. II (New York: United Nations, 1986 and 1990).

TABLE 20

United States Borrowing and Lending Flows, 1989 to 1990 (Billions of Dollars)

	1989	1990
CENTRAL GOVERNMENT		
Net Borrowing	182.5	249.9
Net Lending	−10.4	34.1
Net Financial Saving	−193.1	−215.9
STATE AND LOCAL GOVERNMENT		
Net Borrowing	32.3	17.7
Net Lending	11.2	−20.1
Net Financial Saving	−21.1	−37.8
NONFINANCIAL ENTERPRISES		
Net Borrowing	108.4	69.6
Net Lending	128.1	131.7
Net Financial Saving	19.7	62.0
HOUSEHOLDS		
Net Borrowing	291.2	268.4
Net Lending	435.0	498.7
Net Financial Saving	143.8	230.3

Source: OECD, *Financial Statistics Monthly* (Paris: OECD, April 1991), p. 37.

TABLE 21

Economics in Transition, 1970s and 1980s

	U.S.	FRANCE	GERMANY
UNIT LABOR COSTS IN MANUFACTURING (ANNUAL PERCENTAGE CHANGE)			
1973–79	8.0	11.2	4.9
1979–88	2.2	6.7	2.7
1988	0.3	−1.6	−0.5
CONSUMER PRICE INDEX (ANNUAL PERCENTAGE CHANGE)			
1973–79	8.5	10.7	4.7
1979–88	5.6	7.7	2.9
1988	4.1	2.7	1.3
CURRENT RECEIPTS OF GOVERNMENT (PERCENT OF GDP)			
1974–79	29.8	40.8	43.9
1980–88	31.2	46.6	44.9
1988	31.5	47.1	43.7
NET LENDING OF GOVERNMENT (PERCENTAGE OF GDP)			
1974–79	−1.4	−1.1	−3.0
1980–88	−3.5	−2.2	−2.3
1988	−3.6	−1.4	−2.1
LONG-TERM REAL INTEREST RATES			
1974–79	−0.6	−0.2	2.7
1980–88	5.5	4.7	4.4
1988	5.6	5.8	4.6
VALUE ADDED IN MANUFACTURING (AS PERCENTAGE OF GDP)			
1974–79	23.3	26.7	34.6
1980–88	20.6	22.3	31.7
1988	19.3	21.2	31.4
NET SAVING (AS PERCENTAGE OF GDP)			
1974–79	7.7	13.5	11.5
1980–88	3.6	7.6	9.8
1988	2.9	8.0	12.3

Source: OECD, *Historical Statistics, 1960–1988* (Paris: OECD, 1990), pp. 63, 68–69, 73, 87, 98, 104, 106.

GRAPHS

A1

Federal Budget Balance
in Constant 1982 Dollars
1950–1990

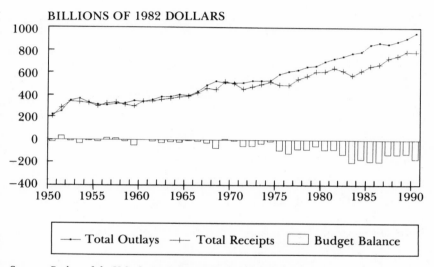

BILLIONS OF 1982 DOLLARS

—•— Total Outlays   —+— Total Receipts   ☐ Budget Balance

Source: *Budget of the U.S. Government, 1992*, Table 1.3, Part Seven: 17.

A2

**Gross Federal Debt
as Percentage of GNP and in 1982 Dollars
1950–1990**

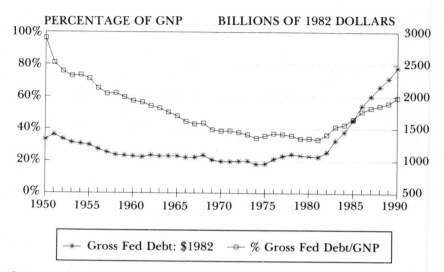

Source: *Budget of the U.S. Government, 1992,* Table 7.1, Part Seven: 71.

A3

Federal Debt and GNP
Annual Increases 1951–1990

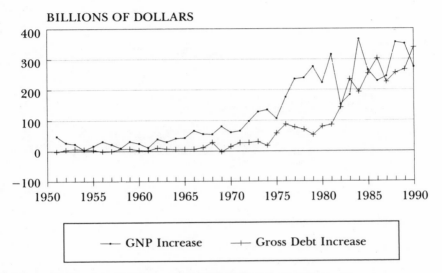

BILLIONS OF DOLLARS

Source: *Budget of the U.S. Government, 1992*, Table 1.2, Part Seven: 15.

B1

Federal Outlays by Superfunction
as Percentage of Total Outlays
1950–1990

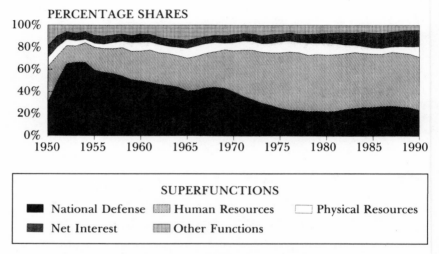

Source: *Budget of the U.S. Government, 1992,* Table 3.1, Part Seven: 31–36.

B2

Federal Outlays by Superfunction in Constant 1982 Dollars 1950–1990

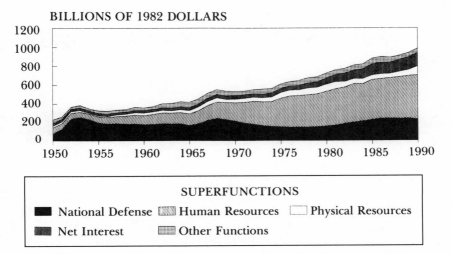

Source: *Budget of the U.S. Government, 1992,* Table 3.1, Part Seven: 31–36. Author's calculations.

c1

**National Defense
Percentage Shares of Functions
1962–1990**

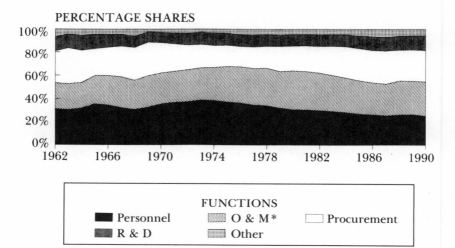

PERCENTAGE SHARES

*Operation and Maintenance
Source: *Budget of the U.S. Government, 1992,* Table 3.1, Part Seven: 31–36.

c2

**National Defense
Outlays by Function
in Constant 1982 Dollars
1962–1990**

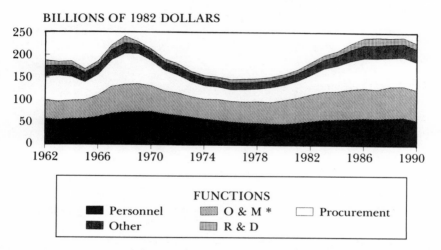

BILLIONS OF 1982 DOLLARS

*Operation and Maintenance
Source: *Budget of the U.S. Government, 1992*, Table 3.1, Part Seven: 31–36.

D1

Human Resources
Percentage Shares of Functions
1950–1990

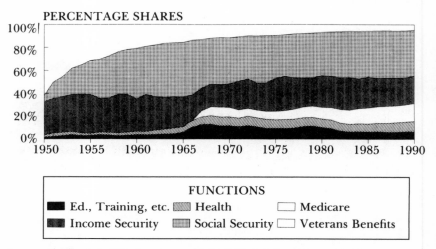

Source: *Budget of the U.S. Government, 1992,* Table 3.1, Part Seven: 31–36.

**Human Resources
Expenditures by Function
in Constant 1982 Dollars
1950–1990**

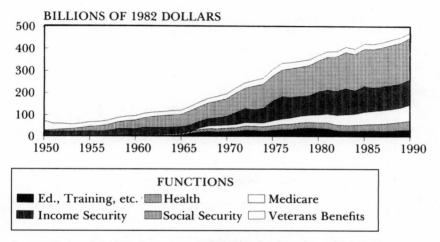

Source: *Budget of the U.S. Government, 1992,* Table 3.1, Part Seven: 31–36.

D3

**Human Resources
Percentage Increases in Constant Outlays,
Total and Per Capita
1950–1990**

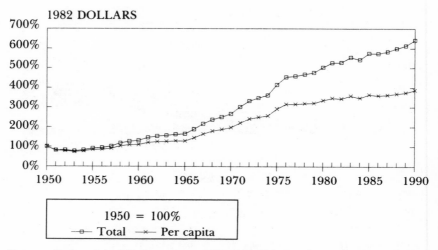

Sources: *Budget of the U.S. Government, 1992*, Table 3.1, Part Seven: 31–36, and *ERP 1991*, p. 321.

D4

**Social Security
Percentage Increases in Constant Outlays,
Total and Per Capita
1950–1989**

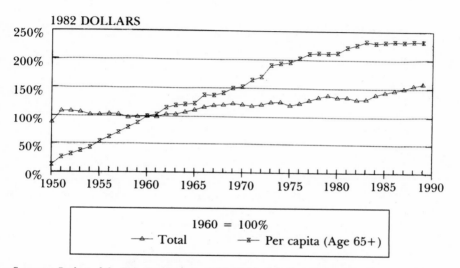

Sources: *Budget of the U.S. Government, 1992*, Table 3.1, Part Seven: 31–36, and *ERP 1991*, p. 321.

D5

Health
Percentage Increases in Constant Outlays,
Total and Per Capita
1950–1990

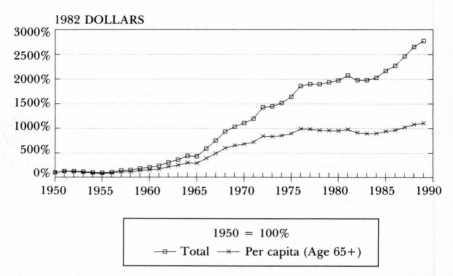

Sources: *Budget of the U.S. Government, 1992,* Table 1.3, Part Seven: 31–36, and *ERP, 1991,* p. 321.

D6

**Medicare
Percentage Increases in Constant Outlays,
Total and Per Capita
1966–1989**

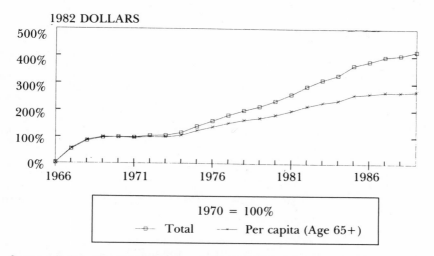

Sources: *Budget of the U.S. Government, 1992,* Table 3.1, Part Seven: 33–36, and *ERP, 1991,* p. 321.

D7

Education, Training, Employment, and Social Services
Percentage Increases in Outlays, Total and Per Capita (Age 5–15)

1982 DOLLARS

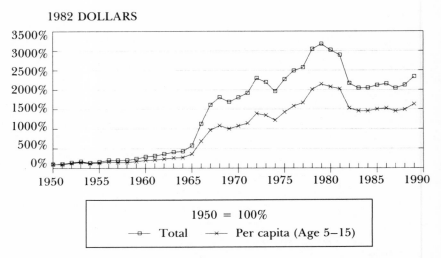

1950 = 100%
—□— Total   —×— Per capita (Age 5–15)

Sources: *Budget of the U.S. Government, 1992*, Part Seven: 31–36, and *ERP, 1991*, p. 321.

E1

Physical Resources
Percentage Shares of Functions
1950–1990

PERCENTAGE SHARES

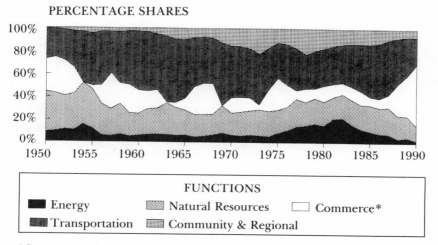

*Commerce and Housing Credit
Source: *Budget of the U.S. Government, 1992,* Table 3.1, Part Seven: 31–36.

E2

**Physical Resources
Outlays by Function
in Constant 1982 Dollars
1950–1990**

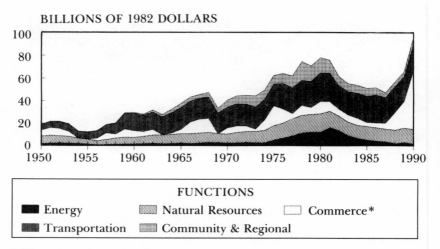

BILLIONS OF 1982 DOLLARS

FUNCTIONS

■ Energy   ▨ Natural Resources   ☐ Commerce*
▨ Transportation   ▦ Community & Regional

*Commerce and Housing Credit
Source: *Budget of the U.S. Government, 1992,* Table 3.1, Part Seven: 31–36.

F1

Other Functions
Percentage Shares of Functions
1950–1990

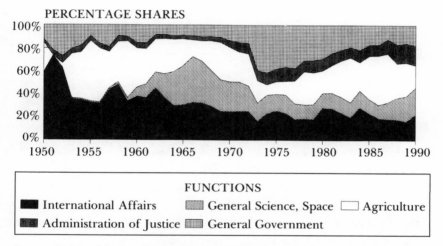

PERCENTAGE SHARES

FUNCTIONS

■ International Affairs ▨ General Science, Space ☐ Agriculture
▨ Administration of Justice ▦ General Government

Source: *Budget of the U.S. Government, 1992*, Table 3.1, Part Seven: 31–36.

F2

**Other Functions
Outlays by Function
in Constant 1982 Dollars
1950–1990**

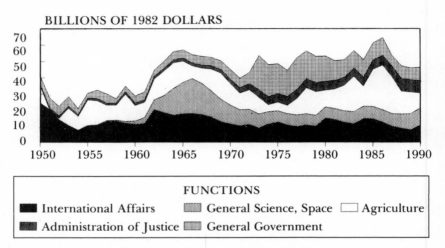

BILLIONS OF 1982 DOLLARS

FUNCTIONS

■ International Affairs   ▨ General Science, Space   ☐ Agriculture
▧ Administration of Justice   ▦ General Government

Source: *Budget of the U.S. Government, 1992*, Table 3.1, Part Seven: 31–36.

STATISTICAL SOURCES

Statistics relating solely to the United States or to the federal government's revenue and outlays, in general, are from the following sources: *Budget of the United States Government* (Washington, D.C.: U.S. Government Printing Office), various fiscal years; *Historical Tables: Budget of the United States Government, Fiscal Year 1990* (Washington, D.C.: U.S. Government Printing Office, 1989); *Economic Report of the President* (Washington, D.C.: U.S. Government Printing Office), various years; U.S. Department of Commerce, *Survey of Current Business,* various issues; U.S. Department of the Treasury, *Treasury Bulletin,* various issues; Board of Governors of the Federal Reserve System, *Federal Reserve Bulletin,* various issues; National Science Board, *Science and Engineering Indicators—1989* (Washington, D.C.: U.S. Government Printing Office, 1989); and Tax Foundation, *Facts and Figures on Government Finance: 1990 Edition* (Baltimore: Johns Hopkins University Press, 1990).

Statistics used for comparing other countries to the United States are primarily from the United Nations (UN), the Organization for Economic Cooperation and Development (OECD), or the International Monetary Fund (IMF). The main sources are as follows: UN, *National Accounts Statistics: Main Aggregates and Detailed Tables,* various years; OECD, *Economic Outlook,* various issues; OECD, *Economic Surveys,* various countries and years; and IMF, *International Financial Statistics,* various years.

Notes

Short titles are used throughout this section as follows: *Budget of the U.S. Government, 1992* for *Budget of the U.S. Government,* Fiscal Year 1992 (Washington, D.C.: Government Printing Office, 1992); and *ERP 1991* for *Economic Report of the President, 1991* (Washington, D.C.: Government Printing Office, 1991).

Chapter 1: Introduction: Budget Deficits and National Decline

1. The estimated 1991 on-budget federal deficit was $378 billion, while the combined on- and off-budget deficit was $318 billion. The $60-billion difference consists of the off-budget portions of social security, commerce and housing credit, net interest, as well as old-age and survivors insurance, and disability insurance contributions. See *Budget of the United States Government, Fiscal Year 1992* (Washington, D.C.: U.S. Government Printing Office, 1991), Part Seven: 14, 18, 20, 28, 36.
2. Between 1989 and 1990, the net foreign purchases of U.S. Treasury securities had declined from $30.0 billion to $1.1 billion. In the fourth quarter of 1990 alone, foreigners were net sellers of $2.2 billion of U.S. Treasury securities. See U.S. Department of Commerce, *Survey of Current Business,* Vol. 71, No. 3 (March 1991), p. 46.

3. For many foreigners, American assets have seemed very cheap. By the middle of 1989, with then current prices and exchange rates, the market value of Japan's overall assets was calculated to be roughly one third greater than those of the United States. Since the United States had more than three times Japan's GNP, twice its population, and nearly twenty-five times its territory, the difference in valuations hardly seemed a sign of American economic health. Japanese assets were doubtless inflated, as the subsequent sharp decline in the Tokyo markets indicated, but the differential over America has nevertheless remained large.

4. For my analysis of America's cycles of security spending, and the economic consequences, see David P. Calleo, *Beyond American Hegemony: The Future of the Western Alliance* (New York: Basic Books, 1987), Chapters 3–6.

5. Only 49.1 percent of the voting-age population cast votes in the 1988 presidential election. *Keesing's Record of World Events* Vol. 34, No. 12 (Longman, December 1988), p. 36341.

Chapter 2: Fiscal Deficits: Definitions and Consequences

1. It has grown customary to limit the term "public good" strictly to those benefits actually supplied by public authority. I use terminology here that permits it to be said that many goods are public, i.e., collectively beneficial and even necessary, but may be better supplied privately. I prefer this conceptual approach because I believe the state has a responsibility to ensure that a wide range of collective goods are provided to the society, but that the state need not and should not always attempt to provide those goods directly. This approach seems to me to correspond to the reality of public belief and behavior in Western societies.

  The question of when state or private supplying of public goods is preferable obviously depends on many particular factors that affect efficiency, as well as the society's general political, economic, and institutional culture.

  Public goods are meant not only to secure the safety, health, and prosperity of citizens but also to provide the foundation for their own individual self-development and freedom. Western democratic societies tend to be sensitive to the tension between state intervention and the broader individual freedom that public goods are meant to make possible. State action always has some element of coercion—if only to acquire funds by taxation.

Discussion of public goods is often confused by the clash of two distinctive philosophical traditions. The first might be called the nominalist-individualist-utilitarian tradition embodied in writers like Bentham and Ricardo. The second is called the Idealist tradition—reflected in continental writers like Rousseau or Hegel—or among British Idealists like Coleridge, Green, Bradley, or Bosanquet. In the first tradition, a public good has to be justified in terms of the aggregated private interests of a majority—however that majority is defined and calculated. In this utilitarian tradition, an individual might vote for providing state education as a public good because he or his children plan to enjoy it, or perhaps because it seems in his own individual self-interest that the general population should be educated. If a majority of other people share this personal interest of his, it is justified to declare it a public good. The Idealist tradition, by contrast, presumes a collective public interest, and even a collective private identity, which it considers as distinct from the sum total of purely individual interests. Thus, while I may not personally need public education, and may personally resent having to pay taxes to support it, as a citizen I share the collective interest in a good society. I recognize that such a society requires, to sustain itself, public provision for education. As a citizen, it is my duty—and interest—to support public education—even though as a purely private individual I might not need it or it might serve me better to be a "free-rider" on its benefits. By intellectual training, most Anglo-Saxon economists are conditioned toward the first approach, a considerable handicap for any realistic analysis of public goods.

2. For a historical survey, see Herbert Stein, *Presidential Economics: The Making of Economic Policy from Roosevelt to Rea-*

gan and Beyond (Washington, D.C.: American Enterprise Institute, 1988).

3. "Recognizing Federal Underwriting Risks," *Budget of the United States Government, Fiscal Year 1991* (Washington, D.C.: Government Printing Office, 1990), pp. 229–55, A-282.

4. This is not to deny the use of other calculations of the budget deficit. A capital budget indicates the government's contribution to the growth in productive resources. A "structural" or "full employment" budget indicates fiscal stimulus to the economy. And a budget that differentiates independent agencies from those controlled by the federal government indicates political accountability. But the net borrowing requirement is the best measure of the deficit's principal impact on the economy. See Alan S. Blinder and Robert M. Solow, "Analytical Foundations of Fiscal Policy," *The Economics of Public Finance* (Washington, D.C.: Brookings Institution, 1974); *Budgetary Finance and Monetary Control,* OECD Economic Series (Paris: OECD, 1982); *Report of the President's Commission on Budgetary Concepts* (Washington, D.C.: U.S. Government Printing Office, 1967).

5. There is a fourth way: A government can also sell its assets, as when Britain sold public housing and publicly owned companies in the 1980s.

6. "Crowding out" is possibly one of the most contentious issues in the economic analysis of fiscal policy. For a good survey of different perspectives, see Richard J. Cebula, *The Deficit Problem in Perspective* (Lexington, Mass.: D.C. Heath and Company, 1987), particularly pp. 7–39.

7. For a survey of the effects of high interest rates in the 1980s, see William Greider, *Secrets of the Temple: How the Federal Reserve Runs the Country* (New York: Simon and Schuster, 1987), Chapters 13 and 16. For an update, see William Greider, *The Trouble with Money* (Knoxville, Tenn.: Whittle Direct Books, Larger Agenda Series, 1989).

8. For effects, see C. Fred Bergsten, "Debtor America and the Budget Deficit," statement before the Committee on the Budget, U.S. House of Representatives, March 2, 1988.

9. Most of the dollar appreciation between 1981 and 1985

can be explained by higher United States real interest rates, compared with other G-7 countries. For later exceptions and a more detailed discussion, see Peter Hooper and Catherine L. Mann, *The Emergence and Persistence of the U.S. External Imbalance, 1980–87,* Princeton Studies in International Finance, No. 65, October 1989.

10. Recent initiatives, such as the Uruguay Round of the GATT negotiations, the United States-Canada Free Trade Agreement, and the EC 1992 project, may reduce the "nontradability" of services, especially in the financial sector.

11. See Stephen Marris, *Deficits and the Dollar: The World Economy at Risk,* updated ed., Analyses in International Economics No. 14 (Washington, D.C.: Institute for International Economics, 1987), pp. xlv–xlvii, 3–13, 42–50.

12. The current account includes net merchandise trade, transport, tourism, and investment income plus net private and official transfers.

13. Consider the following statement from Professor Eisner:
    Fiscal policy was not stimulatory at the end of the 1970s. Appropriate accounting for the inflation tax— the reduction in the real value of outstanding government debt held by the public—meant that the much maligned Carter nominal deficits ($60 billion in 1980) were substantial real structural surpluses! Along with Paul Volcker's suffocating monetary policy, they slowed the economy and, initially prolonged in the Reagan Administration, drove it eventually to collapse in 1982. Robert Eisner, "Debunking the Conventional Wisdom in Economic Policy," *Challenge,* May–June, 1990, pp. 4–11.

14. See Stein, op. cit. pp. 65–133. See also Herbert Stein, *The Fiscal Revolution in America* (Chicago: University of Chicago Press, 1969).

15. See Stein, *Presidential Economics,* op. cit. p. 80.

16. How much later Keynesianism has to do with Keynes is a matter of great argument. There is far from unanimous agreement about the extent to which Keynes adhered to the notion of classical equilibrium. Hyman Minsky, for example, suggests that Keynes saw a fundamental instability in economic relations. See Hyman P. Minsky, *Stabilizing an*

Unstable Economy, a Twentieth Century Fund Book (New Haven: Yale University Press, 1986). Robert Skidelsky, writing a major new study of Keynes's life and ideas, emphasizes a basic commitment to equilibrium. See Robert Skidelsky, "Keynes's Middle Way," a special Ford Lecture delivered at Oxford University, May 3, 1991.

17. For further development of this argument, see David P. Calleo, *The Imperious Economy* (Cambridge, Mass.: Harvard University Press, 1982), p. 13.

18. *Economic Report of the President, 1991* (Washington, D.C.: U.S. Government Printing Office, 1991), pp. 293, 363.

19. Rhetorically, the Reagan administration favored budgetary equilibrium reached through civilian cuts to compensate for its tax cuts and military increases. For a prominent inside view of how rhetoric translated into policy, see David Stockman, *The Triumph of Politics* (New York, Harper and Row, 1986).

20. For a good discussion of the "Laffer Curve," see Stein, *Presidential Economics,* op. cit. pp. 245–49. Also see Victor A. Canto, Douglas H. Joines, and Arthur B. Laffer, *Foundations of Supply-Side Economics, Theory and Evidence* (New York: Academic Press, 1983), Chapter 1.

21. For a discussion of the change toward a more expansionary monetary policy in 1982 and the government's acquiescence in it see Stein, *Presidential Economics,* op. cit. p. 306. Also Paul Krugman, *The Age of Diminished Expectations* (Cambridge, Mass.: MIT Press, 1990), p. 85.

22. David Hume, *Essays, Moral, Political, and Literary* (London: Grant Richards, 1903), p. 289.

23. Ibid., p. 294.

24. See John Hicks, *The Crisis in Keynesian Economics* (New York: Basic Books, 1974), pp. 59–85.

25. See Phillip Cagan, *Persistent Inflation: Historic and Political Essays* (New York: Columbia University Press, 1979). The mechanism may be reversed, as was the intent behind the strong currency policy adopted in France after 1986. Low inflation presumably makes a currency more attractive to domestic and foreign investors and means a stronger exchange rate and lower interest rates. Terms of trade move in a favorable direction and investment thrives as a result

of lower interest rates. Currency appreciation also holds
down the price of imports and decreases inflationary pressures. Thus the economy moves into a virtuous (i.e., self-
reinforcing) cycle of productive investment and growth.
See Patrick McCarthy, "France Faces Reality: Rigueur and
the Germans," in David P. Calleo and Claudia Morgenstern, eds., *Recasting Europe's Economies: National Strategies
in the 1980s* (Lanham, Md.: University Press of America,
1990), pp. 55–58.

26. See John Maynard Keynes, *Essays in Persuasion* (New York:
    W.W. Norton & Co., 1963), pp. 92–96.
27. See Hume, op. cit. p. 366.
28. See Jacques Rueff, *Oeuvres Complètes*, Vol. III, *Politique
    Économique* (Paris: Plon, 1979), pp. 131–49. Walter Eucken,
    Grundsätze der Wirtschaftspolitik, 6th ed. (Tuebingen:
    J.C.B. Mohr, 1990), pp. 355–69.
29. For President Richard Nixon's efforts to stimulate the
    economy while trying to hold back inflation through wage
    and price controls, see Stein, *Presidential Economics*, op. cit.
    pp. 133–207, particularly pp. 176–87.
30. Defining public capital expenditures is a problem in itself.
    The category could be much broader than federal outlays
    for physical investment. See "Technical Perspectives on
    Expenditures, Off-Budget Activities, Capital Outlays, and
    Borrowing," *Budget of the United States Government, Fiscal
    Year 1991*, op. cit. pp. A:83–114.
31. See Robert Eisner, *How Real Is the Federal Deficit?* (New
    York: The Free Press, 1986), pp. 26–40. See also Robert
    Heilbroner and Peter Bernstein, *The Debt and the Deficit:
    False Alarms/Real Possibilities* (New York: W.W. Norton &
    Co., 1989), pp. 57–67.
32. The serious advocates of capital budgeting obviously make
    provision for depreciation but also note the difficulty of
    estimating depreciation and capital allowance for public
    investments. See Heilbroner and Bernstein, op cit. pp. 81–
    85, 96–97; and Eisner, op. cit. p. 32. By my own reckon-
    ing, the heavy federal budgetary cuts for physical re-
    sources in the 1980s and the manifest dilapidation of much
    of the country's existing physical infrastructure, suggest
    little, if any, net investment for some time. Amortization

with realistic depreciation charges could easily increase any deficit. See also Paul Krugman, *The Age of Diminished Expectations* (Cambridge, Mass.: MIT Press, 1990), p. 71. See also Chapter 3, note 30, below.

33. *Budget of the United States Government, Fiscal Year 1991,* op. cit. pp. A:91, A:301. Usually figures representing the government's payment of interest on its debt net out payments kept within the government. In this way, interest is paid from one hand of government to another is treated as "interest earned," even though it is not counted directly in the general revenue.

34. According to Senator Daniel Patrick Moynihan of New York, social security has become a gigantic scam. Since social security's trust fund is merely a part of the federal debt, unsecured by anything but the government's future income, social security's payroll taxes are a form of taxation like any other. And since those payroll taxes fall more heavily on the poor than the rich, increasing them has distorted the whole federal tax system in a regressive direction. Social security, Moynihan argued, should return to a pay-as-you-go system. If the federal government needed additional revenue for other functions, it should raise it from a less regressive form of taxation. In early 1990, he introduced a bill to roll back the 1983 increases. See Joseph White and Aaron Wildavsky, *The Deficit and the Public Interest: The Search for Responsible Budgeting in the 1980s* (Berkeley: University of California Press, Russell Sage Foundation, 1989), particularly pp. 313–15; and for Moynihan's proposal, see Paul Blustein, "Alternate Social Security Plan Gaining: Hill Expected to Take Pension Plan Out of Budget Calculations," *The Washington Post,* February 16, 1990, p. A10.

35. The situation would be essentially the same even if the entire national pension system was private but invested in government obligations.

36. Investing in foreign countries is one possible strategy, seemingly taken up by Japanese pension funds in recent years. Investing abroad transfers intergenerational exploitation to some other country's younger generation. When the money is needed, it will supposedly be pulled out of a

foreign economy, and therefore not be subject to the political revenge of the beleaguered younger generation at
home. But trying to withdraw capital on the scale that demographic trends indicate might cause such economic disruption that the assets would have to be sold at a great
discount, or arouse so much antagonism that the transfer
would be blocked politically.

37. This is not necessarily to recommend investing social security trust funds directly into the economy, which would
put a large pool of federal money into private markets.
The point is that excessive social security contributions invested in the deficit do little to enhance productivity and
are a regressive form of taxation. See White and Wildavsky, op. cit. p. 316.

38. *The New York Times,* June 6, 1990, p. D1.

39. In the S and L crisis, for example, many analysts have
argued that the real costs are only the interest on the borrowing and the charges for administration—both very large
but substantially less than the $500 billion figure that in-
cludes the capital transfers. See Chapter 7, pp. 135–138,
and note 40, p. 263. In this perspective, the government
is simply borrowing from current savers to replace the lost
capital of old savers. The transferred capital will presumably be injected back into credit markets and should
therefore not be counted as consumption on the government's part. The ultimate capital cost will depend on how
much the government can recover from the collapsed real
estate assets. A full assessment would presumably also
include the opportunity costs of having new savings di-
verted to rescue the malinvestment of old, or the consequent disruption of property values and the building
industry.

Chapter 3: Federal Spending Since 1950

1. State and local spending brought the total to approximately $24.5 trillion.

2. Of the total federal spending from 1950 through 1990,
36.6 percent occurred from 1980 through 1989 and 40.9
percent from 1980 through 1990.

3. This calculation uses the *GNP deflator.* Using the *composite*

deflator the increase would be reduced to approximately 200 percent. See notes 10 and 11 below.

4. "Tables and Graphs," Graph A1.

5. As a percentage of GNP, however, the debt decreased from 96.3 percent in 1950 to a low of 33.3 percent in 1981 and then increased to 59.3 percent in 1990. The dynamics of the debt/GNP ratio are such that inflation cuts the real value of earlier debt, while swelling the nominal value of current GNP. Improvement in the ratio can also come, of course, from a faster growth of GNP than of new debt, but that has seldom occurred since 1982. See "Tables and Graphs," Graphs A2 and A3.

6. By 1990, net interest on the debt took up 14.7 percent of the federal budget, a sum of $184.2 billion. From 1952 to 1978, net interest remained between 6 and 8 percent although in 1948 it had been as high as 14.6 percent. *Budget of the United States Government, Fiscal Year 1992* (Washington, D.C.: U.S. Government Printing Office, 1991), Part Seven: 30–36.

7. The GNP is the sum of the GDP plus net factor income from abroad.

8. "Tables and Graphs," Graph B2.

9. Real defense spending doubled from fiscal 1951 to 1953— its highest postwar year, approached but not equaled in 1968 and 1987. Real 1990 levels were roughly those of 1954. *Budget of the United States Government, Fiscal Year 1992,* op. cit., Part Seven: 66–70.

10. These calculations use the *consumer price index* as reported in the *Economic Report of the President, 1991* (Washington, D.C.: U.S. Government Printing Office, 1991). The index is the most commonly used measure of general price inflation in the economy. Nevertheless, other more specific measures may be used in conjunction with different sets of data. In this chapter, for instance, the index of price inflation used to deflate government expenditures is the *composite deflator* as reported in the *Budget of the United States Government, Fiscal Year 1992,* op. cit. On the other hand, the *GNP implicit price deflator* is used to adjust nominal GNP figures for inflation. That index is reported in the *Economic Report of the President, 1991* (Washington, D.C.: U.S.

Government Printing Office, 1991). In general, although the magnitudes of change of the three indices vary somewhat, the overall trends are the same.

11. For discussions of price indices, see Robert J. Barro, *Macroeconomics* (New York: John Wiley and Sons, 1984), pp. 21–23; Franklin M. Fisher and Karl Shell, *The Economic Theory of Price Indices: Two Essays on the Effects of Taste, Quality, and Technological Change* (New York: Academic Press, 1972); and Edwin Mansfield, *Microeconomics* (New York: Norton, 1982), pp. 98–105.

12. National defense accounted for nearly 70 percent of the federal budget during the height of the Korean War between 1952 and 1954.

13. "Tables and Graphs," Graph B1.

14. Other, generally smaller components of the defense budget include military construction, family housing, revolving and management funds.

15. "Tables and Graphs," Graphs C1 and C2. For data on the components of the defense budget starting from 1948, see Alex Mintz, "Guns Versus Butter: A Disaggregated Analysis," *American Political Science Review*, Vol. 83, No. 4 (December 1989), pp. 1285–93.

16. See United States House of Representatives, Committee on Armed Services, *Review of Defense Acquisition in France and Great Britain*, Committee Print No. 5 (Washington, D.C.: U.S. Government Printing Office, August 16, 1989).

17. In 1985, as a percentage of GDP, total R and D expenditure in the United States (2.83 percent) was higher than in Japan (2.81 percent), Germany (2.66 percent), or France (2.31 percent). Moreover, given the relative sizes of those economies, the United States spends much more than the others in absolute terms. See OECD, *Economies in Transition: Structural Adjustment in OECD Countries* (Paris: OECD, 1989), p. 139. However, when defense R and D expenditure is excluded, the United States percentage falls to the bottom of the pack. For example, in 1987, as a percentage of GNP, nondefense R and D expenditure was estimated at 2.8 percent in Japan, 2.6 percent in Germany, and 1.8 percent in both the United States and France. (The figure

for France may be slightly overstated because it is measured as a percentage of GDP instead of GNP.) See National Science Board, *Science and Engineering Indicators—1989* (Washington, D.C.: U.S. Government Printing Office, 1989), p. 288.

18. See Edward N. Luttwak, *The Pentagon and the Art of War* (New York: Simon and Schuster, 1984), especially pp. 89–92; Jacques S. Gansler, *Affording Defense* (Cambridge, Mass.: MIT Press, 1989), Chapter 8; and Andrew Pollack, "In U.S. Technology, a Gap Between Arms and VCR's," *The New York Times*, March 4, 1991, p. A1.

19. See Richard Cohen and Peter A. Wilson, *Superpowers in Economic Decline: U.S. Strategy for the Transcentury Era* (New York: Crane Russak, 1990), Figure 4.6.

20. Putting forces into strategic nuclear and regional categories can be problematic. The navy is particularly difficult. Ballistic missile submarines clearly form part of the nuclear deterrent, but much of the rest of the fleet is not firmly linked to a single region, even if most of it normally covers Eurasian commitments and interests.

21. Figures published in 1990 show 321,300 United States military personnel stationed in Europe, plus some 20,000 afloat. Those figures did not include forces in the United States regularly assigned to NATO, which include six army divisions, thirty-seven air force squadrons, and one marine expeditionary brigade. Those United States-based forces were meant to be in Europe within ten days of the outbreak of hostilities. Elaborate prepositioning of materiel and lift programs have been required.

The same figures show 117,500 troops stationed in the Philippines, Japan, South Korea, and Guam, but do not include the 36,900 troops assigned to Hawaii, the 720 troops in Australia, the 900 troops on Diego Garcia, or the members of the Third and Seventh fleets in the Pacific. International Institute for Strategic Studies, *The Military Balance 1990–1991* (London: Brassey's 1990), pp. 25–26.

22. The first major cycle of defense spending peaked in 1953 and reached its low in 1965. The second significant peak

came in 1968 and the next low in 1976. The third cycle peaked in 1987 while the trend since then has been downward (i.e., through 1990).

23. For the actual text of *NSC-68*, dated April 14, 1950, see U.S. Department of State, *Foreign Relations of the United States 1950*, (Washington, D.C.: U.S. Government Printing Office, 1977), Vol. 1, pp. 236–90. Much of the substance of *NSC-68* can be found in earlier internal memoranda. See Clark M. Clifford's report to President Truman, "American Relations with the Soviet Union," September 24, 1946, in Arthur Krock, *Memoirs: Sixty Years on the Firing Line* (New York: Funk and Wagnall's, 1968), pp. 419–82. For a recent appraisal, see "The Truman Doctrine," *The Economist 302*, No. 7489 (March 14, 1987), pp. 19–22. See David P. Calleo, *Beyond American Hegemony: The Future on the Western Alliance* (New York: Basic Books, 1987); John Lewis Gaddis, "NSC-68 and the Problem of Ends and Means," *International Security*, Spring 1980, pp. 164–70; John Lewis Gaddis, *Strategies of Containment: A Critical Appraisal of Postwar National Security Policy* (New York: Oxford University Press, 1982), pp. 21–24; Paul Y. Hammond, "NSC-68: Prologue to Rearmament," in Warner R. Schilling, Paul Y. Hammond, and Glenn H. Snyder, *Strategy, Politics and Defense Budgets* (New York: Columbia University Press, 1962), pp. 267–378; Leon Keyserling, "The Economic Implications of the Proposed Programs: Required Fiscal, Budgetary, and Other Economic Policies," enclosed in *NSC-68/3*, "United States Objectives and Programs for National Security," December 8, 1950; Paul H. Nitze, "The Development of NSC-68," *International Security*, Spring 1980, pp. 170–76; *NSC-68/1*, "United States Objectives and Programs for National Security," September 21, 1950; and Samuel F. Wells, "Sounding the Tocsin: NSC-68 and the Soviet Threat," *International Security*, Fall 1979, pp. 116–38.

24. The ANZUS Pact of September 1, 1951, committed the United States to defend Australia and New Zealand. In December 1954, a mutual defense pact was signed with Taiwan to protect it from the Chinese communists and to

prevent Chiang Kai-shek from attempting to invade the mainland without United States approval.

25. See Herbert Stein, *Presidential Economics: The Making of Economic Policy from Roosevelt to Reagan and Beyond* (Washington, D.C.: American Enterprise Institute, 1988), p. 421. From 1950 to 1951, federal personal income taxes as a percentage of personal income increased from 7.9 percent to 10.2 percent. In the same period, federal corporate income taxes as percentage of real profits increased from 50.4 percent to 56.1 percent. Also see Herbert Stein, *The Fiscal Revolution in America* (Chicago: University of Chicago, 1969), pp. 284–85.

26. Indeed, the Eisenhower administration, blaming Korea on an ambiguous American commitment, added two precise new regional commitments: the South East Asian Treaty (SEATO) in September 1954 and the Baghdad Pact in early 1955. For a study of some of Eisenhower's early views on containment and the Korean War, see Stephen E. Ambrose, *Eisenhower: Soldier, General of the Army, President-Elect, 1890–1952* (New York: Simon and Schuster, 1983), pp. 497–99, pp. 529–72. Also see Gaddis, *Strategies of Containment,* op. cit. 281–308. See also Ronald W. Pruessen, "John Foster Dulles and the Predicaments of Power," in Richard H. Immerman, ed., *John Foster Dulles and the Diplomacy of the Cold War* (Princeton, N.J.: Princeton University Press, 1990), pp. 21–45.

27. For a study of various recurring phases of United States policy, see Gaddis, *Strategies of Containment,* op. cit. Although Gaddis sometimes focuses narrowly on the intellectual strategic debate as opposed to the economic debate, his work is full of insight, along with superb narration and documentation. Also see Calleo, *Beyond American Hegemony,* op. cit., Chapters 3–5; p. 225, note 1.

28. See *The United States and NATO in an Undivided Europe* (Washington, D.C.: The Johns Hopkins Foreign Policy Institute, 1991).

29. See Chapter 8, note 10, below.

30. Real spending for physical resources rose by a whopping 45.7 percent in fiscal 1990. But that was not the result of

increased infrastructure spending, but of outlays to the Resolution Trust Corporation, the body charged with taking over the disposing of the assets of bankrupt S and Ls. In fiscal 1991, real physical-resources spending is expected to rise a further 37.3 percent for the same reason. *Budget of the United States Government, Fiscal Year 1992,* op. cit., Part Seven: 36.

31. "Tables and Graphs," Graph B2. Real outlays for human resources grew nearly 69 percent during the Eisenhower years (1953–60), another 62 percent during the Kennedy-Johnson years (1961–68), 81 percent in the Nixon-Ford era (1969–76), and 10 percent in Carter's four years, (1977–80). During the eight Reagan years (1981–88), budget share was being cut, but real outlays nevertheless rose by nearly 14 percent.
32. "Tables and Graphs," Graph B1.
33. "Tables and Graphs," Tables 1 and 2; and Graphs D1 and D2.
34. "Tables and Graphs," Graph D3.
35. "Tables and Graphs," Graph D4.
36. See Social Security Administration, Office of Research and Statistics, *Fast Facts and Figures About Social Security* (Washington, D.C.: U.S. Department of Health and Human Resources, 1990).
37. See Chapter 5, note 9, below.
38. "Tables and Graphs," Graphs D5 and D6.
39. Medicare served about 12.0 million in 1975; by 1990, it served 20.3 million. The proportion of those actually served from among those enrolled jumped from 528 per 1,000 to 729 per 1,000 in the same period. Average outlays, in 1982 dollars, rose from $1,892 to $2,995 per patient served. See *1990 Health Care Financing Administration Statistics* (Washington, D.C.: U.S. Department of Health and Human Services, 1990).
40. "Tables and Graphs," Graph D7.
41. In 1986–87, federal aid accounted for only 5.9 percent of the total public elementary and secondary education revenue of $165.9 billion. See Bureau of the Census, *1987 Census of Governments, Government Finances, Finances of Pub-*

lic School Systems (Washington, D.C.: Department of Commerce, 1990).

42. M. Edith Rasell and Lawrence Mishel, *Shortchanging Education: How U.S. Spending on Grades K-12 Lags Behind Other Industrial Nations* (Washington, D.C.: Economic Policy Institute, 1990), p. 2; M. Edith Rasell and Lawrence Mishel, *Measuring Comparative Education Spending: A Response to the Department of Education,* (Washington, D.C.: Economic Policy Institute, 1990); and *Economic Report of the President, 1991,* op. cit. pp. 121–28.

43. "Tables and Graphs," Graphs E1 and E2.

44. "Tables and Graphs," Graphs F1 and F2.

45. Real GNP increased by 198 percent from 1950 to 1990 using the composite deflator (as in the federal spending figures). However, using the implicit GNP deflator the increase was 268 percent. See Chapter 3, notes 10 and 11, above, on different indices of inflation.

46. David E. Sanger, "Seeing a Dependent and Declining U.S., More Japanese Adopt a Nationalistic Spirit." See *The New York Times,* August 4, 1989; Flora Lewis, "Japan's Looking Glass," *The New York Times,* November 8, 1989; and Peter F. Drucker's book review of Shintaro Ishihara, *The Japan That Can Say No,* trans. Frank Baldwin (New York: Simon and Schuster, 1991) in *The New York Times,* January 13, 1991.

Chapter 4: United States Fiscal Policy: An International Perspective

1. See Antonio Pedone, "Public Expenditure," in Andrea Boltho, *The European Economy: Growth and Crisis* (Oxford, U.K.: Oxford University Press, 1982), pp. 390–409.

2. See "Tables and Graphs," Table 3, for national comparisons. Our comparisons use data for West Germany before unification. Reunification lowered German per capita income significantly. Comparisons with other Western states are obviously possible. Britain has high defense spending and many economic and cultural features in common with the United States, including a common language. But Britain is much poorer per capita ($11,765 per capita ver-

sus $18,338 per capita for the United States in 1987). Japan is now richer per capita, but with comparatively minuscule defense spending (in 1987, 1 percent of GNP versus over 6 percent for the United States), as well as a notably different political, economic, and social organization and culture. Italy is as rich per capita as Britain and has a very high fiscal deficit, but, unlike the United States, has very low defense spending, a very high savings rate, and an enormous state-owned industrial sector. Holland and Belgium are rich and capitalist, but substantially smaller and without the same geopolitical roles and military expenses. See OECD, *Economic Survey of Germany, 1989–90* (Paris: OECD, 1990), p. 123; International Institute for Strategic Studies, *Military Balance, 1989–90* (London: Brassey's 1990), pp. 208–10.

3. In 1987, state and local government accounted for 38 percent of total government disbursements in West Germany, 42 percent in the United States, and 16 percent in France. See United Nations, *National Accounts Statistics: Main Aggregates and Detailed Tables, 1987* (New York: United Nations, 1990): detailed tables for France, pp. 474–511; for West Germany, pp. 525–74; and for the United States, pp. 1586–639.

4. OECD, *Public Expenditure on Income Maintenance* (Paris: OECD, 1976), p. 67.

5. The limits of central bank independence in Germany were demonstrated in 1990, when Chancellor Helmut Kohl pushed through the German Monetary Union even though the Bundesbank was fiercely against it. See David Buchan and David Marsh, "Pöhl Says German Monetary Union Is a Disaster," *The Financial Times*, March 20, 1991, p. 1.

6. Significantly, when France adopted a policy of monetary *rigueur* in the 1980s, it tied itself firmly to the European Monetary System, an international regime that obliged maintaining the franc's parity against the deutschemark. In effect, the French devolved their monetary policy-making to the Bundesbank, and thus borrowed its constitutional independence. See Patrick McCarthy, "France Faces Reality: Rigueur and the Germans," in David P. Calleo

and Claudia Morgenstern, eds., *Recasting Europe's Economies: National Strategies in the 1980s,* (Lanham, Md.: University Press of America, 1990), pp. 25–79.

7. See International Institute for Strategic Studies, *Military Balance, 1989–90,* op. cit., pp. 208–10.

8. See OECD, *Health Care Systems in Transition* (Paris: OECD, 1990), p. 10.

9. See United Nations, *National Accounts Statistics: Main Aggregates and Detailed Tables, 1986* (New York: United Nations, 1989), pp. 1559–60.

10. Between 1970 (a year when the United States ran a trade surplus) and 1987, total absorption rose by 3.8 percentage points relative to GDP. Private final consumption expenditure rose from 63 percent of GDP to 66.7 percent in 1987—a rise of 3.7 percentage points relative to GDP. Private consumption expenditure on health increased its share in United States GDP during the same period by 3.9 percentage points. See United Nations, *National Accounts Statistics: Main Aggregates and Detailed Tables, 1987,* op. cit., pp. 1586–639.

11. During the 1980s, France and Germany sustained ground forces at roughly 80 percent of overall American levels, but within military budgets that were, when combined, less than half of America's outlays for its NATO commitment alone. See David P. Calleo, *Beyond American Hegemony: The Future of the Western Alliance* (New York: Basic Books, 1987), pp. 117–18; note 22, p. 256.

12. See Chapter 3, pp. 54–57.

13. OECD, *Health Care Systems in Transition* (Paris: OECD, 1990), p. 91.

14. For a detailed discussion, see *The Changing Health Care Market* (Washington, D.C.: Employee Benefit Research Institute, 1987), pp. 187, 189.

15. OECD, *Health Care Systems,* op. cit. p. 57.

16. U.S. Bipartisan Commission on Comprehensive Health Care (The Pepper Commission), *A Call For Action: Final Report* (Washington, D.C.: U.S. Government Printing Office, 1990).

17. OECD, *Health Care Systems,* op. cit., 67–68.

18. Ibid., pp. 106–9.

19. Ibid., p. 109.
20. Ibid., p. 110.

Chapter 5: Taxes and Incomes in the United States

1. The most common comparative measure of government receipts, percentage of GDP, makes the low United States rates obvious. See "Tables and Graphs," Table 4.
2. See "Tables and Graphs," Table 5.
3. According to International Monetary Fund estimates published in May 1991, the federal budget deficit (including the social security surplus and expenditures for the S and L bailout) will remain at around $300 billion in fiscal years 1991 and 1992 even after the October 1990 budget package. The estimate assumed GNP would grow at 0.2 percent in 1991 and 2.7 percent in 1992. IMF, *World Economic Outlook, May 1991* (Washington, D.C.: International Monetary Fund, May 1991); pp. 101–4. For details about the budget deal of October 1990, see *Omnibus Budget Reconciliation Act of 1990* (Washington, D.C.: U.S. Government Printing Office, 1990). See also Chapter 8, note 8, below.
4. The 1986 tax reform, planned to be revenue-neutral, actually reversed the former erosion of the income-tax base and was the first to increase progressivity since the Kennedy-Johnson tax cut of 1964. Joseph A. Pechman, "The Future of the Income Tax," *Brookings General Series Reprints No. 437* (Washington, D.C.: Brookings Institution, 1990), pp. 1, 10–12. See also Joseph A. Pechman, *Federal Tax Policy* (Washington, D.C.: Brookings Institution, 1987), pp. 132–34.
5. For long-standing United States-European military relations, including budgetary and general economic consequences, see David P. Calleo, *Beyond American Hegemony: The Future of the Western Alliance*, (New York: Basic Books, 1987).
6. See Chapter 4, Table 4.4, p. 73.
7. In fiscal year 1988, 81 percent of overall federal outlays for education, training, employment, and social services and 33 percent of total outlays for health (including Medicare) were tax expenditures. Pechman, *Federal Tax Policy*, op. cit., p. 363.

8. According to the Tax Foundation, individual income taxes yielded 28.4 percent of total (federal, state, and local) government general tax revenue in the United States in 1987. Property and corporate income taxes yielded 7.2 and 6.4 percent, respectively. Tax Foundation, *Facts and Figures on Government Finance: 1990 Edition* (Baltimore: Johns Hopkins University Press, 1990), p. 15.

9. In 1985, French public expenditures on retirement pensions were 12.7 percent of GDP, German 11.8 percent, and American 7.2 percent. In France, the standard of living of retirees using the state pension system appears to be equivalent to that of those still working. OECD, *Economic Survey, France 1989–1990* (Paris: OECD, 1990), pp. 73–77. The West German pension formula has long included a so-called "statutory contingency percentage," meant to ensure a pension appropriate to the standard of living the pensioner enjoyed while working. See P.R. Kaim-Candle, *Comparative Social Policy and Social Security* (London: Martin Robertson Co., 1973), p. 136.

10. An American worker retiring in the 1980s with a preretirement income equal to the taxable maximum (in 1981: $29,700) could expect to receive benefit payments corresponding to about 28 percent of his previous income. The corresponding figure for workers with average and low preretirement incomes was 48 percent and 61 percent, respectively. For a full discussion, see Alicia H. Munnell, *The Economics of Private Pensions* (Washington, D.C.: Brookings Institution, 1982), pp. 23–28.

11. For the poor, a "federal means tested SSI [supplemental security income] program currently provides an inflation indexed income guarantee at 77% of the poverty level for aged individuals and 91% for aged couples. Many states supplement these benefits, but few do so to the poverty level." John L. Palmer, "Financing Health Care and Retirement for the Aged," in Isabel V. Sawhill, ed., *Challenge to Leadership: Economic and Social Issues for the Next Decade* (Washington, D.C.: Urban Institute Press, 1988), p. 193.

12. By 1990, for more than 70 percent of American taxpayers, social security contributions—their own and those of their employers for them—were greater than income taxes.

The CBO's analysis of the 1991 Budget implies that the taxpayer pays the entire contribution (directly or indirectly), surely a contentious proposition. See United States Committee on the Budget, *President Bush's 1991 Budget Review and Analysis* (Washington, D.C.: United States Senate Committee on the Budget, 1991). In any event, given the low ceiling on benefits, the tax seems less regressive for the poor than progressive for the rich. To the extent that social security surpluses finance other government spending, the tax is regressive. See Chapter 2, note 34, above.

13. According to OECD estimates, there is evidence that the net effect of taxes (direct and indirect) in France (1970) and West Germany (1981) reduces the ratio between the average income in the top bracket and the average income in the lowest bracket substantially more than in the United States (1970). See Peter Saunders and Friedrich Klau, "The Role of the Public Sector: Causes and Consequences of the Growth of Government," *OECD Economic Studies*, No. 4, Spring 1985, pp. 205–22.

14. In 1986, the combined federal, state, and local levels of government in the United States received 10.6 percent of their tax revenue from property taxes—in Germany and France only 3.1 percent and 4.8 percent, respectively. Tax Foundation, op. cit., p. 37.

15. For estimates indicating the regressivity of the property tax at the bottom end of the income distribution, see Pechman, *Federal Tax Policy*, op. cit., pp. 273–75.

16. Joseph A. Pechman, *Who Paid the Taxes, 1966–85?* (Washington, D.C.: Brookings Institution, 1985), pp. 63–68.

17. See Pechman, "The Future of the Income Tax," op. cit., p. 4.

18. See Pechman, *Who Paid the Taxes, 1966–85?*, op. cit., p. 66.

19. For a discussion of the anti-property-tax movement in the late 1970s and its legislative consequences in California and other states, see Pechman, *Federal Tax Policy*, op. cit., p. 277.

20. For the politics of social security reform, see Joseph White and Aaron Wildavsky, *The Deficit and the Public Interest: The Search for Responsible Budgeting in the 1980s* (Berkeley: Uni-

versity of California Press, 1989), pp. 310–30. For details about the increases in social security taxes, see Tax Foundation, op. cit., p. 144. See also Chapter 2, note 34, above.

21. For the increases in state and local taxes during the 1970s and 1980s, see Tax Foundation, op. cit., p. 181.

22. See Frank Levy, "Incomes, Families, and Living Standards" in Robert E. Litan et al., eds., *American Living Standards: Threats and Challenges* (Washington, D.C.: Brookings Institution, 1988), p. 136.

23. See Pechman, "The Future of the Income Tax," op. cit., p. 3.

24. See Joseph J. Minarik, "Family Incomes," in Isabel V. Sawhill, ed., *Challenge to Leadership* (Washington, D.C.: The Urban Institute Press, 1988), pp. 33–67. Also Louis Uchitelle, "U.S. Wages: Not Getting Ahead? Better Get Used to It," *The New York Times,* December 16, 1990, Section 4, pp. 1, 6.

25. See *The Economist,* November 10, 1990, pp. 19–22.

26. See Levy, op. cit., pp. 108–53. See also Minarik, op. cit., pp. 37–41.

27. See Chapter 7, pp. 127–28, for a discussion of the link between productivity and wage growth.

28. See Arthur M. Hauptman, *The Tuition Dilemma* (Washington, D.C.: Brookings Institution, 1990).

29. See *The Economist,* November 10, 1990, p. 22.

30. The rapidly rising costs of education were a further factor in the squeeze of family income in the 1980s. Real family incomes increased on average by 7 percent in 1980–86, while inflation-adjusted college tuition went up 30 percent. See Hauptman, op. cit., p. 3.

31. For bracket creep and the Reagan indexing scheme, see Pechman, *Federal Tax Policy,* op. cit., pp. 114–16.

32. For the "revenue-enhancing" measures passed by the Reagan administration in every year after 1981, see *Budget of the United States Government, Fiscal Year 1990* (Washington, D.C.: U.S. Government Printing Office, 1989), Section Four: 4.

33. The public probably would have reacted strongly against a further inflation-induced tax rise no matter who won the 1980 election. For public resentment of "bracket creep"

and the prospect of continuing unlegislated tax increases, see Douglas A. Hibbs, *The American Political Economy: Macroeconomics and Electoral Politics* (Cambridge, Mass.: Harvard University Press, 1987), p. 296.

34. See Daniel P. Moynihan, *Deficit by Default: New York State and the Federal Fisc: XIV, Fiscal Year 1989* (Washington, D.C.: July 31, 1990).

35. "Deficit at 1981 Receipts/GNP Ratio" is the difference between what actual expenditures were as a percentage of GNP and what receipts would have been if federal tax revenues had remained at the 1981 level (20.1 percent of GNP). Projecting actual spending and different tax rates, while assuming the same GNP, can obviously provide only a rough estimate of a hypothetical deficit. The projection, however, probably understates the estimated hypothetical deficit, since the higher tax rates it uses would probably have had a comparatively depressing effect on immediate GNP—and hence on revenue. But these additional considerations further reinforce the argument that a substantial part of Reagan's actual deficits should be attributed to his spending increases as well as to his tax cuts.

36. "Tables and Graphs," Graph B2.

37. Note that this was before the actual increases in social security payments.

38. "Tables and Graphs," Table 6.

Chapter 6: Financing the Deficit: The International Dimension

1. For my more extended discussion of hegemonic theory applied to America's world role, see *Beyond American Hegemony: the Future of the Western Alliance* (New York: Basic Books, 1987). For a discussion of other writings that have influenced my own, see ibid p. 259, note 2.

2. For a detailed discussion of the international monetary system and its geopolitical implications during various periods, see my *The Imperious Economy* (Cambridge, Mass.: Harvard University Press, 1982), Chapters 3–5; and *Beyond American Hegemony,* op. cit., Chapters 6 and 8.

3. The balance of payments can be measured at any one of several places. The measurements contrasted here are the

balance on current account (the balance on the exchange of goods and services) and the "basic balance" (the balance on the exchange of goods, services, and long-term capital flows). For a discussion of various balance of payments measurements, see "Measuring Equilibrium in the Balance of Payments," in Charles P. Kindleberger, *International Money: A Collection of Essays* (London: George Allen and Unwin, 1981), pp. 120–38.

4. The dollar's role as the key currency made it the obvious choice for conducting the growing number of international transactions, which required liquid, short-term credit. In addition, since dollars, unlike gold, earned interest, central banks themselves were encouraged to hold dollars. See Susan Strange, "International Monetary Relations," in Andrew Shonfield, ed., *International Economic Relations of the Western World, 1959–1971,* Vol. II (London: Oxford University Press, 1976), pp. 176–77; Jacques Rueff, *The Monetary Sin of the West* (New York: Macmillan Company, 1972), p. 22.

5. In 1970, the estimated net size of the Eurodollar market was $57 billion, compared with total gold reserves in the United States of $11 billion and total gold reserves of all countries of $37 billion. BIS, *Annual Report,* No. 41 (Basel: Bank for International Settlements, 1971), pp. 127, 157. For a historical account and analysis of the development and effects of the Eurodollar market see Strange, op. cit., pp. 176–94.

6. For a discussion of the reasons for the large capital flows from the United States to Europe during the 1950s and 1960s, see "Capital Movements and International Payments Adjustment" in Kindleberger, op. cit., pp. 209–22.

7. De Gaulle's favorite economist, Jacques Rueff, was a major critic of Bretton Woods, which he linked to the interwar gold-exchange standard set up in 1923, which had collapsed in the early 1930s. As a conservative who basically approved of America's hegemonic world role, Rueff concentrated his attack on the system's inflationary potential. As dollars were exported, he noted, the central banks that were America's creditors added the dollars to their reserves, thus increasing their own national money sup-

plies. But since the expatriate dollars were held in the form of U.S. Treasury securities and thus merely added to the American national debt, there was no corresponding automatic reduction in the United States money supply. Demand was exported to Europe without being reduced in America. As a result, the classic adjustment mechanism of the gold standard no longer functioned, so far as American deficits were concerned. For his analysis of various aspects of the Bretton Woods system, see Rueff, op. cit. For a comprehensive view of his economic and social theory, see Jacques Rueff, *Oeuvres Complètes* (Paris: Plon and The Lehrman Institute, 1979).

8. Charles de Gaulle, *Major Addresses, Statements and Press Conferences of General Charles de Gaulle,* Vol II (New York: French Embassy and Information Division, 1967), pp. 179–81. For an analysis of the inflationary role of the United States in the Bretton Woods system, see Harold van Buren Cleveland and W.H. Bruce Brittain, *The Great Inflation: A Monetarist View* (Washington, D.C.: National Planning Association, 1976), pp. 13–16.

9. For a contemporary look at the extent of American overseas investment and the European response, see Jean-Jacques Servan-Schreiber, *Le défi américain* (Paris: Éditions Denoël, 1967).

10. See Strange, op. cit., pp. 278–95.

11. The Belgian-American economist Robert Triffin was among the prominent analysts who focused on liquidity, pointing out that the consistent United States balance of payments deficits provided between two thirds and three fourths of the liquidity requirements of the international system. Triffin, citing the impossibility of sustaining those deficits in the long term, urged reforms to prevent the dollar's use as a reserve currency and to place the International Monetary Fund at the center of the system. See Robert Triffin, *Gold and the Dollar Crisis: The Future of Convertibility* (New Haven, Conn.: Yale University Press, 1960). For his views on the current system, see his *IMS: International Monetary System or Scandal?* (San Domenico: European University Institute, 1991). See also Chapter 6, note 46, below.

12. For my analysis of American stagflation in the 1960s, see Calleo, *Imperious Economy,* op. cit., pp. 25–44.

13. In fact, the dollar's effective rate of exchange rose during the 1960s despite the persistent deficit in the basic balance. This revaluation occurred because of devaluations of other currencies. Peter G. Peterson, *The United States in the Changing World Economy,* Vol. II (Washington, D.C.: U.S. Government Printing Office, 1971), pp. 29–30.

14. For a discussion of the Johnson administration's failure to adjust fiscal and monetary policies to reconcile full employment and stable prices, including the effects of the temporary surtax on income taxes enacted in 1968, see Joseph A. Pechman, *Federal Tax Policy* (Washington, D.C.: Brookings Institution, 1987), pp. 28–29.

15. Between 1966 and 1972, expenditures for human resources nearly doubled in 1982 dollars—from $138.6 billion to $245.2 billion. Medicare, which began in 1966, was absorbing 3.1 percent of federal outlays by 1969. *Historical Tables: Budget of the United States Government, Fiscal Year 1990* (Washington, D.C.: U.S. Government Printing Office, 1989), pp. 41–42; author's calculations.

16. Female and black unemployment more than doubled during the 1970s, as overall unemployment rose from below 4 percent in the late 1960s to 8 percent by 1975. Total unemployment remained above 5 percent throughout the 1980s. *Economic Report of the President, 1991* (Washington, D.C.: Government Printing Office, 1991), p. 331.

17. In 1969, state and local governments received only 16.7 percent of their funds from the federal government. By 1973, the year after the enactment of revenue sharing, that figure was 20.6 percent. For statistical data, see Tax Foundation, *Facts and Figures on Government Finance: 1990 Edition* (Baltimore: Johns Hopkins University Press, 1990), p. 180. For analysis of federal economic relations, see George F. Break, *Financing Government in a Federal System* (Washington, D.C.: Brookings Institution, 1980), pp. 123–86; J. Richard Aronson and John L. Hilley, *Financing State and Local Governments* (Washington, D.C.: Brookings Institution, 1986), pp. 10–30, 48–74.

18. Price data from December to December. *Economic Report*

of the President, 1990 (Washington, D.C.: Government
Printing Office, 1990), p. 363. The export of inflation
continued. In the mid-1960s, world consumer prices were
inflating at 2.5 percent per annum in the industrial world
and less than 1.5 percent in the United States. In the eight
years from the first quarter of 1968 to the fourth quarter
of 1975, consumer prices rose 62 percent in the United
States and Canada, 127 percent in Britain, 85 percent in
France, 92 percent in Italy, 106 percent in Japan, and 47
percent in Germany. American credit inflation was heavily
responsible. See Cleveland and Brittain, op. cit., p. 26. See
also Calleo, op. cit., p. 107. For exporting inflation, see
W. Max Corden, *Inflation, Exchange Rates, and the World
Economy* (Chicago: University of Chicago Press, 1986),
pp. 88–94.

19. Behind the increase in money and credit that was directly
    responsible for inflation lay changes and pressures in the
    real economy that monetary increases were accommodat-
    ing. W.W. Rostow has attributed the price rises prior to
    the oil shock to rising agricultural prices caused by popu-
    lation outpacing increases in agricultural productivity, rapid
    industrial expansion that drew down energy reserves, an-
    ticipation of continuing high employment pushing up
    money wages faster than productivity increases, and pres-
    sure on the dollar caused by declining United States com-
    petitiveness and continuing overseas security outlays.
    W.W. Rostow, *The World Economy: History and Prospect*
    (Austin: University of Texas Press, 1978), p. 286. For a
    monetarist interpretation of the inflation of the 1960s and
    early 1970s, see Cleveland and Brittain, op. cit., pp. 8–11.
    For my own more extended discussion of the Nixon rev-
    olution and the subsequent shocks, see my *The Imperious
    Economy,* op. cit. Chapters 4–7.

20. "Transcript of President's Address on Moves to Deal with
    Economic Problems," *The New York Times,* August 16, 1971,
    p. 14.

21. Herbert Stein, *Presidential Economics: The Making of Eco-
    nomic Policy from Roosevelt to Reagan and Beyond* (Washing-
    ton, D.C.: American Enterprise Institute, 1988), pp.
    148–68.

22. From 1971 to 1979, the dollar depreciated 47 percent against the deutschemark and 23 percent against the French franc. Exports increased, but were more than offset by increases in imports—for reasons explained in the following paragraphs. *Economic Report of the President, 1991,* op. cit., pp. 402, 410.

23. Two interpretations of monetary policy during the Nixon years are offered by Edward R. Tufte, *Political Control of the Economy* (Princeton, N.J.: Princeton University Press, 1978), pp. 45–50; and Andrew Brimmer, *Politics and Monetary Policy: The Federal Reserve and the Nixon White House,* a paper presented before the tenth annual meeting of the Eastern Economics Association, New York City, March 6, 1984.

24. *Economic Report of the President, 1991,* op. cit. p. 410.

25. Lewis E. Lehrman, "The Creation of International Monetary Order," in David P. Calleo, ed., *Money and the Coming World Order* (New York: New York University Press and The Lehrman Institute 1976), pp. 112–13.

26. *Economic Report of the President, 1991,* op. cit., p. 355.

27. The balance on merchandise trade showed a $8.9-billion surplus, with the current-account balance showing a surplus of over $18.1 billion (current dollars). *Economic Report of the President, 1990,* op. cit., p. 410.

28. M2 grew 5.5 percent in 1974, 12.6 percent in 1975, and 13.7 percent in 1976. The federal funds rate, after reaching a record high of 10.5 percent in 1974, fell to 5.82 percent in 1975 and to 5.04 percent in 1976. The current account, in a huge surplus in 1975, fell dramatically in 1976 and went into deficit—the largest of postwar history to that point—in 1977. *Economic Report of the President, 1991,* op. cit., pp. 363, 368, 402.

29. For such an analysis, see Paul McCracken, ed., *Towards Full Employment and Price Stability* (Paris: OECD, 1977), pp. 66–74, 133–39.

30. The deflated demand for other products following the oil shock was particularly devastating for developing countries, often deeply in debt to finance capital infrastructure. The high oil price raised their costs at the same time as it cut demand drastically for their products. The United

States defended its own inflation by arguing that rich developed countries should, in this situation, be bankers and buyers of last resort for the third world, freely supplying credit to keep weaker producers from being ruined. For an analysis of locomotive theory and the positive and negative spillover effects associated with it, see W.M. Corden, *Inflation, Exchange Rates, and the World Economy* (Chicago: University of Chicago, 1986), pp. 150–54.

31. The United States pressed the locomotive theory particularly before and during the Downing Street economic summit in May 1977. See Robert D. Putnam and Nicholas Bayne, *Hanging Together: The Seven-Power Summits* (Cambridge, Mass.: Harvard University Press, 1984), pp. 69–71.

32. As a result, they were badly hit by the second oil "shock" in 1979, when the OPEC producers sought to restore the 1973 oil prices that had been badly eroded by the falling dollar. See Stanley W. Black, "Learning from Adversity: Policy Responses to Two Oil Shocks," in *Essays in International Finance*, No. 160, (Princeton, N.J.: Princeton University Press, 1985), pp. 13–16.

33. Volcker brought the money supply from the double-digit growth rates of the 1970s to below 4.5 percent. Real interest rates on twenty-year government bonds went from an average of 0.6 percent in 1979 to 5.4 percent during the recession of the early 1980s. Historically, the government bonds have yielded 2 percent or less. See William Greider, *Secrets of the Temple: How the Federal Reserve Runs the Country* (New York: Simon and Schuster, 1987), pp. 76–77, 562.

34. For a discussion of bracket creep's effects on government revenue and the policy changes made in the 1980s to address the problem, see Pechman, op. cit., pp. 114–17.

35. Among the major provisions of the Economic Recovery Tax Act of 1981 were reductions of marginal tax rates for individuals and the maximum marginal tax rate (to 50 percent) for individuals; indexation of income tax brackets to the CPI beginning in 1985; increases in the amount deductible for charitable contributions and for foreign earned income; acceleration of capital expenditure write-offs; reductions in windfall profit taxes and corporate in-

come below $50,000; addition of savings incentives such as the exclusion of interest and dividend payments from taxation and extension of eligibility for individual retirement accounts; and a decrease in estate and gift taxes. *Budget of the United States Government, Fiscal Year 1983* (Washington, D.C.: U.S. Government Printing Office, 1982), Section Four: 3–8. Indexing occurred in stages, however, with revisions scheduled in both 1989 and 1990. Pechman, op. cit., p. 116.

36. The 1982 deficit, measured in constant (1982) dollars, was surpassed only by the wartime deficits in 1943–45. *Historical Tables: Budget of the United States Government, Fiscal Year 1990* (Washington, D.C.: U.S. Government Printing Office, 1989), pp. 19–20.

37. Measurements of real interest rates are inexact by nature, since they depend on assessments of general expectations and investor choices. The OECD calculates both short- and long-term real interest rates by using three-month Treasury bills or government bonds with maturities of more than five years and dividing by the annual inflation rate. According to those calculations, short-term real interest rates were negative for more than four years before turning positive in 1979. Long-term real interest rates, however, were negative only in 1974–75 and 1979, staying barely positive for the rest of the decade but becoming strongly so throughout the 1980s. OECD, *Economic Outlook: Historical Statistics, 1960–1988* (Paris: OECD, 1990), pp. 105–6.

38. For an analysis of the risks and problems the Mexican debt crisis posed to the United States banking system and policymakers, see Greider, op. cit., pp. 483–87.

39. In 1984, the federal funds rate, a general indicator of the Fed's tightening and loosening, rose to 10.23 percent from 9.09 percent in 1983. Similar jumps followed in short-term rates for Treasury bills and commercial paper. *Economic Report of the President, 1991*, op. cit., p. 368.

40. For much of the 1980s, Belgium and Spain were the only OECD countries with corporate tax rates lower than those of the United States. By 1988, most OECD countries had lowered their corporate tax rates, but the 1986 Tax Re-

form Act kept corporate taxes in the United States among the lowest of industrial countries. OECD, *Economies in Transition: Structural Adjustment in OECD Countries* (Paris: OECD, 1989), p. 182.

41. See Harold van Buren Cleveland, "Europe in the Economic Crisis of Our Time: Macroeconomic Policies and Microeconomic Constraints," in David P. Calleo and Claudia Morgenstern, eds., *Recasting Europe's Economies: National Strategies in the 1980s* (Lanham, Md.: University Press of America, 1990), pp. 160–68.

42. For an analysis of how the United States borrowed from German and Japanese savings, see Cleveland, "Europe in the Economic Crisis of Our Time," op. cit., pp. 160–63.

43. See Gottfried Haberler, "Further Thoughts on International Policy Coordination," in Paul A Volcker, et al. *International Monetary Cooperation: Essays in Honor of Henry C. Wallich.* Essays in International Finance, No. 169. (Princeton, N.J.: Princeton University, December 1987), pp. 23–27.

44. See Cleveland, "Europe in the Economic Crisis of Our Time," op. cit., pp. 165–67.

45. This failure of exchange rates to reflect a parity of purchasing power has sparked a significant revision among monetary theorists. See James M. Boughton, *The Monetary Approach to the Exchange Rate: What Now Remains?* Essays in International Finance No. 171 (Princeton: N.J.: Princeton University, October 1988).

46. Robert Triffin, "The Paper-Exchange Standard: 1971– 19??," in *International Monetary Cooperation,* op. cit., pp. 74–75, and *IMS: International Monetary System—or Scandal?,* op. cit., pp. 3–15.

Chapter 7: Fiscal Deficits, Public Goods, and the Real Economy

1. By October 1, 1990, Japan's Nikkei share index plunged 48 percent from its all-time high at the end of 1989. The government bond market lost 15 percent of its value in the first nine months of 1990 and the property market began to seem shaky. "A Survey of Japanese Finance," *The*

Economist, December 8, 1990; and OECD, *Economic Surveys: Japan, 1989–1990* (Paris: OECD, 1990).

2. See Chapter 7, Table 7.1, p. 127; "Tables and Graphs," Tables 7 and 12.

3. For changing techniques of production and their significance for the future of industrial society, see Michael J. Piore and Charles F. Sabel, *The Second Industrial Divide: Possibilities for Prosperity* (New York: Basic Books, 1984).

4. William R. Cline, *Exports of Manufactures from Developing Countries* (Washington, D.C.: Brookings Institution, 1984), p. 23.

5. "Tables and Graphs," Tables 8–10.

6. See Margaret M. Blair and Robert Litan, "Corporate Leverage and Leveraged Buyouts in the Eighties," in John B. Shoven and Joel Waldfogel, eds., *Debts, Taxes, and Corporate Restructuring* (Washington, D.C.: Brookings Institution, 1990), pp. 68–70. During the period 1978–87, the authors' rankings show comparatively low profitability for transportation, electrical and electronic equipment, and machinery.

7. See Michael L. Dertouzos et al., *Made in America: Regaining the Productive Edge* (Cambridge, Mass.: MIT Press, 1989), especially Chapters 1 and 2; Sylvia Nasar, "American Revival in Manufacturing Seen in U.S. Report," *The New York Times*, February 5, 1991, p. A1; and Sylvia Nasar, "Boom in Manufactured Exports Provides Hope for U.S. Economy," *The New York Times*, April 21, 1991, p. A1.

8. Annual business failures rose rapidly from their post-1948 low in 1978 of 23.9 per 10,000 listed enterprises, to a high of 120.0 in 1986. In 1990, the figure was at 75.0 after having fallen to 65.0 in 1989. The data beginning in 1984 is based on a new methodology making comparisons with earlier years problematic, but our general trends do not seem altered by the change. *Economic Report of the President, 1991* (Washington, D.C.: U.S. Government Printing Office, 1991), p. 394; and U.S. Department of Commerce, *Survey of Current Business*, Vol. 71, no. 3 (March 1991), p. S–5.

Effects on domestic manufacturing were not distributed evenly among the nation's regions. Between 1970 and 1987, the share of total United States earnings from manufacturing, mining, construction, and agriculture in the "Rust Belt"—comprising the New England, Middle Atlantic, East North Central, and West North Central regions of the United States—dropped from 60.6 to 50.6 percent. During the same period, the "Sun Belt"—comprising the South Atlantic, East South Central, West South Central, Mountain, and Pacific regions—saw an increase in its share from 39.4 to 49.4 percent. For comparable employment patterns, see note 10, below. Also see Robert W. Crandall, "The Regional Shift of U.S. Economic Activity," in Robert E. Litan et al., eds., *American Living Standards: Threats and Challenges* (Washington, D.C.: Brookings Institution, 1988), p. 159.

9. See Barry P. Bosworth, "Taxes and the Investment Recovery," in *Brookings Papers on Economic Activity,* No. 1 (Washington, D.C.: Brookings Institution, 1985), pp. 1–47. Bosworth shows the investment recovery in 1980–84 taking place primarily in office equipment, business automobiles, and commercial buildings. The investment boom in business automobiles and commercial real estate was linked to changes in tax treatment, while falling prices seem to have fueled the purchases of new office equipment.

   Between 1980 and 1987, the capital investment portion of the national defense budget increased from 1.2 to 2.0 percent of GNP. By 1990, the figure had been reduced to 1.6 percent. See *Budget of the United States Government, Fiscal Year 1992* (Washington, D.C.: U.S. Government Printing Office, 1991), Part Seven: 89.

10. In 1979, some 21 million people worked in manufacturing—the highest total for the postwar period. After dropping to 18.5 million in 1983, the total employment for manufacturing recovered to 19.4 million in 1989—a figure roughly equal to the total for 1967. However, by 1990, the total was back down to 19.1 million. By contrast, service-producing industries employed 63.4 million in 1979, 83.0 million in 1989, and 85.3 million in 1990. *Economic Report of the President, 1991,* op. cit., pp. 334–35.

    Regional patterns of employment in manufacturing

magnify the effects of the decline. The Rust Belt has lost manufacturing jobs steadily since 1967. Some of those lost jobs have been matched by new job creation in the Sun Belt. In 1967, total Rust Belt employment in manufacturing was 12.3 million, while the Sun Belt provided 7.2 million. By 1988, 9.3 million were employed in manufacturing in the Sun Belt and 9.7 million in the Rust Belt. See Crandall, op. cit., pp. 160–61.

11. See Kurt H. Biendenkopf, "The Federal Republic of Germany; Old Miracles and New Challenges," in David P. Calleo and Claudia Morgenstern, eds., *Recasting Europe's Economies: National Strategies in the 1980s* (Lanham: University Press of America, 1990), pp. 90–93. For data references, see Kurt H. Biedenkopf and Meinhard Miegel, *Investieren in Deutschland: Die Bundesrepublik als Wirtschaftsstandort* (Stuttgart Poller-Verlag, 1989).

12. For earnings, see *Economic Report of the President, 1991,* op. cit., p. 336. Figures are for total weekly earnings of production or nonsupervisory workers in private, nonagricultural industries. Figures are in 1982 dollars, using the CPI for urban wage-earners and clerical workers. For saving, see "Tables and Graphs," Table 14.

13. For detailed movements of the money supply, see *Federal Reserve Bulletin* (Washington, D.C.: Board of Governors of the Federal Reserve System), Table 1.10, various issues.

14. Chapter 4, Table 4.6a, p. 75.

15. See C. Eugene Steuerle, "Federal Policy and the Accumulation of Private Debt," in Shoven and Waldfogel, eds., op. cit., pp. 21–43, especially p. 26.

16. Note that in 1980–87, the share of private final consumption rose by 4.2 percent of United States GDP, while the share of public consumption rose by 5.7 percent of the GDP. See United Nations, *National Accounts Statistics: Main Aggregates and Detailed Tables, 1987* (New York: United Nations, 1990), Table 1.1, pp. 1586–639.

17. During World War II, the debt increased even more dramatically. Specifically, between 1941 and 1946, gross federal debt increased from 50.9 to 127.3 percent of GDP. From 1980 to 1989, the debt increased from 34.0 to 55.9 percent of GNP. *Budget of the United States Government, Fis-*

cal Year 1992, op. cit., Part Seven: 71. See also Chapter 6, note 42.

18. See United Nations, *National Accounts Statistics,* op. cit., Tables 1.1 and 1.2, pp. 1586–639. In 1980–87, United States government consumption expenditure earmarked for defense rose by 1.3 percent of the GDP, while at the same time overall private and public consumption rose by 4.3 percentage points relative to GDP.

19. See ibid., Tables 1.1 and 2.5, pp. 1586–639. In 1980–87, private final consumption expenditures on health care rose to consume an additional 2.7 percentage points of the GDP; the same increase as for overall private consumption.

20. See Steuerle, op. cit., p. 26. United States net outstanding corporate debt had fallen between 1968 and 1981, a trend that was sharply reversed from 1981 to 1988.

21. See R. Dan Brumbaugh, Jr., Andrew S. Carron, and Robert Litan, "Cleaning Up the Depository Institutions Mess," *Brookings Papers on Economic Activity,* No. 1 (Washington, D.C.: Brookings Institution, 1989), pp. 243–97, especially pp. 250–58.

22. For this classification of financing structures, see Hyman P. Minsky, *Stabilizing an Unstable Economy,* a Twentieth Century Fund Book (New Haven, Conn.: Yale University Press, 1986), pp. 206–13, 335–41. See also Chapter 8, note 17.

23. Margaret M. Blair, "A Surprising Culprit Behind the Rush to Leverage," *The Brookings Review,* Winter 1989/1990, pp. 19–26.

24. See Steuerle, op. cit., pp. 33–35.

25. Roy C. Smith, *The Money Wars: The Rise and Fall of the Great Buyout Boom of the 1980s* (New York: Dutton, 1990).

26. Some creditors have brought "fraudulent conveyance" suits against debtors who have gone bankrupt after leveraged buyouts. Bankruptcy law sets criteria for the fraudulent transfer of assets (e.g., transfer while the firm is insolvent or transfers that render the firm insolvent). See "Is There Sweet Revenge for Deals That Go Sour?" *Business Week,* March 19, 1990, pp. 132–33; and Richard E. Cherin and Margaret E. Zaleski, "Leveraged Buyouts: The Fraudu-

lent Transfer Risk," *Journal of Commercial Bank Lending,* March 1985, pp. 41–51.

27. For a list of major bankruptcies, see "The Price of Distress," *The Economist,* April 27, 1991, survey, 24.

28. See Department of the Treasury, *Modernizing the Financial System: Recommendations for Safer, More Competitive Banks* (Washington, D.C.: U.S. Treasury Department, February 1991), especially pp. XVIII, 23–32. In June 1990, foreign-controlled banking offices accounted for 20.4 percent of United States banking assets and about 29.4 percent of commercial and industrial loans, up from 14 and 20 percent, respectively, in 1983.

29. See *Economic Report of the President, 1991,* op. cit., p. 388. Figures are for profits of Federal Reserve banks, with inventory valuation adjustment, without capital consumption adjustment, and deflated by the implicit GNP deflator.

30. See Department of the Treasury, *Modernizing the Financial System,* op. cit., pp. 1–10. For financial innovation and the banking industry, see Ralph C. Bryant, *International Financial Intermediation* (Washington, D.C.: Brookings Institution, 1987), Chapters 6–8; Robert A. Eisenbeis, "Regulatory Policies and Financial Instability," in *Debt, Financial Stability, and Public Policy,* a symposium sponsored by the Federal Reserve Bank of Kansas City in Jackson Hole, Wyoming, August 27–29, 1986, pp. 107–32; and Minsky, op. cit. For the dangers posed by recession, see Stephen Rousseas, "Can the U.S. Financial System Survive the Revolution?" *Challenge,* March–April 1989, pp. 39–43.

31. For a pioneering survey of the development and dangers of the new world financial structure and the absence of efficient government policy and regulation, see Susan Strange, *Casino Capitalism* (Oxford, U.K.: Basil Blackwell, 1986). See also R. Dan Brumbaugh, Jr., and Robert E. Litan, "The Banks Are Worse Off Than You Think," *Challenge,* January–February 1990, pp. 4–12; and Felix G. Rohatyn, *The Twenty-Year Century: Essays on Economics and Public Finance* (New York: Random House, 1983), Chapter 8.

32. A list of troubled institutions of the 1970s and early 1980s

included: Penn Central, W. T. Grant, Lockheed, International Harvester, U.S. Steel, Ford, Chrysler, General Motors, as well as the city of New York. For a knowledgeable commentary on the financial troubles of the period, see Rohatyn, op. cit.

33. For the age-old tension between the need for a "lender of last resort" and the danger of encouraging "moral hazard," see Charles P. Kindleberger, *Manias, Panics, and Crashes* (New York: Basic Books, 1989), Chapters 8–10.

34. In early 1991, the Department of the Treasury published plans for reforming the United States financial system. Those plans included structural reforms to the financial system (i.e., removing barriers to interstate banking and permitting corporations to own banks), supervisory and regulatory modernization, and recapitalizing the Bank Insurance Fund. See Department of Treasury, *Modernizing the Financial System*, op. cit.; and "American Banking Reform," *The Economist*, June 29, 1991, pp. 66–68. See also Chapter 7, note 53, below.

35. See Robert E. Litan, *What Should Banks Do?* (Washington, D.C.: Brookings Institution, 1987), pp. 33–60, 99–144.

36. Walter B. Wriston, "Banking Against Disaster," *The New York Times*, September 14, 1982.

37. During much of the 1940s, 1951, and 1958, commodity price inflation was also higher than short-term interest rates. See *Economic Report of the President, 1991*, op. cit., 356, 368.

38. For a comprehensive study of third world debt, see Jeffrey D. Sachs, ed., *Developing Country Debt and Economic Performance*, a National Bureau of Economic Research Project Report (Chicago: University of Chicago Press, 1989). The chapter by Rudiger Dornbusch, "Debt Problems and the World Macroeconomy," pp. 331–57, examines the role of interest rates, commodity prices, and growth in the debt crisis of 1979–82.

39. For real interest rates in the United States, see "Tables and Graphs," Table 11. For bank earnings, see Jeffrey D. Sachs and Harry Huizinga, "U.S. Commercial Banks and the Developing-Country Debt Crisis," *Brookings Papers on Economic Activity*, No. 2 (1987), pp. 555–606; and Brum-

baugh, Carron, and Litan, op. cit., pp. 243–97, especially pp. 255–58.

40. The GAO broke down the cost as follows:

> Losses of insolvent S and Ls—*$155 billion
> Interest payments on bonds—$105 billion
> Interest on short-term working capital—$28 billion
> Administrative and other costs—$37 billion
> *Amount by which assets of insolvent S and Ls fail to cover their insured deposits.

See David E. Rosenbaum, "A Financial Disaster with Many Culprits," *The New York Times,* June 6, 1990, p. A1.

41. *U.S. News and World Report,* April 9, 1990, pp. 37–38.
42. The Resolution Trust Corporation, with which the government is funding the losses, is being financed by 40-year bonds.
43. See Peter Rossi, *Without Shelter: Homelessness in the 1980s* (New York: Priority Press, 1989).
44. See William Greider, *The Trouble with Money,* Larger Agenda Series (Knoxville, Tenn.: Whittle Direct Books, 1989), pp. 35–46.
45. See Steuerle, op. cit., pp. 27–29.
46. See *The New York Times,* June 6, 1990, p. A1 for an explanation of the "3-6-3 rule" (i.e., pay depositors 3 percent, receive 6 percent on mortgages, and tee off on the golf course at 3 o'clock).
47. R. Dan Brumbaugh, Jr., and Andrew S. Carron, "The Thrift Industry Crisis: Causes and Solutions," *Brookings Papers on Economic Activity,* No. 2 (Washington, D.C.: Brookings Institution, 1987), p. 354.
48. Average interest return on mortgages and cost of funds are for insured savings associations. After 1978, the construction rate of new homes was declining rapidly and homeowners holding nonassumable low-rate mortgages were unable or unwilling to sell their residences, resulting in a plummeting rate of mortgage repayment. Thus, the spread between new mortgage rates and the average rates on existing mortgage portfolios began to widen markedly. See Andrew S. Carron, *The Plight of the Thrift Institutions*

(Washington, D.C.: Brookings Institution, 1982), pp. 15, 18–20. For later developments, see *Economic Report of the President, 1991,* op. cit., pp. 368–69; and Brumbaugh, Carron, and Litan, "Cleaning Up the Depository Institutions Mess," op. cit., pp. 281–82.

49. See Brumbaugh, and Carron, "The Thrift Industry Crisis," op. cit., pp. 349–89, especially pp. 355–56.

50. *The New York Times,* June 6, 1990, p. A1.

51. For the text released by the Senate Ethics Committee after its hearings on the "Keating Five" senators, see *Congressional Quarterly Weekly Report,* March 2, 1991, pp. 563–66. Further information is contained on pp. 517–27 of the same issue. See also *The New York Times,* June 6, 1990, A1; and Peter Riddell, "Cranston Case to Go Before Full U.S. Senate," *The Financial Times,* February 28, 1991, p. 6.

52. As I write, Allied-Lyons, a British firm, reports a £150-million loss. UBS Phillips and Drew and the Midland Bank, both experienced players in financial markets, have also recently reported large losses from trading currency options and speculating on interest rates. For an excellent analysis of the difference between routine hedging and speculation, see Anthony Harris, "Measuring Options for the Future," *The Financial Times,* March 25, 1991, p. 22. Also see Chapter 7, note 34, above.

53. See Henry Kaufman, "Don't Let Business Own Banks," *The Washington Post,* February 17, 1991, p. C7.

Chapter 8: The Future According to Present Trends

1. *Budget of the United States Government, Fiscal Year 1992,* (Washington, D.C.: U.S. Government Printing Office, 1991), Part Seven: 17.

2. See "Tables and Graphs," Table 15.

3. The Council of Economic Advisers was predicting a budget deficit of $318 billion, not including the cost of the Gulf war. *Economic Report of the President, 1991* (Washington, D.C.: U.S. Government Printing Office, 1991), p. 375.

4. In 1990, the merchandise trade deficit fell and the surplus on services and investment income rose, but unilateral transfers associated with the Gulf war more than offset the gains. Ignoring those unilateral transfers, the current-

account deficit was $78 billion. Faith in United States international transactions accounts was shaken, however, by the growth of its "statistical discrepancy" category. The 1990 statistical discrepancy was $73 billion, equal to 5.2 percent of total current-account flows. According to recorded capital-account statistics, recorded foreign inflows were insufficient to balance the capital-account deficit. The discrepancies were blamed on, among other things, the inability of the United States statistical system to keep pace with technological and innovative changes in the world's capital markets. In February 1991, the federal government launched the 1992 Economic Statistics Initiative to improve its accounting. See "U.S. International Transactions, Fourth Quarter and Year 1990," U.S. Department of Commerce, *Survey of Current Business,* Vol. 71, No. 3, (March 1991) pp. 4–5, 34–68.

5. United States net oil imports per unit of real GDP rose by nearly 13 percent from 1973 to 1978, fell by almost 50 percent between 1978 and 1985, and then rose by 33 percent in the following three years. By comparison, French and German net oil imports have steadily declined since 1973. In France, they fell about 24 percent from 1973 to 1978, 36 percent between 1978 and 1985, and a further 3 percent between 1985 and 1988. German net oil imports fell by 13.5 percent from 1973 to 1978, by 31 percent from 1978 to 1985, and by 3 percent from 1985 to 1988. OECD, *Economic Outlook, 48* (Paris: OECD, 1990), p. 35.

6. The 1984 *Economic Report of the President* described the structural deficit as the deficit that would exist even if the unemployment rate was at its inflation threshold, i.e., the minimum level of unemployment that can be sustained without raising the rate of inflation. It also predicted that by 1989 the structural deficit would grow to $197 billion. *Economic Report of the President, 1984* (Washington, D.C.: U.S. Government Printing Office, 1984), pp. 35–36.

7. *Budget of the United States Government, Fiscal Year 1992,* op. cit., Part Seven: 17. For Ponzi finance, see note 17 below.

8. In October 1990, Congress passed a budget package designed to reduce the federal deficit by a cumulative $492

billion over a five-year period. However, the package op-
timistically assumed average annual real GNP growth rates
of 3.3 percent and a fall in both nominal and real interest
rates. In addition, the package excluded the capital
spending of the Resolution Trust Corporation and the costs
of the Gulf war. Even with those exclusions, the budget
deficit was still expected to increase in fiscal years 1991
and 1992. OECD, *Economic Outlook, 48,* op. cit. p. 50; and
Martin Feldstein, "Bush's Budget Deal Made the Deficit
Bigger," *The Wall Street Journal,* November 29, 1990,
p. A12.

9. The administration's 1992 budget proposed cutting
spending for national defense by $97 billion in nominal
terms through 1995 in comparison with 1990 spending
projections. *Budget of the United States Government, Fiscal Year
1992,* op. cit., Part Two: 183–84.

10. The term "cost" in calculating such military operations is
ambiguous, since it normally includes only the operational
cost of the actual engagement and ignores the huge annual outlays to build and sustain the forces used over the
years. Official estimates apparently do not even include
any depreciation, an issue clouded, of course, by plans to
cut back inventories in the future. For a knowledgeable
interim assessment, see United States Congressman Les
Aspin, "Sharing the Burden of the Gulf: Are the Allies
Paying Their Fair Share?" a report issued from his office
and dated April 8, 1991. As for reconstruction, the cost
for Kuwait alone has been estimated at between $50 bil-
lion and $100 billion. "Large-scale Foreign Borrowing Ex-
pected," *Financial Times,* February 27, 1991, p. 2.

11. For an early and prescient analysis of the weakness of the
banking industry, see R. Dan Brumbaugh, Jr., Andrew S.
Carron, and Robert E. Litan, "Cleaning Up the Depository Institutions Mess," *Brookings Papers on Economic Activity,* No. 1 (Washington, D.C.: Brookings Institution, 1989),
pp. 250–58. For a later survey, see "The Future of Banking," *Business Week,* April 22, 1991, pp. 72–76. Several other
government-guaranteed financial agencies were also short
of funds. Student loan defaults, for example, forced Sally
Mae, the Student Loan Marketing Association, to ask

Congress for more funds. In short, future bailouts on the scale of the S and L debacle, or beyond, are easily imaginable. Indeed, outstanding federal guarantees totaled $1.4 trillion as of September 30, 1990. *Treasury Bulletin,* March 1991, pp. 67–69.

12. Energy Department estimates in 1990 placed the total research and cleanup costs for nuclear weapons plants at $200 billion over thirty years. Keith Schneider, "New Mission at Energy Department: Bomb Makers Turn to Cleanup," *The New York Times,* August 17, 1990, pp. A1 and A17.

13. Real spending for physical resources rose by a whopping 45.7 percent in fiscal 1990. But this was not the result of increased infrastructure spending, but of outlays to the Resolution Trust Corporation, the body charged with taking over and disposing of the assets of bankrupt S and Ls. See Chapter 3, note 30.

14. State and local budgets were hit by a combination of trends and shocks in the 1980s. During the early 1980s, federal grants to states declined in nominal terms. Federal grants declined from 25 to 17 percent of state and local budgets and tax collections slowed with decreases in growth and corporate profits. Meanwhile, spending demands mounted with deteriorating infrastructure, escalating health care costs, and rising concerns about the quality of education combined with increasing school enrollments. In 1990, twenty-six state legislatures enacted tax hikes, 41 percent of localities raised property tax rates, 43 percent created new fees, and 76 percent raised the level of existing fees and charges. Tax revolts were numerous. Laura S. Rubin, "The Current Fiscal Situation in State and Local Governments," *Federal Reserve Bulletin* (Washington, D.C.: Board of Governors of the Federal Reserve System, December 1990), pp. 1009–18.

15. Federal spending measured in constant (1982) dollars for the function "Education, training, employment and social services" fell from $37.7 billion in 1980 to $29.2 billion in 1989, a drop of 22.6 percent. Removing the spending on employment and social services shows a drop of 29 percent. *Budget of the United States Government, Fiscal Year 1992,*

op. cit. Part Seven: 35–36; author's calculations.

16. According to data compiled by the U.S. Senate Special Committee on Aging, federal spending on pensions and health care for the elderly rose from 4.4 percent of GNP in 1965 to 9.7 percent in 1990, and will reach 13.5 percent in 2030. As a percentage of federal outlays, this spending program is expected to surpass the 50-percent mark shortly after 2020—compared with 24.9 percent in 1965 and 40.4 percent in 1990. See *Aging America: Trends and Projections,* annotated, an Information Paper to the Special Committee on Aging, United States Senate (Washington, D.C.: U.S. Government Printing Office, 1990), pp. 1–23, 125–30.

17. Ponzi finance may be said to occur in the government sector when interest payments regularly exceed income growth. Thus, an ever larger part of government borrowing is devoted to interest payments on existing debt. In other words, debt rises faster than the means to service it. Harold van Buren Cleveland, "Europe in the Economic Crisis of Our Time: Macroeconomic Policies and Microeconomic Constraints," in David P. Calleo and Claudia Morgenstern, eds., *Recasting Europe's Economies: National Strategies in the 1980s* (Lanham, Md.: University Press of America, 1990), p. 165.

18. According to the OECD, the aggregate marginal rate of income tax in the United States rose nearly two thirds from the mid-1950s to the end of the 1970s. OECD, *Economies in Transition: Structural Adjustment in OECD Economies* (Paris: OECD, 1989), pp. 170–71.

19. See *Budget of the United States Government, Fiscal Year 1990* (Washington, D.C.: U.S. Government Printing Office, 1989), Part Four: 4.

20. For a discussion of inflation, interest payments, and government deficits, see Rudiger Dornbusch, *Dollars, Debts, and Deficits* (Cambridge, Mass.: MIT Press, 1986), pp. 184–92.

21. Some analysts argue that demographics will naturally solve the savings shortage in the United States. One argument is that as the "baby boomers" reach middle age, they will begin to save more in preparation for retirement. While

that may be the case, the trend will likely be reversed early in the next century as the baby boomers hit retirement age and consequently begin dissaving. Furthermore, there is statistical evidence showing that generations born after 1939 save substantially less than those born earlier. These arguments are summarized in Bijan B. Aghevli et al., *The Role of National Saving in the World Economy: Recent Trends and Prospects* (Washington, D.C.: International Monetary Fund, March 1990), pp. 17–18. For a comparison of United States savings and needs, see "Tables and Graphs," Table 14.

22. The reconstruction of eastern Germany is expected to require a net investment of between $1.5 trillion and $1.9 trillion in 1990 prices for the period 1991 to 2000. See Leslie Lipschitz and Donogh McDonald, eds., *German Unification: Economic Issues,* IMF Occasional Paper No. 75 (Washington, D.C.: International Monetary Fund, 1990), p. 77.

23. Some analysts, however, see a very different outcome. According to their reasoning, the war helped dampen domestic demand, lower oil prices (after the victory), and boost foreign demand as a result of reconstruction efforts in Kuwait. For a summary of their views, see Sylvia Nasar, "Economy Benefits from Gulf War," *The New York Times,* March 13, 1991, p. D1.

24. Financial analysts in early 1991 predicted that global capital demand for Eastern Europe, the Middle East, and Latin America would exceed supply by more than $200 billion a year through 1993 and by about $100 billion a year through 1996. The supply of capital would likely be restricted by the domestic economic preoccupations of two of the world's major capital exporters: Germany and Japan. As a result, some analysts expected interest rates to rise by as much as two percentage points. See Steven Greenhouse, "World's Finances Facing Strains As Troubled Areas Try to Rebuild," *The New York Times,* March 26, 1991, pp. A1, D11.

25. The "soft landing"—and its counterpart the "hard landing"—was at the heart of Stephen Marris's study of the

United States and the world economy, *Deficits and the Dollar: The World Economy at Risk* (Washington, D.C.: Institute for International Economics, 1987).

26. After four years of negotiations, the Uruguay Round of the GATT reached a deadlock over the United States-European dispute concerning agricultural subsidies. In May 1991, President Bush received congressional permission for fast-track negotiating authority, which means Congress will not review the final agreement on a line-by-line basis but will accept or reject it with a single vote. See *The Year in Trade, 1990,* Annual Report of the Export Task Force of the U.S. House of Representatives (Washington, D.C.: U.S. Government Printing Office, 1991), p. 18; "GATT's Last Chance," *The Economist,* June 1, 1991, p. 65.

27. News that the recession had worsened in the first quarter—with mounting layoffs and falling orders for manufactured goods—led the Federal Reserve to cut both the discount rate and the federal funds rate at the end of April. John M. Berry, "Fed Reduces Rates to Boost Economy," *The Washington Post,* 1 May 1991, pp. A1, A4.

28. The weak pound and the low level of foreign exchange reserves forced Britain in 1976 to turn to the IMF for standby credit of $3.9 billion, which was granted once Britain agreed to restrict its domestic credit expansion for a two-year period. See Geoffrey E.J. Dennis, "Money Supply and its Control," in W. Peter J. Maunder, ed., *The British Economy in the 1970s* (London: Heinemann Educational Books, 1980), pp. 49–53.

29. For a discussion of debt maturity and inflation, see Dornbusch, op. cit., pp. 184–89.

30. The average maturity of interest-bearing public debt held by private investors in September 1990 was six years and one month. That compares with the postwar low of two years and five months achieved in December 1975. See Department of the Treasury, *Treasury Bulletin,* December 1990 (Washington, D.C.: U.S. Government Printing Office, 1990), pp. 32–33.

31. Throughout the 1970s, the United States exported capital to other countries, giving it a capital-account deficit. In

the 1980s, however, the capital account turned dramatically positive as foreign funds financed the huge United States current-account deficit. IMF, *International Financial Statistics, Yearbook, 1989* (Washington, D.C.: International Monetary Fund, 1989), pp. 724–25.

32. For America's early postwar geopolitical and economic policy, see David P. Calleo and Benjamin M. Rowland, *America and the World Political Economy* (Bloomington: Indiana University Press, 1973), pp. 3–15.

33. Lessons could be drawn from early postwar experience, when the reconstruction of Europe and the expansion of international trade were largely responsible for the continued and dramatic growth rates of the European and American economies. For a discussion of that period, see Andrew Shonfield, *Modern Capitalism: The Changing Balance of Public and Private Power* (New York: Oxford University Press, 1965), pp. 61–67.

Chapter 9: Decline Revisited

1. Joseph A. Schumpeter, *Capitalism, Socialism, and Democracy* (New York: Harper and Row, 1950), pp. 81–86.

2. For a survey of the "long wave" debate from Nikolai Kondratieff and Joseph Schumpeter to the 1970s and 1980s, see Joshua S. Goldstein, *Long Cycles: Prosperity and War in the Modern Age* (New Haven, Conn.: Yale University Press, 1988), especially Chapters 2 and 3. Also see David P. Calleo, *The Imperious Economy* (Cambridge, Mass.: Harvard University Press, 1982), pp. 110–11; p. 246, note 21.

3. Much of the financial sector had been nationalized since 1945–46. By 1980, the three largest public institutions accounted for 62 percent of deposits. After the nationalization of two large investment banks and the majority of the commercial banking sector in 1982, public enterprises accounted for 93 percent of deposits. See William James Adams, *Reconstructing the French Economy: Government and the Rise of Market Competition Since World War II* (Washington, D.C.: Brookings Institution, 1989), pp. 59–72. See also OECD, *Economic Surveys: France, 1986/87* (Paris: OECD, 1987), pp. 39–55.

4. See Patrick McCarthy, "France Faces Reality: Rigueur and the Germans," in David P. Calleo and Claudia Morgenstern, eds., *Recasting Europe's Economies: National Strategies in the 1980s* (Lanham, Md.: University Press of America, 1990), p. 63.

5. On the role of German and Japanese banks, see Andrew Shonfield, *Modern Capitalism: The Changing Balance of Public and Private Power* (New York: Oxford University Press, 1965), pp. 239–64; J. Andrew Spindler, *The Politics of International Credit: Private Finance and Foreign Policy in Germany and Japan* (Washington, D.C.: Brookings Institution, 1984), pp. 21–28, 110–14; and John Zysman, *Governments, Markets, and Growth: Financial Systems and the Politics of Industrial Change* (Ithaca, N.Y.: Cornell University Press, 1983), pp. 233–65.

6. "Tables and Graphs," Tables 7 and 10; Chapter 7, Table 7.1, p. 127.

7. Harold van Buren Cleveland, "Europe in the Economic Crisis of Our Time: Macroeconomic Policies and Microeconomic Constraints," in Calleo and Morgenstern, eds., op. cit., pp. 187–89, 193–5.

8. Ibid., p. 186.

9. For early statistical signs, see "Tables and Graphs," Table 21. See also Tables 4.1a and b, Chapter 4, p. 70.

10. "Tables and Graphs," Table 14.

11. See Susan Strange, "The Persistent Myth of Lost Hegemony," *International Organization*, Vol. 41, No. 4 (Autumn 1987), pp. 551–74; *"Cave! Hic Dragones:* A Critique of Regime Analysis," *International Organization,* Vol. 36, No. 2 (Spring 1982), pp. 337–54; *States and Markets: An Introduction to International Political Economy* (London: Printer Publishers, 1988), especially Chapter 11; and "The Future of the American Empire," *Journal of International Affairs,* Vol. 42, No. 1 (Fall 1988), pp. 1–17.

12. See Raymond Vernon, "International Investment and International Trade in the Product Cycle," *Quarterly Journal of Economics,* May 1966, pp. 190–207.

13. See "Refashioning IBM," *The Economist,* November 17, 1990, pp. 21–24.

14. "Tables and Graphs," Table 19. Also see Michael L. Der-

touzos et al., *Made in America: Regaining the Productive Edge* (Cambridge, Mass.: MIT Press, 1989).

15. Barry Bluestone and Bennett Harrison, *The Deindustrialization of America: Plant Closings, Community Abandonment, and the Dismantling of Basic Industry* (New York: Basic Books, 1982).

16. Figures for 1988 reveal the scale. Of the total Ph.D.s in all science and engineering fields, 24 percent were earned by non-United States citizens on temporary visas. In both mathematical sciences and engineering, temporary visa holders accounted for more than 41 percent. Including non-United States citizens on permanent visas puts the ratios even higher—29 percent in all science and engineering fields, 46 and 50 percent in the mathematical sciences and engineering. National Science Board, *Science and Engineering Indicators—1989* (Washington, D.C.: U.S. Government Printing Office), pp. 225, 227.

17. See Richard J. Murnane, "Education and Productivity of the Workforce: Looking Ahead," in Robert E. Litan et al., eds., *American Living Standards: Threats and Challenges* (Washington, D.C.: Brookings Institution, 1988), pp. 215–45.

18. For an outline of the direct and indirect costs and benefits of military spending on the United States economy see Dertouzos et al., op. cit., pp. 114–16.

19. Surveys of employers show a higher growth rate of jobs than do surveys of households. That implies either more multiple job-holding or an increase in the employment of illegal aliens. Moreover, the number of apprehensions of illegal aliens increased from about 0.9 million in 1980 to about 1.8 million in 1986. Those figures suggest an "undetected" gross inflow "well above a half million" per year between 1985 and 1988. See Paul O. Flaim, "How Many New Jobs Since 1982? Data from Two Surveys Differ," *Monthly Labor Review*, Vol. 112, No. 8 (August 1989), pp. 10–15.

20. A growing percentage of the population under age eighteen lives in families classified as poor (i.e., 20 percent in 1986 versus 16 percent in 1979). Equity issues aside, the trend toward impoverishment of the young has negative

implications for United States productivity. Evidence suggests that children who grow up in poverty typically do poorly in school and encounter difficulties in the labor market. Frank Levy, "Incomes, Families, and Living Standards," and Richard J. Murnane, "Education and the Productivity of the Work Force: Looking Ahead," in Litan et al., op. cit., 226–29.

21. The United States, however, seems better off in this respect than its major competitors. In Europe, generous welfare benefits perhaps make unemployment preferable to low-paying service jobs. See "Tables and Graphs," Tables 9 and 17.

22. From 1980 to 1987, the United States securities industry—the high-flying segment of the financial services sector—doubled its employment to 261,000. Since 1987, jobs have been reduced by 40,000. See Dominic Ziegler, "In Search of the Crock of Gold: A Survey of the International Capital Markets," *The Economist,* July 21, 1990. The remainder of the financial sector, although still creating jobs through 1989, was not doing so as rapidly as in the mid-1980s. See *Monthly Labor Review,* statistics in various issues in the 1980s.

23. There are numerous ways to rank the world's banks. The most common methods are to compare their total assets or shareholders' equity. Recent rankings of these types are found in "Tables and Graphs," Table 18. For a ranking of the world's banks by quality—solvency, capital adequacy, profitability, and management quality—see "Leaders of the Pack," *Euromoney,* December 1990.

24. Robert B. Reich, *The Work of Nations: Preparing Ourselves for 21st Century Capitalism* (New York: Alfred A. Knopf, 1991), pp. 98–102.

25. Ibid., p. 81.

26. Reich believes these functional categories cover more than three out of four American jobs. The rest are farmers and miners—or government employees, including public school teachers, or those working in regulated or defense industries sheltered from global competition. Ibid., pp. 173–80.

27. Ibid., p. 184.

28. Ibid., pp. 185–95.
29. Ibid., p. 209, including note 1.
30. Paul Kennedy, *The Rise and Fall of the Great Powers: Economic Change and Military Conflict from 1550 to 2000* (New York: Random House, 1987), p. 531.

Selected Bibliography

A complete bibliography on the subjects covered in this book would be a major work in itself. Listed here are some general secondary sources particularly useful in shaping my own general analysis. More specific studies are mentioned in the Notes.

Aging America: Trends and Projections, annotated. An Information Paper to the Special Committee on Aging, United States Senate. Washington, D.C.: U.S. Government Printing Office, 1990.

Bergsten, C. Fred. "Debtor America and the Budget Deficit." Statement before the Committee on the Budget, U.S. House of Representatives, March 2, 1988.

Biedenkopf, Kurt H. "The Federal Republic of Germany: Old Miracles and New Challenges." In David P. Calleo and Claudia Morgenstern, eds., *Recasting Europe's Economies: National Strategies in the 1980s.* Lanham, Md.: University Press of America, 1990.

Blair, Margaret M., and Robert Litan. "Corporate Leverage and Leveraged Buyouts in the Eighties." In John B. Shoven and Joel Waldfogel, eds., *Debt, Taxes, and Corporate Restructuring.* Washington, D.C.: Brookings Institution, 1990.

Blinder, Alan S., and Robert M. Solow. "Analytical Foundations of Fiscal Policy," *The Economics of Public Finance*. Washington, D.C.: Brookings Institution, 1974.

Bluestone, Barry, and Bennett Harrison. *The Deindustrialization of America: Plant Closings, Community Abandonment, and the Dismantling of Basic Industry*. New York: Basic Books, 1982.

Bosworth, Barry P. "Taxes and the Investment Recovery." In *Brookings Papers on Economic Activity*, No. 1 (Washington, D.C.: Brookings Institution, 1985), pp. 1–47.

Brittan, Samuel. "Can Democracy Manage an Economy?" In Robert Skidelsky, ed., *The End of the Keynesian Era: Essays on the Disintegration of the Keynesian Political Economy*. New York: Holmes and Meier, 1977.

Brumbaugh, R. Dan, Jr., and Andrew S. Carron. "The Thrift Industry Crisis." In *Brookings Papers on Economic Activity*, No. 2 (1987), pp. 349–89.

Bryant, Ralph C. *International Fiscal Intermediation*. Washington, D.C.: Brookings Institution, 1987).

Cagan, Phillip. *Persistent Inflation: Historic and Political Essays*. New York: Columbia University Press, 1979.

Calleo, David P. *Beyond American Hegemony: The Future of the Western Alliance*. New York: Basic Books, 1987.

———. *The Imperious Economy*. Cambridge, Mass.: Harvard University Press, 1982.

———, and Claudia Morgenstern, eds. *Recasting Europe's Economies: National Strategies in the 1980s*. Lanham, Md.: University Press of America, 1990.

———, and Benjamin M. Rowland. *America and the World Political Economy*. Bloomington: Indiana University Press, 1973.

Carron, Andrew S. *The Plight of the Thrift Institutions*. Washington, D.C.: Brookings Institution, 1982.

Cleveland, Harold van Buren. "Europe in the Economic Crisis of Our Time: Macroeconomic Policies and Macroeconomic Constraints." In David P. Calleo and Claudia Morgenstern, eds.,

Recasting Europe's Economies: National Strategies in the 1980s. Lanham, Md.: University Press of America, 1990.

————, and W. H. Bruce Brittain. *The Great Inflation: A Monetarist View.* Washington, D.C.: National Planning Association, 1976.

Corden, W. Max. *Inflation, Exchange Rates, and the World Economy.* Chicago: University of Chicago Press, 1986.

Crandall, Robert W. "The Regional Shift of U.S. Economic Activity." In Robert E. Litan et al., eds., *American Living Standards: Threats and Challenges.* Washington, D.C.: Brookings Institution, 1988.

Dertouzos, Michael L., et al. *Made in America: Regaining the Productive Edge.* Cambridge, Mass.: MIT Press, 1989.

Dornbusch, Rudiger. *Dollars, Debts, and Deficits.* Cambridge, Mass.: MIT Press, 1986.

Eisner, Robert. "Debunking the Conventional Wisdom in Economic Policy." *Challenge,* May–June 1990, pp. 4–11.

————. *How Real Is the Federal Deficit?* New York: The Free Press, 1986.

Friedman, Benjamin M. *Day of Reckoning: The Consequences of American Economic Policy Under Reagan and After.* New York: Random House, 1988.

Gaddis, John Lewis. *Strategies of Containment: A Critical Appraisal of Postwar National Security Policy.* New York: Oxford University Press, 1982.

Goldstein, Joshua S. *Long Cycles: Prosperity and War in the Modern Age.* New Haven, Conn.: Yale University Press, 1988.

Greider, William. *Secrets of the Temple: How the Federal Reserve Runs the Country.* New York: Simon & Schuster, 1987.

————. *The Trouble with Money.* Knoxville, Tenn.: Whittle Direct Books, Larger Agenda Series, 1989.

Haberler, Gottfried, "Further Thoughts on International Policy Coordination," in Paul V. Volcker, et al., *International Mon-*

etary Cooperation: Essays in Honor of Henry C. Wallich. Essays in International Finance, No. 169. Princeton, NJ: Princeton University, December, 1987, 23–30.

Heilbroner, Robert, and Peter Bernstein. *The Debt and the Deficit: False Alarms/Real Possibilities.* (New York: W.W. Norton & Co., 1989.

Hicks, John. *The Crisis in Keynesian Economics.* New York: Basic Books, 1974.

Hooper, Peter, and Catherine L. Mann. *The Emergence and Persistence of the U.S. External Imbalance, 1980–87.* Princeton Studies in International Finance, No. 65, October 1989.

Hume, David. *Essays, Moral, Political, and Literary.* London: Grant Richards, 1903.

Kaim-Candle, P. R. *Comparative Social Policy and Social Security.* London: Martin Robertson Co., 1973.

Kennedy, Paul. *The Rise and Fall of the Great Powers: Economic Change and Military Conflict from 1550–2000.* New York: Random House, 1987.

Keynes, John Maynard. *Essays in Persuasion.* New York: W.W. Norton & Co., 1963.

Kindleberger, Charles P. *Manias, Panics, and Crashes.* New York: Basic Books, 1989.

Krugman, Paul. *The Age of Diminished Expectations.* Cambridge, Mass.: MIT Press, 1990.

La Malfa, Giorgio. "Italy: New Dilemmas and Old Evasions." In David P. Calleo and Claudia Morgenstern, eds., *Recasting Europe's Economies: National Strategies in the 1980s.* Lanham, Md.: University Press of America, 1990.

Litan, Robert E. *What Should Banks Do?* Washington, D.C.: Brookings Institution, 1987.

———, et al., eds. *American Living Standards: Threats and Challenges.* Washington, D.C.: Brookings Institution, 1988.

Luttwak, Edward N. *The Pentagon and the Art of War.* New York: Simon and Schuster, 1984.

Marris, Stephen. *Deficits and the Dollar: The World Economy at Risk,* updated ed. Analyses in International Economics No. 14. Washington, D.C.: Institute for International Economics, 1987.

McCarthy, Patrick. "France Faces Reality: Rigueur and the Germans." In David P. Calleo and Claudia Morgenstern, eds., *Recasting Europe's Economies: National Strategies in the 1980s.* Lanham, Md.: University Press of America, 1990.

Minarik, Joseph J. "Family Incomes." In Isabel V. Sawhill, ed., *Challenge to Leadership.* Washington, D.C.: The Urban Institute Press, 1988.

Minsky, Hyman P. *Stabilizing an Unstable Economy.* A Twentieth Century Fund Book. New Haven, Conn.: Yale University Press, 1986.

Moynihan, Daniel P. *Deficit by Default: New York State and the Federal Fisc: XIV, Fiscal Year 1989,* 14th annual ed. Washington, D.C.: July 31, 1990.

Murnane, Richard J. "Education and Productivity of the Workforce: Looking Ahead." In Robert E. Litan et al., eds., *American Living Standards: Threats and Challenges.* Washington, D.C.: Brookings Institution, 1988, pp. 215–45.

Organization for Economic Cooperation & Development (OECD). *Economic Surveys, France, 1986/1987.* Paris: OECD, 1987.

————. *Economic Surveys of France, 1989/1990.* Paris: OECD, 1990.

————. *Economic Surveys of Germany, 1989/1990.* Paris: OECD, 1990.

————. *Economies in Transition: Structural Adjustment in OECD Countries.* Paris: OECD, 1989.

————. *Health Care Systems in Transition.* Paris: OECD, 1990.

————. *The Role of the Public Sector.* Paris: OECD, 1985.

———. *Public Expenditure on Income Maintenance.* Paris: OECD, 1976.

Pechman, Joseph A. *Federal Tax Policy.* Washington, D.C.: Brookings Institution, 1987.

———. "The Future of the Income Tax," *Brookings General Series Reprints No. 437.* Washington, D.C.: Brookings Institution, 1990.

———. *Who Paid the Taxes, 1966–85?* Washington, D.C.: Brookings Institution, 1985.

Pedone, Antonio. "Public Expenditure." In Andrea Boltho, *The European Economy: Growth and Crisis.* Oxford, U.K.: Oxford University Press, 1982, pp. 390–409.

Piore, Michael J., and Charles F. Sabel. *The Second Industrial Divide: Possibilities for Prosperity.* New York: Basic Books, 1984.

Rasell, M. Edith, and Lawrence Mishel. *Shortchanging Education: How U.S. Spending on Grades K-12 Lags Behind Other Industrial Nations.* Washington, D.C.: Economic Policy Institute, 1990.

"Recognizing Federal Underwriting Risks," *Budget of the United States Government: Fiscal Year 1991.* Washington, D.C.: U.S. Government Printing Office, 1990.

Reich, Robert B. *The Work of Nations: Preparing Ourselves for 21st Century Capitalism.* New York: Alfred A. Knopf, 1991.

Rohatyn, Felix G. *The Twenty-Year Century; Essays on Economics and Public Finance.* New York: Random House, 1983.

Rostow, W.W. *The World Economy: History and Prospect.* Austin: University of Texas Press, 1978.

Rousseas, Stephen. "Can the U.S. Financial System Survive the Revolution?" *Challenge,* March–April 1989, pp. 39–43.

Rubin, Laura S. "The Current Fiscal Situation in State and Local Governments." *Federal Reserve Bulletin,* December 1990, pp. 1009–18.

Rueff, Jacques. *The Monetary Sin of the West.* New York: Macmillan, 1972.

———. *Oeuvres Complètes,* Vol. III, *Politique Économique.* Paris: Plon and Lehrman Institute, 1979.

Sachs, Jeffrey D., ed. *Developing Country Debt and Economic Performance.* National Bureau of Economic Research Project Report. Chicago: University of Chicago Press, 1989.

Saunders, Peter, and Friedrich Klau. "The Role of the Public Sector: Causes and Consequences of the Growth of Government." *OECD Economic Studies,* No. 4, Spring 1985.

Schumpeter, Joseph A. *Capitalism, Socialism, and Democracy.* New York: Harper and Row, 1950.

Shonfield, Andrew. *Modern Capitalism: The Changing Balance of Public and Private Power.* New York: Oxford University Press, 1965.

Skidelsky, Robert. "Britain: Mrs. Thatcher's Revolution." In David P. Calleo and Claudia Morgenstern, eds., *Recasting Europe's Economies: National Strategies in the 1980s.* Lanham, Md.: University Press of America, 1990.

———. "The Political Meaning of the Keynesian Revolution." In Robert Skidelsky, ed., *The End of the Keynesian Era: Essays on the Disintegration of the Keynesian Political Economy.* New York: Holmes and Meier, 1977.

———. "The Revolt Against the Victorians." In Robert Skidelsky, ed., *The End of the Keynesian Era: Essays on the Disintegration of the Keynesian Political Economy.* New York: Holmes and Meier, 1977.

Smith, Roy C. *The Money Wars: The Rise and Fall of the Great Buyout Boom of the 1980s.* New York: Dutton, 1990.

Stein, Herbert. *The Fiscal Revolution in America.* Chicago: University of Chicago, 1969.

———. *Presidential Economics: The Making of Economic Policy from Roosevelt to Reagan and Beyond.* Washington, D.C.: American Enterprise Institute, 1988.

Steuerle, C. Eugene. "Federal Policy and the Accumulation of Private Debt." In John B. Shoven and Joel Waldfogel, eds.,

Debt, Taxes, and Corporate Restructuring. Washington, D.C.: Brookings Institution, 1990.

Stockman, David. *The Triumph of Politics.* New York: Harper and Row, 1986.

Strange, Susan. *Casino Capitalism.* Oxford, U.K.: Basil Blackwell, 1986.

————. "International Monetary Relations." In Andrew Shonfield, ed., *International Economic Relations of the Western World, 1959–1971,* Vol. II. London: Oxford University Press, 1976.

Triffin, Robert. *Gold and the Dollar Crisis: The Future of Convertibility.* New Haven: Yale University Press, 1960.

————. "The Paper-Exchange Standard: 1971–19??," in Paul A. Volcker, et al., *International Monetary Cooperation: Essays in Honor of Henry C. Wallich.* Essays in International Finance, No. 169. Princeton, NJ: Princeton University, December 1987, 70–85.

Vernon, Raymond. "International Investment and International Trade in the Product Cycle." *Quarterly Journal of Economics,* May 1966, pp. 190–207.

White, Joseph, and Aaron Wildavsky. *The Deficit and the Public Interest: The Search for Responsible Budgeting in the 1980s.* Berkeley: University of California Press, Russell Sage Foundation, 1989.

Zysman, John. *Governments, Markets, and Growth: Financial Systems and the Politics of Industrial Change.* Ithaca, N.Y.: Cornell University Press, 1983.

Index

Page numbers in **boldface** refer
    to tables and graphs.

absorption:
    consumption and, 31–32, 73–
        74, 77
    defined, 31
    inefficiency and, 84
    investment and, 31–32
    overseas, 105
    as percentage of GDP, **74**
    redefined, 105
    twin deficits and, 31–33
Adenauer, Konrad, 190
agriculture, 64–65, **223, 224**
    employment in, **202**
Allied–Lyons, 264n
ANZUS Pact, 238n
Arab-Israeli War (1973), 111
arbitrage, monetary instability
        and, 138
Aristotle, 66
arms race, third world and, 56
assets:
    foreign, 16–17, 155–156
    fraudulent transfer of, 260n

Japanese vs. U.S., 227n
of social security fund, 44–45
Atomic Energy Commission, 148
Australia, 237n, 238n

baby boomers, 268n–269n
Baghdad Pact, 239n
balance of payments (external)
        deficit(s), 102–121, 248n–
        249n, 250n
    Bretton Woods formula and,
        104–109
    with current-account surplus,
        104–105
    Nixon formula and, 109–116
    Reagan formula and, 116–120
    in twin deficits, 31–33
balance of power, 57
Bank of France, 71
bankruptcy, economic role of, 161
banks, banking:
    crisis in, 115
    ranking of, 274n
    world's largest, **203**
    see also finance industry
Belgium, 242n, 255n
Bentham, Jeremy, 184, 228n

borrowing, 13–15, 16, 27, 29, 39,
    70, 77, 119, 125, 158
  domestic, 30, 36–37, 42
  flow of U.S., **205**
  foreign, 30–31, 33, 37, 42,
    120–121
  Gulf War and, 143–144
  national, **201**
  Ponzi finance and, 150, 151
  private, "crowding out" of, 30,
    42, 229n
  "recycled" funds and, 115
  speculative financing and, 130–
    131
  takeovers and, 131
  tax laws favoring, 131
  see also fiscal deficit
Bosanquet, Bernard, 228n
Bosworth, Barry P., 258n
bracket creep, 99, 100, 109, 150,
    151
  inflation and, 92, 96, 109
  tax revolt and, 91–92
Bradley, Francis Herbert, 228n
Brady, Nicholas, 135
Bretton Woods formula, 103–
    109, 110, 154, 187, 249n
  balance of payments deficits
    and, 104–109
  collapse of, 107–109
  Nixon formula and, 111, 113
  offshore capital markets and,
    106
  reserve currency and, 105–106
  Vietnam War and, 108
budget(s), 13
  capital, 229n, 232n
  current dollars used in, 49
  fiscal politics and, 26–29
  full-employment, 35–36, 229n
  percentage breakdown of fed-
    eral, **50**
  Ponzi factor of, 145
  recession and balancing of, 35
  state and local, in 1980s, 267n
  see also civil budget; defense
    budget

Bundesbank, 71, 140, 242n
burden-sharing, defense expen-
    ditures and, 59, 155, 156–
    157, 176
bureaucracy, 55, 83, 182
Burke, Edmund, 181
Bush, George, 86
  GATT and, 270n
  new taxes and, 147
Bush administration, 16, 139, 144

Canada, 107
capital, 28, 32, **162,** 269n
  current expenditures and, 28,
    43–44
  flight of, 38
  future European need for,
    152–153
capital-account deficit, 32, 265n,
    270n–271n
capital-account surplus, 32, 271n
capital budget, 229n, 232n
capitalism, European, 69
Carter, Jimmy, 14, 98, 230n
  Volcker appointed by, 116
Carter administration, 11, 115
central government financial bal-
    ances, **70**
central government spending, **72,
    73**
Chiang Kai-shek, 239n
China, People's Republic of, 58
Chrysler Corporation, 135, 262n
civil budget, 60–65, 148–150
  demography and, 61, 149
  education and, 60, 62–63, 149
  environment and, 64, 148
  general government and, 64–
    65
  health care and, 60–61, 62, 63
  human resources and, 60–61,
    63–64
  infrastructure and, 148
  Medicare and, 60–61, 62
  physical resources and, 60, 64,
    148
  social security and, 60, 61–62

technology and, 64–65
see also budget
cold war, 123, 176, 178
    end of, 148
    Soviet Union and, 57, 58, 189–
        190
Coleridge, Samuel Taylor, 228n
Common Market (European Eco-
    nomic Community), 17,
    103
composite deflator, 235n
compound interest, 151
Congress, U.S., 26, 58, 265n–
    266n, 267n
    budget process and, 183
    GATT and, 270n
    S and L deregulation and, 137
    social security tax increased by,
        91–92, 116
    tax increase resisted by, 86
    weapon procurement and, 55
conscription, 56
constant dollars, 47–48
    current dollars vs., 49–51
consumer price index (CPI), 96,
    113, **206,** 235n
consumption, 31, 33, 85, 90
    absorption and, 31–32, 73–74,
        77
    debt and, 129
    defense spending and, 129
    expenditures for, **75**
    tax on, 90
containment policy, 57, 58
Continental Illinois, 129
controls, 41, 59, 111, 113
cost-plus contracts, 55
cost trends, 53, 54, 55
Cray Research, 165
"creative financing," 130
credit, 14, 117, 252n
    demand for, 29
    federal spending and, 64
    financial industry and, 133
    foreign, 12, 155–156
    inflation of, 33–40, 108, 112,
        113, 130, 151

investment and, 129, 150
    outflow of, 106
    speculation and, 130
"crowding out," 30, 42, 229n
currency, 231n–232n
    balance of payments and, 105
    depreciation of, 38–39
    gold-exchange standard and,
        105–107
    hedging and, 138–139
    reserve, 105–106
    tight, 114
    see also dollar, U.S.
current-account balance, 114,
    248n–249n
current-account deficit, 31–32,
    84, 120, 125, 143, 264n–
    265n
current-account surplus, 104–105
current dollars, constant dollars
    vs., 49–51

debt, 13, 16, 73, 163, 171, 270n
    compound interest and, 151
    consumption and, 129
    Europe and, 148, 154
    federal, GNP and, **208, 209**
    in finance industry crisis, 129–
        132
    foreign savings and, 151, 152
    GDP relative to, 83
    GNP and, 13, 119, 150, **208,
        209,** 235n
    growth of, 129, 143
    income and, 128
    inflation and, 33, 40, 154–155
    in Latin American crisis, 133
    in Mexican crisis, 117, 129
    overhang and, 106
    servicing of, 13
    social security and, 28, 233n
    third world, 134, 148, 154,
        262n
    in World War II, 259n
defense budget, 54–60
    components of, 54
    manpower costs and, 57

defense budget (*continued*)
  military strategy and, 56–57
  NATO and, 57
  Soviet Union and, 158, 176,
    177
  spending and, 54–57
  technology and, 56, 124–125
  U.S. world role and, 59–60
  weapon procurement and, 55
  weapons systems and, 58
  see also budget
Defense Department, U.S.:
  business culture of, 56
  procurement procedures of,
    54–55
defense spending, 13, 48, **50,** 69,
    84, **99,** 116, 210*n*, 211*n*,
    213*n*
  burden-sharing and, 59, 155,
    156–157, 176
  consumption and, 129
  cost of, 76–78
  cycles of, 58, 237*n*–238*n*
  GDP and, 75–76
  GNP and, 18, 21, 175, **199**
  growth of, 145, **146**
  Gulf War and, 59, 143–144,
    152–153, 155, 156–157
  by Japan, **199,** 241*n*–242*n*
  Reagan deficit and, 99, 100–
    101
  structural improvements in,
    147–148
  U.S. world role and, 59–60,
    77–78, 144, 147–148, 175
  weapon procurement and, 55
  see also spending
deficit(s):
  capital-account, 32, 265*n*,
    270*n*–271*n*
  current-account, 31–32, 84,
    120, 125, 143, 264*n*–265*n*
  see also balance of payments
    deficit; fiscal deficit
deflation, 111
de Gaulle, Charles, 107, 108, 190,
    249*n*

Democratic party, U.S. 86
Depression, Great, *see* Great
    Depression
deregulation, 130, 133, 137, 180–
    181
de Tocqueville, Alexis, 181
direct taxes, 90
"disintermediation," 132
dissaving, 21, 32, 173, 269*n*
dividends, 131
dollar, U.S., 14, 15, 32, 71, 87,
    101, 118, 249*n*, 250*n*
  constant, 47–48
  current vs. constant, 49–51
  declining, 153
  floating, 104, 108–109, 111–
    112, 139, 187
  foreign capital and, 117
  Germany and, 107–108
  gold and, *see* gold-exchange
    standard
  Gulf War and, 154
  inflation and depreciation of,
    155
  Japan and, 107–108
  Nixon formula and, 111–113
  overvalued, 31, 108, 109, 119,
    120
  Reagan formula and, 126
  as reserve currency, 105–106
  trade and collapse of, 155
  unstable, 125
Dukakis, Michael S., 86

Economic Recovery Tax Act
    (1981), 254*n*
Economic Report of the President
    (1984), 144, 265*n*
Economic Statistics Initiative,
    265*n*
economy, U.S.:
  chronic imbalances in, 124–125
  "identity problem" of, 167
  new jobs and, 126–127
  political power and, 41
education, 13, 14, **20,** 21, 26, 27,
    29, 66, **75,** 77, 90, 109–

110, 172, 173, 214n, 215n,
    228n
civil budget and, 60, 62–63,
    149
family income and, 95
federal spending for, 267n
GNP and spending on, 63–64
outlays for, **192, 220,** 267n
technology and, 166–167
Eisenhower, Dwight D., 59, 109
Eisenhower administration, 239n
election of 1972, 113
employment:
    in agriculture, **202**
    civilian, **202**
    classification of, 169
    deficits and, 35, 144
    in finance industry, 168, 274n
    in France, **197, 202**
    in Germany, **197, 202**
    immigrants and, 167–168
    inflation and, 33–34, 150
    investment and, 126–127
    in Japan, **202**
    in manufacturing, **196,** 258n–
        259n
    new jobs and, 126–127
    productivity and, 123–124
    service sector and, 167–168
    total, **197**
energy, 64, **221, 222**
Energy Department, U.S., 267n
"enterprise web," 169
entitlements, 19, 23, 89
environment, 14, 19
    civil budget and, 64, 148
Eurodollar market, 106, 109,
    249n
Europe, 15, 57, 58, 78, 87, 89,
    100, 120, 123, 125, 132,
    139, 143, 151, 171, 177,
    188, 190–191, 250n
    attitude toward public spend-
        ing in, 21
    capitalism in, 69
    capital needs of, 152–153
    consumption taxes in, 90

declining dollar and, 126
Eastern Europe and future of,
    152
entitlement policy in, 19
"Eurosclerosis" in, 123
exported credit and, 106
global economy and, 157–158
gold-exchange standard re-
    sented by, 107
health care system in, 21–22,
    82
import policy of, 114
investment potential of, 151–
    153
nineteenth-century debts to, 13
oil shock and, 115
pensions in, 89–90
public spending in, 71–73, 75,
    88, 95
social security in, 62
Soviet Union and future of, 152
unemployment in, 162
U.S. fiscal deficit and, 117–118
U.S. tax policy vs. tax policies
    of, 20–22
U.S. tax rates and, 88
U.S. troops in, 237n
U.S. world role and, 152–153,
    177
welfare benefits in, 274n
Europe, Eastern, 16, 59, 134, 188
    capital demand vs. supply in,
        269n
    debt and, 148, 154
    economic potential of, 159
    Europe's future and, 152
    Western Europe contrasted
        with, 189
European Community (EC), 15,
    16, 140, 151–152, 163,
    177, 188–189, 190, 191
    unified Germany and, 156
    U.S. hegemony and, 157–158
European Economic Community
    (Common Market), 17, 103
European Monetary System
    (EMS), 15, 140, 163, 242n

European Monetary System (*cont.*)
France and, 242*n*
exchange rates, 12, 15, 120, 256*n*
fixed, 103–104, 105, 106, 109
floating, 104, 108–109, 111–112, 139, 187
exported inflation, 110–111
export market shares, **204**
external deficits, *see* balance of payments deficits

family income:
median, **93,** 94
single wage-earner, 94
two wage-earner, 94–95
Federal Deposit Insurance Corporation, 148
Federal Reserve, 71, 113, 114, 117, 120, 128, 130, 154, 155, 270*n*
inflation and, 96
Johnson's criticism of, 108
Nixon's reliance on, 112
Volcker appointed to, 116
federal spending, *see* budget; civil budget; defense spending; spending
feminist movement, 95
finance industry:
bank failures in, 148
changing technology and, 132
credit and, 133
debt crisis in, 129–132
deregulation and, 130, 133
employment in, 168, 274*n*
erratic dollar and, 125
government policy and, 138–139
hedging and, 130–131
interest rates and, 139–140
monetary instability and, 138–139
monetary policy and, 133–134
speculation practiced by, 130–131
structural problems of, 132–134

takeovers and, 130–131
technology and, 132
treatment of federal guarantees to, 28–29
world interest rates and, 139–140
fiscal deficit(s):
accounting arguments and, 27–28
arguments for complacency about, 12–23
benefits of, 12, 13
Bush administration and, 16
capital vs. current expenditures and, 43–44
creating money (monetization) and, 33–40, 42, 112
domestic borrowing and, 30, 36–37, 42
economy and, 14
employment and, 144
Europe and, 117–118
Federal Reserve and, 112
federal spending and, 65–67
foreign borrowing and, 30–31, 33, 37, 42
foreign competition and, 16–17
foreign savings and, 117–119, 157–158
of France, Germany, U.S. contrasted, 70–71, 83–84
global economy and, 157–158
growth in, **110**
inflation and, 33–40
of Italy, 242*n*
Japan and, 117–119
as not mattering, 12, 13–17
off-budget expenditures and, 28, 44–46
oscillating monetary policy and, 15
power and, 40–41
raising taxes as solution to, 12, 20–23
recession and, 144
savings and, 117–119, 157–158

self-generating character of, 65
social security and, 44–45, 234n
spending less as solution to, 12,
    18–20
stagflation and, 39
state and local governments
    and, 148–149
structural nature of, 144–146
tax cuts and, 20, 34–37
in theory, 42–43
in twin deficit, 31–33, 84, 142
Uruguay Round and, 153
U.S. political system and, 22, 23
way out of, 23–24
fixed exchange rates, 103–104,
    105, 106, 109
floating exchange rates, 104,
    108–109, 111–112, 139,
    187
Ford Motor Company, 262n
foreign labor, 164–172
in U.S., 167–168
foreign savings, 117–119, 151,
    152, 157–158, 187
France, 15, 17, **19**, 22, 78, 80,
    89, 127, 128, 173, 177,
    188, 190–191, **206,** 243n,
    246n
civilian employment in, **202**
current receipts of, **194**
defense industry of, 55
European Monetary System
    and, 242n
export market shares of, **204–
    205**
fixed capital formation of, **162**
GDP of, 74, 75, 76
gold-exchange standard re-
    sented by, 107
health care in, 84
industrial restructuring in,
    161–163, 167
infant mortality rate in, **79**
key statistics for, **193**
long-duration unemployment
    in, **202**
military expenditures of, **199**

monetary policy of, 71, 118,
    163, 231n, 242n
oil imports of, 265n
public spending of, 71–73, 84,
    245n
R and D expenditures of,
    236n–237n
real GDP of, **197**
social security tax in, 89–90
statism in, 140–141
supply-side policy adopted by,
    117–118, 163
total employment in, **197**
unemployment rates of, **197**
U.S. and German fiscal deficits
    vs. fiscal deficit of, 70–71,
    83–84
U.S. GNP vs. GNP of, 69
U.S. monetary policy vs. mon-
    etary policy of, 164
free-riders, 102, 228n
full-employment   (structural)
    budget, 35–36, 229n

General   Accounting   Office
    (GAO), 135
General Agreement on Tariffs
    and Trade (GATT), 270n
general government financial
    balances, **70**
General Motors Corporation,
    262n
German Monetary Union, 242n
Germany, Federal Republic of
    (West), 15, 57, 78, 80, **89,**
    119, 171, 172, 173, 188,
    190–191, **206,** 241n, 243n,
    246n, 269n
civilian employment in, **202**
current-account surplus of, 32
current receipts of, **194**
export market shares of, **204–
    205**
fixed capital formation of, **162**
GDP of, 74, 75, 76
health care in, 82, 84

Germany, Federal Rep. of (*cont.*)
  industrial restructuring in, 161–163, 167
  infant mortality rate of, **79**
  inflation in, 71
  key statistics for, **193**
  long-duration unemployment in, **202**
  military expenditures of, **199**
  monetary policy of, 71, 118, 163
  oil imports of, 265*n*
  productivity in, 127, 128
  public spending by, 71–73, 84, 245*n*
  R and D expenditures of, 236*n*
  real GDP of, **197**
  social security tax in, 89–90
  statism in, 140–141
  supply-side policy adopted by, 117–118, 163
  total employment in, **197**
  unemployment rates of, **197**
  U.S. and French fiscal deficits vs. fiscal deficit of, 70–71, 83–84
  U.S. dollar and, 107–108
  U.S. GNP vs. GNP of, 69
  U.S. monetary policy vs. monetary policy of, 164
Germany, unified, 16, 17, **19**, 22, 141, 151–152, 188
  burden-sharing and, 155
  European Community and, 156
Glasnost, 188
gold-exchange standard, 104, 249*n*
  currency and, 105–107
  European resentment of, 107
  see also Bretton Woods formula government final consumption expenditure, **20**
government outlays and receipts, **20, 71**
Great Britain, 14, 17, 108, 177, 229*n*, 242*n*

health care costs controlled by, 82
IMF and, 154, 270*n*
U.S. contrasted with, 241*n*
Great Depression, 33, 34, 107, 115
  Schumpeter's view of, 161
Great Society, 36
Gross Domestic Product (GDP), **20**, 49, **127**
  absorption as percentage of, **74**
  consumption expenditure as percentage of, **75,** 76
  debt relative to, 83
  defense spending and, 75–76
  of France, 74, 75, 76
  of Germany, 74, 75, 76, **197**
  government financial balances and, **70**
  government spending and, 88
  growth of, **114**
  growth rate and, 125
  Japan's real, **197**
  manufacturing shares of, **196**
  price deflator for, **76**
  real, **197**
  spending and taxes as percentage of, **73**
  tax rate and, 86
  tax receipts as percentage of, **92**
  U.S. receipts and outlays as percentage of, **194**
"gross fixed capital formation," 74
Gross National Product (GNP), 49, 53, 92, 98, **99,** 100, 241*n*, 248*n*
  budget functions and, 51
  debt and, 13, 119, 150, **208, 209,** 235*n*
  defense spending and, 18, 21, 175, **199**
  deflator for, 50, 235*n*
  federal deficit and, 143, 153
  government financial balances and, **70**
  growth of, 47, **114, ** 129, **145**

human resources and, 63–64
inflation and, 150
military expenditures as percentage of, **199**
of 1989, 28, 46
social security and, 61–62, 63
and spending on education, 63–64
state and local taxes and, 91
technology and, 56
U.S. receipts and outlays as percentage of, **194**
"Group of Seven," 179
Guam, 237n
Gulf War, see Persian Gulf War

health care, 13, **20,** 21, 26, 75, **75, 76,** 90, **146,** 173, **214, 215**
civil budget and, 60–61, 62, 63
cost of, 22, 76, 80–81
deregulation and, 83
European system of, 21–22, 82
federal spending for, 268n
in France, 21–22, 84
in Germany, 21–22, 82, 84
in Great Britain, 82
increases in outlays for, **218**
inefficiency in, 22
infant mortality and, 78–79
insurance coverage and, 80–81
market system and, 81–83
outlays for, **192,** 268n
in Scandinavia, 82
technology and, 79, 81
health insurance, **80**
hedge financing, 130–131
currency and, 138–139
investment and, 138–139
Hegel, G.W.F., 228n
hegemony, nature of, 102–103
Hitler, Adolf, 14, 41
Hobbes, Thomas, 40
home ownership, 136
household taxes, **73**
human resources, 48–49, **50, 146,** 149
civil budget and, 60–61, 63–64

defense outlays and, 145
GNP and, 63–64
increases in outlays for, **216**
outlays for, **192, 210, 211, 215**
shares of functions for, **193, 214**
human rights, 181
Hume, David, 37, 38, 40
hyperinflation, 38–40

IBM, 165
Idealist tradition, 228n
IMF, see International Monetary Fund
immigrant labor, 168–171, 273n
income, 14, 51
debt and, 128
education and, 95
median, **93,** 94, 96
productivity and, 127–128
saving and, 128
tax on, 89, 91, 93–96
working-class, 128
indirect taxes, 90
industrial restructuring, 161–163, 167
infant mortality, 78–79, **79**
inflation, 14, 15, 16, 47, 93, 120, 125, **145,** 156, 159, 162, 163, 173, 187, 231n, 252n
addiction to, 37–40
bracket creep and, 92, 96, 109
of credit, 33–40, 108, 112, 113, 130, 151
debt and, 33, 40, 154–155
dollar depreciation and, 155
employment and, 33–34, 150
exported, 110–111
Federal Reserve and, 96
federal spending and, 49–50
fiscal deficit and, 33–40
as form of tax, 42
general revolt against, 116
in Germany, 71
GNP and, 150
investment and, 129, 150

inflation (*continued*)
  measurement of, 50–51
  monetary policy and, 36–37, 108
  money illusion and, 37, 38, 42, 150
  oil market and, 111
  overvalued dollar and, 109
  price lag and, 37–38
  of prices, 36, 38, 39, 49–50, 108, 110–111, 112, 113, 114, 126
  prolonged, 38–40, 42–43
  stagflation and, 39, 43
  stimulation by, 37–40
  by tax cuts, 34–37
  tax revolt and, 91, 96
  trade affected by, 38–39
  trade balance and, 39
  wage and price controls and, 59
in-person services, 169
interest, interest rates, 13, 15, 29, 117, 146, 150, 162–163, 187, 231n, 266n
  compound, 151
  finance industry and, 139–140
  foreign borrowing and, 30–31
  long-term, **198**
  measurements of, 255n
  monetary policy and, 31
  mortgage, 88
  net, *see* net interest
  Reagan formula and, 126
  S and L crisis and, 135–136
  speculation and, 130
International Harvester, 262n
International Monetary Fund (IMF), 244n, 250n
  Great Britain and, 154, 270n
international trade, *see* trade
investment, 11–12, 13, 14, 30, 74, 95, 105, 118, 119, 156, 163, 164, 172, 231n, 258n
  absorption and, 31–32
  credit and, 129, 150
  employment and, 126–127
  Europe's potential for, 152–153

  in foreign countries, 233n–234n
  hedging and, 138–139
  inflation and, 129, 150
  monetary policy and, 15, 138
  private vs. public, 43–44
  productivity and, 128, 171
  recession and, 16
  savings and, 31–33, 42
  speculation and, 15–17
  stagflation and, 39
Iran, 153
Iraq, 59, 144, 153, 156
isolationism, 18, 109
  new plural world and, 178–179
Italy, 17
  fiscal deficit of, 242n

Japan, 15, 16, 59, 132, 139, 141, 151, 152, 153, 159, 171, 172, 190, 256n, 269n
  burden-sharing and, 155
  civilian employment in, **202**
  current-account surplus of, 32
  current receipts of, **194**
  declining dollar and, 126
  export market shares of, **204–205**
  fixed capital formation in, **162**
  import policy of, 114
  industrial productivity of, 166
  long-duration unemployment in, **202**
  military expenditures by, **199,** 241n–242n
  pensions in, 68–69
  productivity in, 127, 128, 166
  R and D expenditures by, 236n
  real GNP of, **197**
  total employment in, **197**
  unemployment rates of, **197**
  U.S. assets vs. assets of, 227n
  U.S. dollar and, 107–108
  U.S. fiscal deficit and, 117–119
  U.S. growth vs. growth in, 125
  U.S. relationship with, 57–58

U.S. troops in, 237n
welfare capitalism and, 123
jobs, *see* employment
Johnson, Lyndon B., 36, 186
    Federal Reserve criticized by,
        108
Johnson administration, 37, 107,
    109, 251n
junk bonds, 15, 130, 131, 148

Kennedy, John F., 35–36, 108,
    186
Kennedy administration, 107, 109
Kennedy, Paul, 41, 178
Keynes, John Maynard, 33, 34–
    35, 36, 186, 230n
Keyserling, Leon, 58
Kohl, Helmut, 242n
Korea, People's Republic of
    (North), 58
Korea, Republic of (South), 57,
    237n
Korean War, 58, 116, 239n
Kuwait, 59, 144, 153, 180, 269n

labor:
    costs of, **196**
    foreign, *see* foreign labor
    immigrant, 168–171, 273n
    technology and, 166
"Laffer Curve," 36
Latin America:
    capital demand vs. supply in,
        269n
    debt crisis of, 133
libertarian tradition, 181–182,
    185
Lockheed Corporation, 135, 262n
locomotive theory, 115, 254n
long-duration unemployment,
    202
long-term, interest rates, **198**
"long wave" debate, 271n
Louis XIV, king of France, 41

manufacturing, **196,** 258n–259n
Marshall Plan, 64, 135

Marx, Karl, 170, 185
median family income, **93,** 94, 96
medical care, *see* health care
Medicare, 44, 99, 109, **146, 214,
    215,** 240n
    civil budget and, 60–61, 62
    increases in outlays for, **219**
    outlays for, **192**
Mexico, debt crisis of, 117, 129
middle class, 21, 22, 101
    decline of, 93–96
    pensions and, 90
    public spending as perceived
        by, 88
    tax revolt and, 91–96
Middle East, 146
    capital demand vs. supply in,
        269n
    future capital needs of, 153
Midland Bank, 264n
military personnel, 54, 56, **212,
    213**
military procurement,   54–55,
    212, 213
military spending, *see* defense
    spending
military strategy, 56–57
Minsky, Hyman, 230n
"missile gap," 59
Mondale, Walter F., 86
monetary policy:
    deficit and, 15, 33–34, 70–71
    finance industry and, 133–134
    floating rates and, 108
    of France, 71, 118, 163, 231n,
        242n
    of Germany, 71, 118, 163
    inflation and, 36–37, 108
    interest rates and, 31
    investment and, 15, 138
    loose, 14–15
    Nixon's reflationary, 108–109
    oil shock and, 115
    oscillating, 15
    Reagan formula and, 117–119
    speculation and, 138
    states and, 71

monetary policy (*continued*)
  statism and, 140–141
  stop-go, 15, 39, 109, 150, 162, 164
  taxes and, 36–37
  tight, 14–15, 96, 108, 125, 130, 134
  of U.S., 71, 164
money illusion, 37, 38, 42, 150
money supply, 37–38, 39, 70, 187
mortgage interest, 88
Moynihan, Daniel Patrick, 28, 233n
M2, **200,** 253n

national security, 57–60
National Security Council, *NSC-68* of, 58–59, 186, 238n
NATO (North Atlantic Treaty Organization), 58–59, 88, 179, 237n, 243n
natural resources, 64, **221, 222**
neofederalist policy, 110
neoisolationism, 109, 111
  new plural world and, 178–179
  Vietnam War and, 186–187
neo-Keynesianism, 186–187
Netherlands, 17, 242n
net interest, 48, **50,** 65, 145, **146,** 151
  federal outlays for, **210, 211**
net national product (NNP), 96–97, **97**
"New Economic Policy," 111
"New World Order," 144
New York, N.Y., 133, 180, 262n
New Zealand, 238n
Nietzsche, Friedrich Wilhelm, 40
Nixon, Richard M., 117, 155
  Federal Reserve relied upon by, 112
  problems facing, 109–111
  reflationary policy of, 108–109
Nixon formula, 103, 104, 111–116, 125, 134
  bank bonanza and, 115

  Bretton Woods formula and, 111, 113
  fall of, 115–116
  floating dollar and, 112–113
  oil crisis and, 113–115
  stagflation and, 154–155
North Atlantic Treaty Organization (NATO), 58–59, 88, 179, 237n, 243n
  defense budget and, 57
NSC-68, 58–59, 186, 238n
nuclear deterrence, 57, 78
nuclear retaliation strategy, 59

off-budget spending, 28, 44–46
"offshore" capital market, 106
oil, oil market, 118, 134, 253n–254n
  French imports of, 265n
  German imports of, 265n
  inflation and, 111
  locomotive theory and, 115
  monetary policy and, 115
  Nixon formula and, 113–115
  U.S. banks and, 115
  U.S. dependence on, 144
operation and maintenance (O and M), 54
Organization of Petroleum Exporting Countries (OPEC), 111, 115, 116, 134, 168, 254n
overabsorption, 32, 105, 156, 164
  production and, 105
  world's industrial structure and, 158–159
overconsumption, 73–74
  public vs. private, 75–76
overhang, 106–107
oversaving, 115
overseas absorption, 105
overvalued dollar, 31, 108, 109, 119, 120

Pan-Europe, 152
Pax Americana, 58, 102, 156, 158, 177

peace dividend, 18, 23, 59–60, 153, 173, 178
  Gulf War and, 147, 149
  Soviet Union and, 59
Penn Central Corporation, 135, 262n
Pentagon, see Defense Department, U.S.
Perestroika, 188
Persian Gulf War, 18, 56, 264n
  borrowing and, 143–144
  burden-sharing and, 59, 155, 156–157
  cost of, 266n
  dollar and, 154
  peace dividend and, 147, 149
  U.S. military spending and, 59, 143–144, 152–153, 155, 156–157
personnel, military, 54, 56, **212, 213**
Philippines, 237n
"Phillips Curve," 34
physical resources, 48, **50,** 99, **146,** 232n, 267n
  civil budget and, 60, 64, 148
  federal outlays for, **210, 211**
  outlays by function for, **222**
  percentage shares of functions for, **221**
  real spending for, 239n–240n
Plato, 66
Ponzi finance, 130, 150–151, 268n
  budget and, 145
population:
  civil budget and, 61, 149
  health insurance and, **80**
  income brackets and, 94
  increase in, 61
  school age, 62–63, 149
  social security and, 61
poverty, 94
power:
  money and, 40–41
  national vs. international, 41, 174–175

price-fixing, 15
price inflation, 36, 38, 39, 49–50, 108, 110–111, 112, 113, 114, 126
price lag, 37–38
private sector, public sector vs., 26–27
procurement, military, 54–55, **212, 213**
product-cycle theory, 165–167, 169, 172, 185
production, productivity, 11–12, 14, 32, 92, 94, 95, 118, 126, **127,** 162, 173, **196**
  employment and, 123–124
  German, 127, 128
  global approach to, 164–165
  income and, 127–128
  investment and, 128, 171
  Japanese, 127, 128, 166
  overabsorption and, 105
  social security deficit and, 45
  technological change and, 124
property tax, 90–91, 246n
protectionism, 15, 17, 109, 140
  world economy and, 159
public good, 227n–228n
public sector, private sector vs., 26–27
public spending, 71–73
purchasing power parity, 120

R and D, see research and development
Reagan, Ronald W., 14, 21, 86, 96, 97, 117, 120, 125, 129, 176, 186
  deficit of, 98–100, 145
  tax cuts by, 92
Reagan administration, 11, 37, 137, 230n, 231n
Reagan formula, 103, 104, 116–120, 125–127, 134, 151, 154
  dollar and, 126
  European monetary policy and, 117–119

Reagan formula (*continued*)
  foreign savings and, 117–118
  interest rates and, 126
  soft landing and, 153
Reaganomics, 36, 187
  see also supply-side economics
Reagan Revolution, 92, 100
real estate, 15–16, 148, **206**
  S and L crisis and, 136–137
  tax on, 90, 91
recession, 31, 33, 36, 91, 108, 113,
    114, 115, 116, 117, 120,
    147, 153, 154, 155, 270n
  balanced budget and, 35
  bank failures and, 148
  fiscal deficit and, 144
  investment and, 16
reflation, 108–109
Reich, Robert, 168–170, 274n
Republican party, U.S., 86
research and development (R and
    D), 54, **212, 213**
  Germany's expenditures for,
    236n
  Japan's expenditures for, 236n
  as percentage of GDP, 236n–
    237n
reserve currencies, 105–106
Resolution Trust Corporation,
    240n, 266n, 267n
Revenue Act (1964), 91
Ricardo, David, 228n
Rostow, W. W., 252n
Rousseau, Jean Jacques, 228n
routine production services, 169
Rueff, Jacques, 249n
Rust Belt, 258n, 259n

Sally Mae (Student Loan Mar-
    keting Association), 266n–
    267n
saving(s), 14–15, 16, 30, 90, 105,
    129, 156, **206**
  baby boom and, 268n–269n
  fiscal deficit and, 117–119,
    157–158

foreign, 117–119, 151, 152,
    157–158, 187
  income and, 128
  investment and, 31–33, 42
  national, **201**
  Reagan formula and, 117–118
  S and L industry and, 135
  in U.S., 33
savings and loan (S and L) in-
    dustry, 46, 143–144, 146,
    149, 240n, 267n
  bailout cost for, 28–29, 135,
    234n
  Congress and deregulation of,
    137
  deficit and, 28–29, 135
  fraud and, 137
  interest rates and, 135–136
  political system and, 137–138
  real estate industry and, 136–
    137
  savings and, 135
  speculation and, 137
Scandinavia, health care costs
    controlled by, 82
Schumpeter, Joseph, 161, 164
SEATO (South East Asian Treaty
    Organization), 239n
Senate Special Committee on
    Aging, 268n
service industry, 167–168
Smith, Adam, 40
social market economy of Ger-
    many, 69
social security, **20,** 86, **89, 214,
    215,** 245n–246n
  assets of, 44–45
  civil budget and, 60, 61–62
  Congress and, 91–92, 116
  debt and, 28, 233
  fiscal deficit and, 44–45, 234n
  in France, 89–90
  in Germany, 89–90
  GNP and, 61–62, 63
  increases in taxes for, 91–92
  Moynihan and, 28, 233n
  outlays for, **192**

percentage increases in outlays
    for, **217**
population and, 61
production and, 45
surplus in, 44–45, 70
taxes for, 28, 44, 91–92
Western European states and,
    62
soft landing, 153–154, 269*n*
sound money, 122
South East Asian Treaty Orga-
    nization (SEATO), 239*n*
"sovereign borrowers," 134
Soviet Union, 56, 78, 102, 147,
    178, 188
cold war and, 57, 58, 189–190
declining economy of, 123
U.S. defense budget and, 158,
    176, 177
Soviet Union, postcommunist, 16,
    18, 158, 188, 189
economic potential of, 152, 159
Europe's future and, 152
peace dividend and, 59
Spain, 255*n*
special interests, 52
speculation, 130–131
spending, 12, **48, 49, 50, 71, 72,
    73,** 112, 173, 175
capital vs. current, 43–44
civil vs. military, 14, 18–19, 21,
    73, 88
credit and, 64
criteria for comparing trends
    in, 53–54
cutting of, as cure for deficits,
    18–20
decline in civil, 149–150
defense budget and, 54–57
deficit, 29
for education, **192, 200,** 267*n*
Europe vs. U.S., 71–73
GDP and, 88
GNP deflator for, 50
for health care, **192,** 268*n*
inflation and, 49–50
Keynes's preference for, 34–35

middle-class perception of, 88
national security and, 57–60
since 1950, 46–47
off-budget, 28, 44–46
for physical resources, 239*n*–
    240*n*
political marketplace and, 52–
    53
U.S. world role and, 59–60
see also budget; civil budget;
    defense spending
Sputnik, 59
stagflation, 108, 150–151
inflation and, 39, 43
Nixon formula and, 154–155
standard of living, 95, 101
statism, 180, 184
in France, 140–141
in Germany, 140–141
libertarianism and, 181–182
monetary policy and, 140–141
stock market crash (1987), 119–
    120, 129
stop-go monetary policy, 15, 39,
    150, 162, 164
Strategic Defense Initiative (SDI),
    176
structural   (full-employment)
    budget, 35, 229*n*
Student Loan Marketing Associ-
    ation (Sally Mae), 266*n*–
    267*n*
Sun Belt, 258*n*, 259*n*
supply-side economics, 36, 116,
    186
effects abroad of, 117–118, 119
France and, 117–118, 163
Germany and, 117–118, 163
social security and, 44–45, 70
symbolic-analytic services, 169

Taiwan, 238*n*–239*n*
takeovers, 16, 148
borrowing and, 131
finance industry and, 130–131
taxes, taxation, 12, 18, 71, 84, 86–
    102, 173

taxes, taxation (*continued*)
  borrowing and, 131
  bracket creep and, 91
  Bush and, 147
  on consumption, 90
  cultural factors and, 88–89
  direct vs. indirect, 90
  of dividends, 131
  effective rates of, **98**
  European vs. U.S., 20–22
  fiscal deficit and, 20, 34–37
  GDP and, 86, **92**
  household, **73**
  impediments to higher, 89–91
  inadequate public spending
    and, 88–89
  on income, 91, 93–96
  inflation and cuts in, 34–37
  inflation as form of, 42
  middle class and, 93–96
  monetary policy and, 36–37
  1964 reduction of, 35–36
  1968 increase in, 109
  in 1980s, 96–98, **97**
  1981 reform of, 36, 92, 96, 100,
    116
  1986 reform of, 96, 97–98,
    244*n*
  as political issue, 86–87
  on property, 90, 91, 246*n*
  raising of, as cure for deficits,
    20–23
  Reagan and, 92
  Reagan deficit and, 98–100
  on real estate, 90, 91
  rearmament and, 59
  social security, 28, 44, 91–92
  sources of, **89**
  standard of living and, 95
  unlegislated increases in, *see*
    bracket creep
  see also tax revolt
Tax Foundation, 245*n*
Tax Reform Act (1986), 255*n*–
  256*n*
tax revolt, 87, 90, 93, 267*n*
  inflation and, 91, 96

  middle class and, 91–92
technology, 66, 138
  cheap labor and, 166
  civil budget and, 64–65
  defense budget and, 56, 124–
    125
  education and, 166–167
  finance industry and changes
    in, 132
  GNP and, 56
  health care and, 79, 81
  industrial restructuring and,
    161
  military vs. civilian, 167
  product-cycle theory and, 165
  productivity and, 124
Thailand, 185
third world, 115, 157, 169
  arms race and, 56
  debt and, 134, 148, 154, 262*n*
  U.S. as model for, 172
total employment, **197**
trade, 12, 31, 102–121
  collapse of dollar and, 155
  inflation's effect upon, 38–39
  surplus, 104
  "voluntary agreements" and, 41
trade balance, 114, 158
  inflation and, 39
trade deficit, 77, 125, 154, 264*n*
  fiscal deficit and, 73
transportation, 64, **221, 222**
Treasury Department, U.S., 44,
  262*n*
Triffin, Robert, 250*n*
Truman, Harry S, 58–59
trust funds, off-budget, 29, 44–
  45
twin deficit, 31–33, 142
  inefficiency and, 84
two-tier work force, 168, 171

unemployment, 92, 110, 118, 124,
  145, 164, 251*n*, 274*n*
  in Europe, 162
  in France, **197, 202**

in Germany, **197, 202**
in Japan, **197, 202**
long-duration, **202**
United States:
economic indicators for, **145**
inefficient political system of,
    21–22
job creation in, 167–168
legal system of, 183–184
national vs. international power
    of, 40–41, 174–175
new plural world and, 176–180
receipts and outlays of, **194–
    195**
tax policy conflict in, 86–87
trade and current accounts of,
    201
world role of, 18, 23, 40–41,
    59–60, 77–78, 102–103,
    144, 147–148, 152–153,
    175–180
Uruguay Round, 153, 230*n*, 270*n*
U.S. Steel, 262*n*
utilitarianism, 184

veterans benefits, 60, **192, 214,
    215**

Vietnam War, 36, 56, 100, 109,
    116
    Bretton Woods system and, 108
    neoisolationism and, 186–187
Volcker, Paul, 96, 97, 117, 125,
    134, 230*n*, 254*n*
    Carter's appointment of, 116
"voluntary agreements," 41

wage and price controls, 41, 111,
    113
    inflation and, 59
Watergate scandal, 113
weapons systems, 54, 58
welfare, 61, 67, 124
welfare capitalism, 123
welfare state, 19, 69
Work of Nations, The (Reich), 168–
    169
World War II, 18, 58, 77, 78, 100,
    113, 177, 179
    Bretton Woods agreement in,
    103–104
    debt in, 259*n*
W. T. Grant, 262*n*

Yugoslavia, 188